Katherine Strand Holkeboer has designed
and built costumes for more than 100
professional, university, television, dance,
civic theatre, summer stock, and high school
groups. Currently a costuming instructor
and designer at Eastern Michigan
University, she has also taught costuming at
Boston University and the University of
Michigan.

Prentice-Hall, Inc.,
Englewood Cliffs, New Jersey 07632

Katherine Strand Holkeboer

Garments, Trims, and Accessories from Ancient Egypt to 1915

Patterns for Theatrical Costumes

Library of Congress Cataloging in Publication Data

Holkeboer, Katherine Strand.
    Patterns for theatrical costumes.

    "A Spectrum Book."
    Bibliography: p.
    Includes index.
    1. Costume.   2. Sewing.   I. Title.
TT633.H65   1984   646'.47   83–27057
ISBN 0-13-654278-6
ISBN 0-13-654260-3 (pbk.)

1 2 3 4 5 6 7 8 9 10

ISBN 0-13-654278-6

ISBN 0-13-654260-3 {PBK.}

Editorial production/supervision by Peter Jordan
Interior design by Maria Carella
Cover design by Hal Siegel
Manufacturing buyers: Edward J. Ellis & Doreen Cavallo

This book is available at a special discount when ordered in
bulk quantities. Contact Prentice-Hall, Inc., General
Publishing Division, Special Sales, Englewood Cliffs, N.J. 07632.

Prentice-Hall International, Inc., *London*
Prentice-Hall of Australia Pty. Limited, *Sydney*
Prentice-Hall Canada Inc., *Toronto*
Prentice-Hall of India Private Limited, *New Delhi*
Prentice-Hall of Japan, Inc., *Tokyo*
Prentice-Hall of Southeast Asia Pte. Ltd., *Singapore*
Whitehall Books Limited, *Wellington, New Zealand*
Editora Prentice-Hall do Brasil Ltda., *Rio de Janeiro*

Contents

Preface

Every costumer knows the frustration of trying to create imaginative and appropriate costumes when time is short and skilled help is unavailable. It is this frustration that *Patterns for Theatrical Costumes* is intended to relieve. The patterns included, which represent a wide range of periods and styles, are illustrated in three basic sizes, and are typical rather than specific, allowing the costumer to adapt them imaginatively. Construction techniques are expressed simply and clearly, step by step.

Experienced costumers who have lamented the hours consumed in training students and apprentices and volunteers may use this book as a teaching guide for basic tasks such as enlarging a pattern or taking a facial cast.

Many period pattern books yield a highly specific costume since they are taken from actual garments in museum collections. The patterns in this book have been adapted to fit the modern figure. They are intended to be representative and in some cases have been simplified in order to allow freedom in the design process. These patterns can be used to achieve the basic silhouette of a given period, but the choices of fabric, trim, sleeve, and neckline details are left to the designer and director.

The decorative patterns are designed to give a feeling of textile patterning in a given era. The illustrations may be used as a guide in selecting appropriate fabrics and trims, or they may be enlarged and used directly as stencil patterns.

Patterns for simple undergarments, hats, and men's suits are included even though many costumers prefer to rent or borrow suits, and to avoid using corsets, hoops, and hats altogether. Men's suits after 1800 require tailoring, and ladies' corsets and hoops, though not particularly difficult to make, are frequently vetoed by directors who fear they may restrict the freedom of the actor. I have included instructions for creating corsets, hoops, and hats, since they are fairly easy to make. Tailoring instruction, on the other hand, could easily fill another book.

Many of the patterns, methods, and use of materials described in this book were developed and refined over many years with the assistance and uncomplicated insights of my students. We continue to learn together.

I am especially grateful to my family for their help in completing this book: to my mother, Dorothy Strand, for typing; to my father, John Strand for technical and graphics assistance; to my husband, Bob, for editing and proofreading the manuscript; and to my children, John and Maja for continuing to love and support a mother whom they saw too seldom. I would also like to thank my colleagues at Eastern Michigan University for providing the time and atmosphere in which to write this book, and my teachers, Zelma Weisfeld, Barbara Costa, Robin Lacy, and Jim Harris, for opening the door to theatrical costume design for me.

Patterns for
Theatrical Costumes

Using The
Patterns

The patterns in this book are drawn to 1/8" = 1" scale unless otherwise noted. They are drawn and aligned on 1/8 inch graph paper to indicate straight of grain as well as scale.

Seam allowance has not been added to the patterns, and allowances for closures (lacings, hooks and eyes, buttons and plackets) are added only when they are an integral part of the design of that garment (a double-breasted dress coat, for example). The patterns are illustrated in three basic sizes (see page 3) unless "one size fits all." These sizes correspond approximately to commercial pattern standard measurements as follows:

Female

	Small (Size 8–10)	Medium (Size 12–14)	Large (Size 16–18)
Bust	31–33 inches	34–37 inches	38–40 inches
Waist	24–26 inches	27–29 inches	30–32 inches
Hip	33–35 inches	36–39 inches	40–43 inches

Male

	Small (Size 34–36)	Medium (Size 38–40)	Large (Size 42–44)
Chest	34–36 inches	38–40 inches	42–44 inches
Waist	30–32 inches	34–36 inches	38–40 inches
Hip	35–37 inches	39–41 inches	43–45 inches

In some cases, patterns show a variety of sleeve styles which can be substituted into a basic pattern for a given period. This is intended to encourage freedom in the manipulation of these patterns and creativity on the part of the costumer. Although a variety of changes have been illustrated, these are only a sampling of the changes possible through alteration in the cut.

Notation on the patterns has been kept to a minimum, and diagrams to help in the understanding of the construction and drape of garments have been included. If the front and back of a garment are illustrated together, the lower neckline refers to the front neckline, and the longer hem indicates a train. Two-piece sleeves are illustrated in like manner with the upper curve indicating the cut of the top part of the sleeve and the lower curve indicating the curve of the undersleeve (see page 4).

ENLARGING THE PATTERNS

There are several ways to enlarge patterns. The method you choose will depend on the specific pattern as well as available space and equipment.

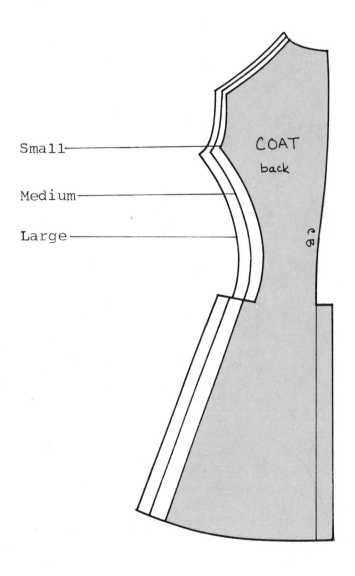

Small

Medium

Large

COAT
back

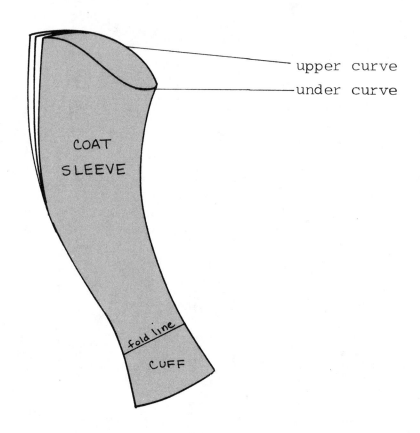

Optical Projection

If an opaque projector is available, as well as a large room with a smooth unbroken wall, this may be the most trouble-free method of enlargement.

1. Situate the opaque projector in such a way that when the pattern is in focus each square of the projected pattern grid measures one inch. (The specific position of the projector may be marked on the floor with masking tape for future enlargement sessions.)
2. Secure a large piece of paper (newspaper, craft or butcher paper) to the wall and outline each pattern piece along with all identifying labels and construction markings.
3. Remove paper from wall and cut out pattern pieces.

Grid Method

The grid method of enlargement is a method with which many are familiar from childhood, and one which produces a fairly accurate enlargement.

1. Draw a 1/8″ grid on top of the book pattern.
2. On a large piece of paper draw a grid of 1″ squares.
3. Following the patterns in this book, transfer the lines, square by square, to the 1″ grid, paying special attention to the corners, curves, and the intersection of pattern and grid lines (see page 6).
4. Label each piece with all markings from the book before cutting out the patterns.

Radial Projection

For this method, a sharp pencil and accurate measurements are essential. With care and a little practice, this method is faster than the grid method.

1. Trace the pattern piece from the book and tape it to the lower left-hand section of a large piece of paper. The paper should be at least eight times the height and width of the pattern piece.
2. From any point (x) in the lower left section of the pattern, extend a series of lines through all critical pattern points (see page 7). Use as many radiating lines as necessary to establish the outline of the pattern piece accurately.
3. Measure the distance from the original point (x) to each intersection in the pattern (a,b,c, etc.) and multiply that distance by eight. Mark that distance on the same line extending beyond the pattern (A,B,C, etc.) (see page 8).

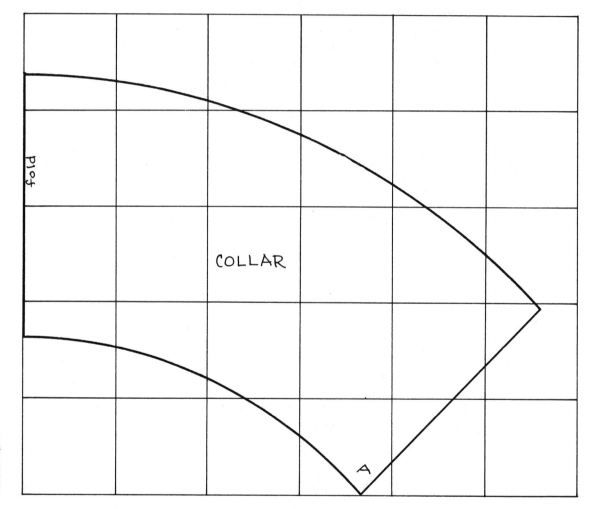

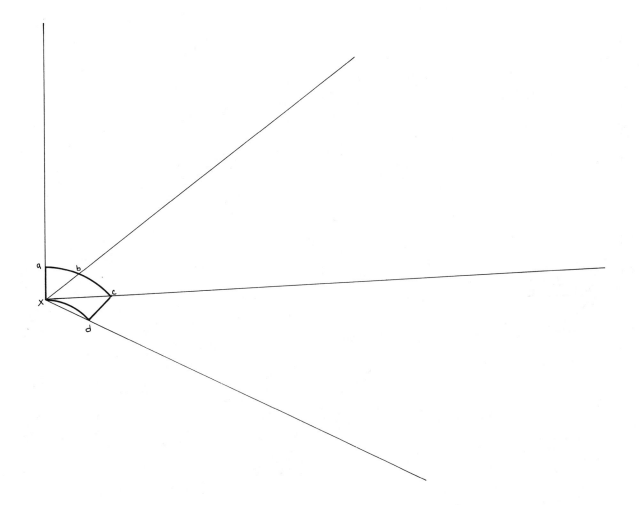

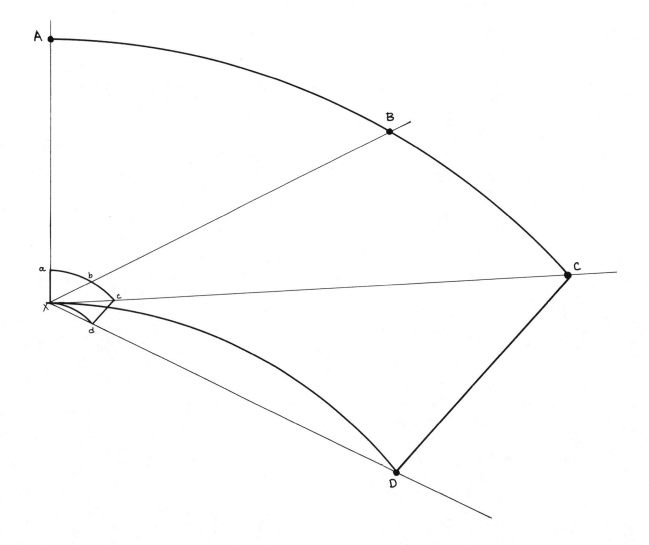

4. Connect outer points of the pattern referring to original pattern for the shape of curves.

5. Label all pieces completely and cut them out.

After the patterns have been enlarged, labeled, and cut out, they are ready to be used. Remember to add seam allowances and extra allowance for overlap closures. It is a good idea to check sleeve and hem length before cutting since the height and arm length of the actor may vary a great deal. Because no two bodies are alike, and because these patterns are based on standard general sizes, refinements will have to be made in the fitting process.

FITTING

Fittings are critical to the success of any costume. Most costumes can be finished successfully with three fittings.

The first fitting should be used to adjust those garments which fit close to the body, such as a coat, breeches, bodice, or doublet. This should be done before collar, sleeves, waistband, kneebands, or closures have been stitched in place. It is a good idea to baste seams for this initial fitting since it is likely that many will require alteration for a perfect fit.

1. Baste seams of garment without locking the ends of the seams.

2. Put together sleeves, skirt, cuffs, and collars, but do not stitch them to the garment.

3. Place garment on the body the way it will be worn (not inside out).

4. Pin garment closed along marked closure line (see top left of page 11).

5. If the garment is too tight, remove darts or seams to relieve the strain.

6. If the garment pulls around the neckline or armhole, clip the curve to just within the seam line (see top right of page 11).

7. Adjust the shoulder seams if necessary. Remove original seam and repin if necessary to achieve a smooth fit.

8. Check the chest area and take in or let out seams as needed. Again, remove the entire seam if necessary to make the garment fit well. Try to make even adjustments to both sides of the garment and at the same time so the garment retains a symmetrical appearance.

9. Fit garment to waistline by adjusting darts and seams evenly around the body. Pay attention to the lines being created by the seams and darts. Make certain that they are where you want them, and that they are the same on both sides of the garment.

10. After the garment fits comfortably and attractively, mark closing, neckline, sleeve position, waistline, and so on. These markings may be made on only one side of the garment and

transferred to the other side after the garment has been removed.

11. For any type of trousers, the first thing to consider is the waistline in relationship to the crotch. First pull the breeches to a comfortable position so the crotch seam is neither too high nor too low. It may be helpful to tie an elastic around the waist to hold this position while other adjustments are being made (see bottom of page 11).

12. Pin along the marked closing line and take in or let out side seams, darts, gathers, or pleats as necessary to achieve the comfort and appearance desired.

13. Mark all adjustments including the new waist placement if necessary.

14. Check sleeves, waistband, collar, cuffs, and so on, separately.

The second fitting occurs after the addition of sleeves, waistband, collar, and skirt, and so on. The purpose of this fitting is to check previous alterations and to mark sleeve length, hem length, and closings wherever they occur (neck, center back, waist, knee, and so on).

The last fitting is a final check to make sure that all adjustments have been made accurately and that the final costume is trimmed and finished properly.

Not every fitting problem can be anticipated and covered in this book. Developing a feeling and skill for fitting comes with practice. When a problem seems insoluble, do not hesitate to rip out all the seams and repin the garment back together on the actor, or to change the placement of armhole and neck openings and to clip to these new seam lines. What you are essentially doing in these two steps is called draping on the body, which is a method many designers use to create patterns in the first place. Do not feel bound to a pattern which fails to work on a particular body. Do not feel obligated to retain the integrity of a flat pattern if the style looks bad on the actor. Finally, do not feel obliged to take in or let out both halves of a seam equally. If the back looks better with three inches of seam allowance removed, and the front with only one half inch, you have effectively moved the seam line. Do what you have to do through ripping and clipping to make the costume look the way you want it to look.

Draping

Draping is the process of fitting and molding fabric to a dress form or directly to the human body. Patterns are thus altered or created directly on a three-dimensional form rather than on a flat table. Draping requires a sensitivity to fabric, a knowledge of fiber weave and weight, and some practice.

Many costumers develop most of their patterns by draping, but even if this method is used exclusively it is helpful to study the shape of a flat pattern or to begin with fabric cut in the basic flat pattern shape before draping for a perfect fit on a form. To see the way an historical garment is laid out in cloth and to study the grain line and shape of the individual pattern pieces will enable the costumer to understand the nature of that garment. This is research which goes beyond the library or museum. The better a costumer understands flat pattern, the better that individual will understand draping.

Draping is really a way of fitting before any sewing occurs, and principles of fitting are applicable to draping. Either dress forms or human bodies may be used as the base for the draping process. If a garment is draped on the actor who will wear the costume, the fitting and draping process are essentially one operation. This is not always possible or desirable, however, since draping may take a considerable amount of time and is easier if the draper can pin directly into the form. Most people lack the endurance to subject themselves to a lengthy draping session.

Certain garments do not lend themselves to draping. Most foundation garments such as corsets, hoops, and padding are intended to distort or confine the human form, so to use a dress or human form as a base does not work. Likewise, tailored garments have a structure of their own, requiring special stitching and padding techniques within the garment and are most successfully created from flat-pattern sources.

ALTERING THE BASIC FORM

Whether the draping is to take place on a dress form or on the human body, it is essential that the form be molded into the shape appropriate to the final costume before the draping occurs. Both the body and the dress form should be clothed in whatever foundation garments the character will eventually wear. The shape of the dress form should imitate the shape of the actor as closely as possible. This may require a combination of padding and corsetry. A polyurethane dress form is particularly easy to mold into a new shape by corsetry, but any dress form may be altered by padding.

DRAPING PROCESS

Materials Needed

1. Dress form (or human form)
2. Muslin (or any inexpensive fabric which imitates the weave and weight of the final fabric)

3. Straight pins
4. Tailor's chalk
5. Pattern

Draping Upper Body Garments

1. Cut pattern pieces in fabric with generous seam allowances.
2. Working on only half of the body, pin the center front of garment in place on the form (see top left of page 17).
3. Work the pattern piece up and around the neck, clipping neckline seam allowance to establish a smooth curve (see top right of page 17).
4. Smooth fabric from chest up and across the shoulder.
5. Pin appropriate garment piece in the center back and establish neck opening as in the front.
6. Pin the shoulder seam in place, checking the pattern for placement.
7. If you are working with a multiple-piece garment, pin side pieces in place, smoothing fabric toward the underarm. Clip armhole seam allowance if necessary to allow a smooth curve (see bottom left of page 17).
8. Pin darts, tucks, or pleats in place, checking pattern for general placement, size, and direction of dart.
9. Connect front and back pieces, checking pattern for the placement of seams.
10. Stand back and observe the results.
11. If necessary, make corrections by repinning pieces, moving seam lines, darts, tucks, and so on, and pinning more fabric in places where the garment is not large enough.
12. When the garment fits correctly mark neckline, armhole, waist position, center front and center back.
13. Remove the pattern pieces from the form and mark pin placement to establish seam lines, tucks, pleats, and so on.
14. Transfer all new markings to the other side of the garment. (Although most human bodies are not perfectly symmetrical, it is usually a good idea to make all garments as symmetrical as possible.)

Draping Skirts

1. Cut skirt pattern pieces from fabric.
2. Pin center front and center back to dress form at waist.
3. Pin pleats, gathers and tucks, in place.
4. Add additional skirt pieces, checking the way the folds and seams hang.
5. Readjust gathers or pleats and seams to fall as desired. Lifting the inside of a pleat will sometimes correct the look of an awkwardly falling pleat.

Draping Pants

1. Cut pants pattern pieces from fabric.

2. Working on only half of the body, pin the center front to the pants form at the waist. (This process may be done on an actor wearing a leotard, or snug swim suit if a pants form is not available.)

3. Establish the proper crotch placement by checking the pattern illustration for shape and placement. Smooth the pants pattern down the center front and around to the inseam, clipping excess fabric if necessary to allow the proper curve around the leg (see bottom right of page 17).

4. Do the same thing with the back of the garment and pin the inseam.

5. Adjust the crotch placement for style and comfort by raising or lowering the fabric at the waist.

6. Pin darts, pleats, and gathers in place, checking the pattern for placement and checking the form for effect.

7. Pin side seam.

8. Pin waistband, knee bands, and so on in place and adjust for fit.

9. Remove pattern from form and transfer all pin markings to the other side.

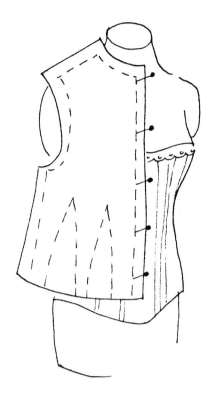

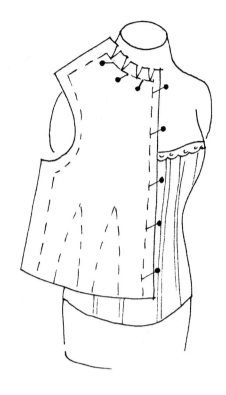

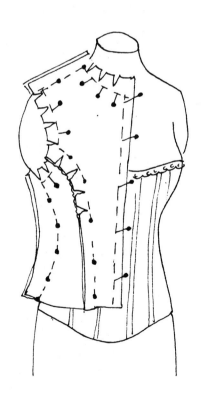

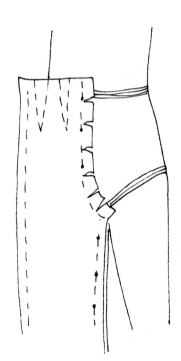

Historic Patterns

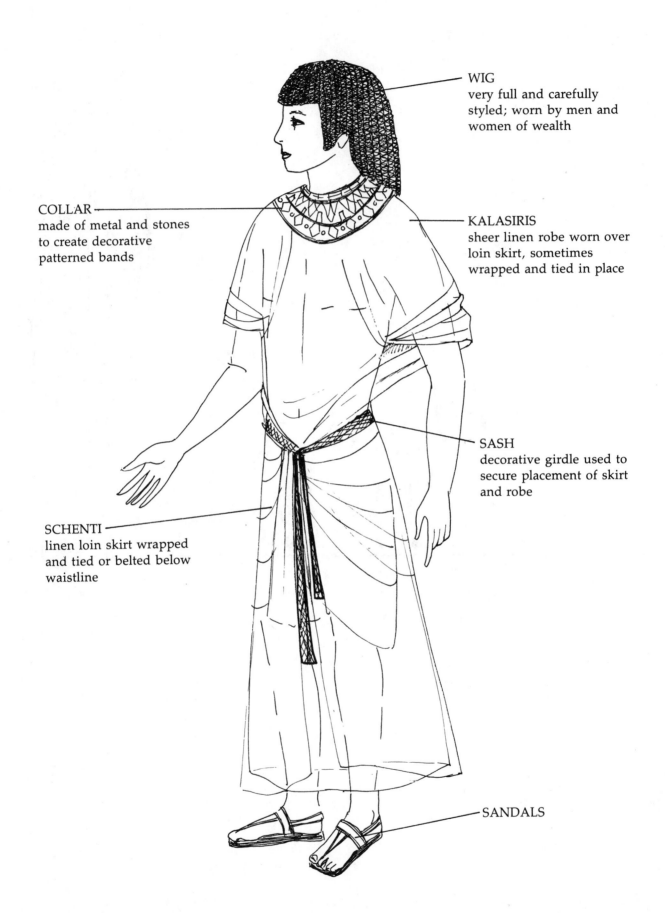

WIG
very full and carefully
styled; worn by men and
women of wealth

COLLAR
made of metal and stones
to create decorative
patterned bands

KALASIRIS
sheer linen robe worn over
loin skirt, sometimes
wrapped and tied in place

SASH
decorative girdle used to
secure placement of skirt
and robe

SCHENTI
linen loin skirt wrapped
and tied or belted below
waistline

SANDALS

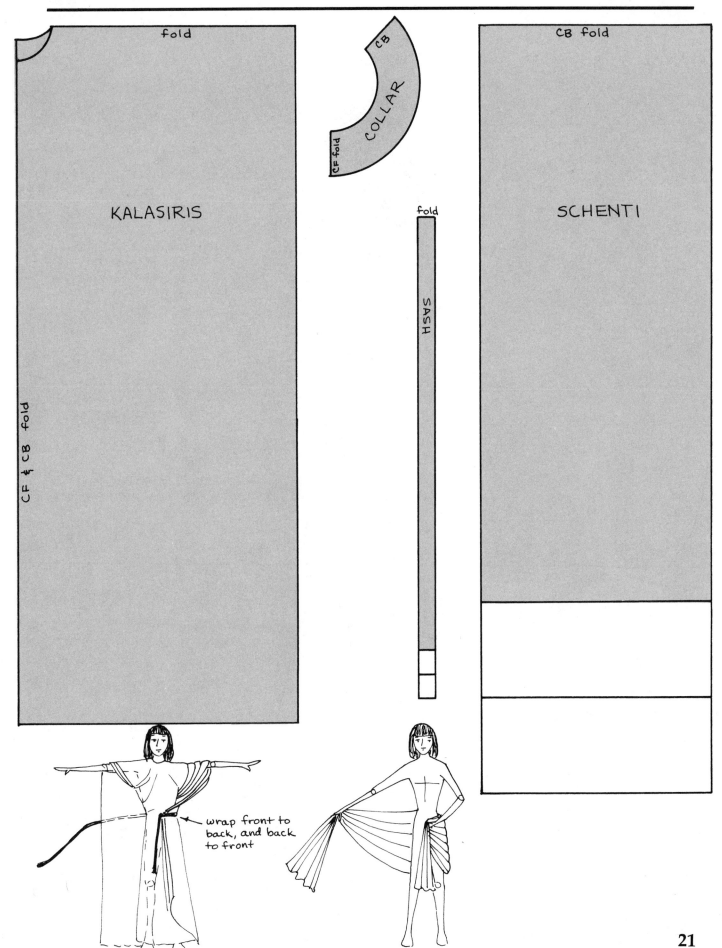

fold

KALASIRIS

CF ξ CB fold

CB

COLLAR

CF fold

fold

SASH

CB fold

SCHENTI

wrap front to
back, and back
to front

CB

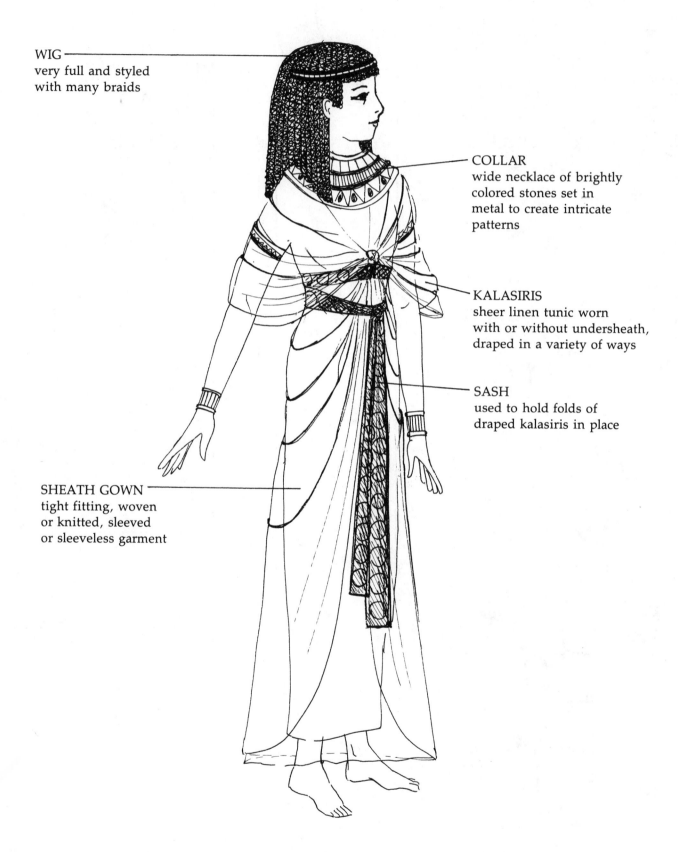

WIG
very full and styled
with many braids

COLLAR
wide necklace of brightly
colored stones set in
metal to create intricate
patterns

KALASIRIS
sheer linen tunic worn
with or without undersheath,
draped in a variety of ways

SASH
used to hold folds of
draped kalasiris in place

SHEATH GOWN
tight fitting, woven
or knitted, sleeved
or sleeveless garment

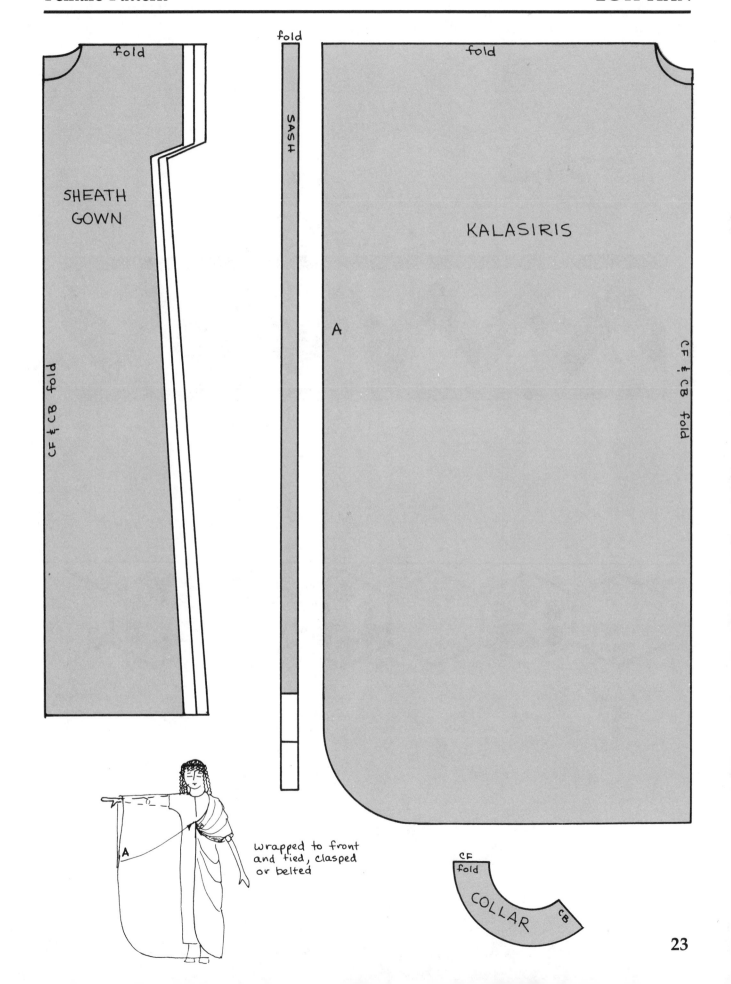

fold

SHEATH GOWN

CF & CB fold

fold

SASH

fold

KALASIRIS

A

CF & CB fold

A

wrapped to front
and tied, clasped
or belted

CF
fold

COLLAR

CB

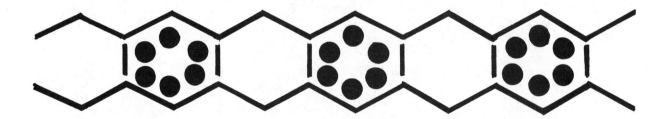

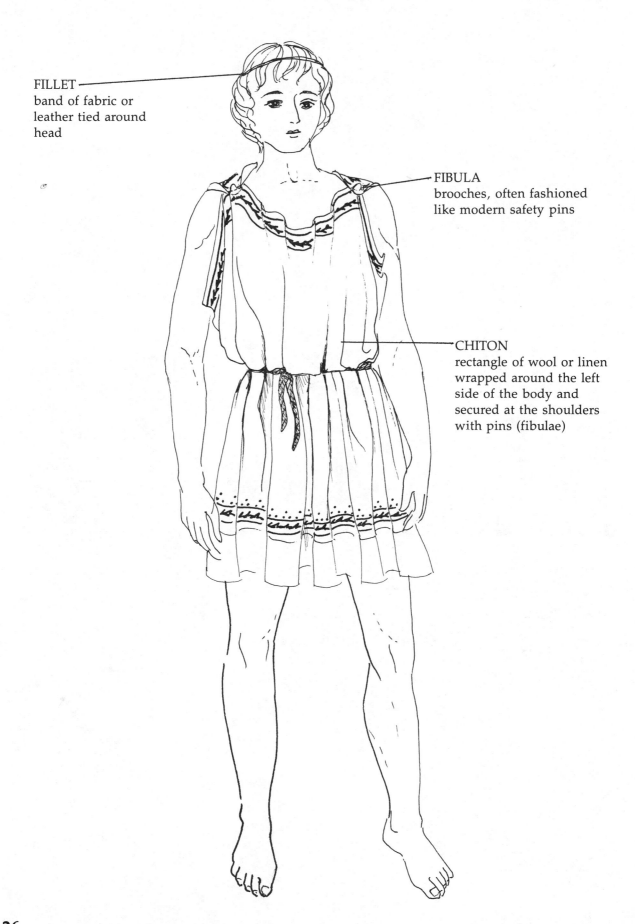

FILLET
band of fabric or
leather tied around
head

FIBULA
brooches, often fashioned
like modern safety pins

CHITON
rectangle of wool or linen
wrapped around the left
side of the body and
secured at the shoulders
with pins (fibulae)

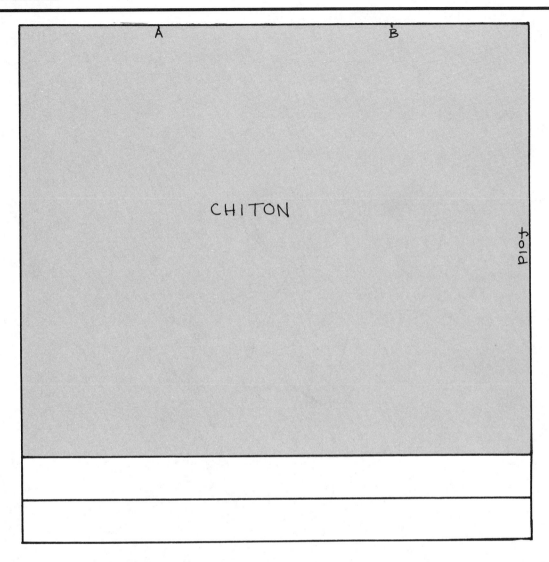

CHITON

fold

open on right side,
fold around left side

pin at A & B

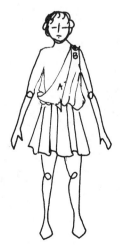

EXOMIS—
chiton unfastened
on one shoulder

HIMATION
rectangular woolen mantle 12 to 18 feet long and four to six
feet wide worn by both men and women, draped in a variety of
ways, usually leaving the right arm free. Could be worn with
or without chiton by men.

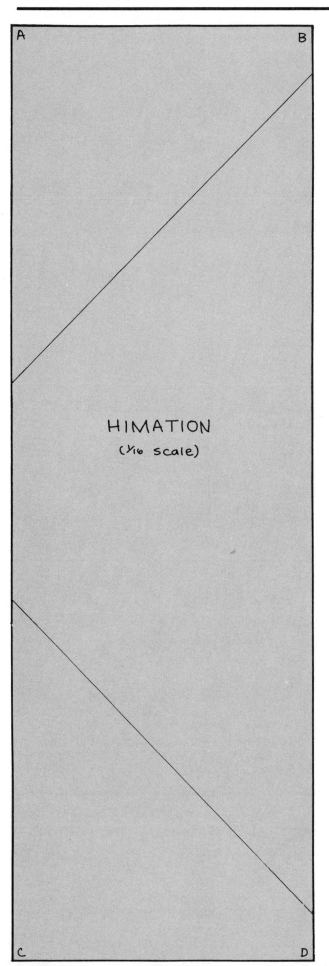

HIMATION

(¹⁄₁₀ scale)

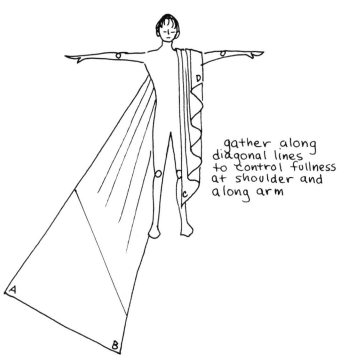

gather along
diagonal lines
to control fullness
at shoulder and
along arm

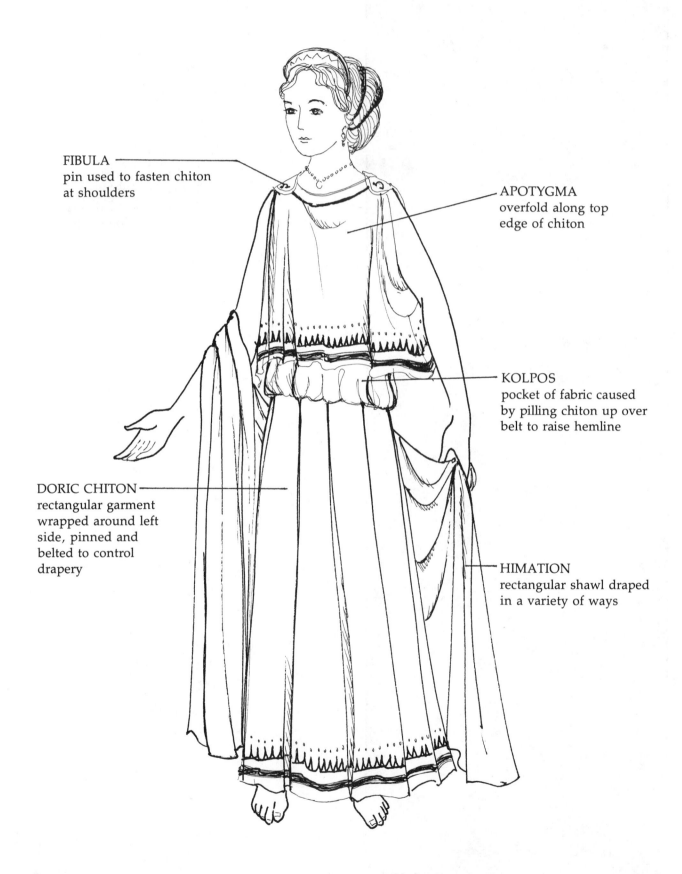

FIBULA
pin used to fasten chiton
at shoulders

APOTYGMA
overfold along top
edge of chiton

KOLPOS
pocket of fabric caused
by pilling chiton up over
belt to raise hemline

DORIC CHITON
rectangular garment
wrapped around left
side, pinned and
belted to control
drapery

HIMATION
rectangular shawl draped
in a variety of ways

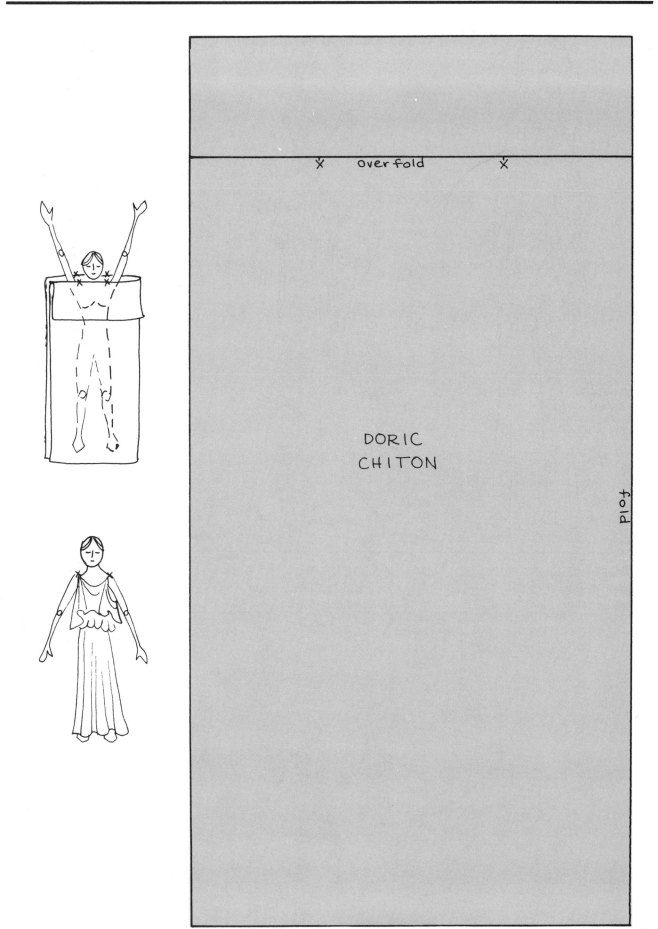

overfold

DORIC
CHITON

fold

DORIC CHITON
with belt over deep
apotygma

IONIC CHITON
very wide chiton pinned
along arm to form sleeves

GATHERED CHITON
similar to Ionic chiton
but gathered and sewn
rather than pinned along
arm

BACK VIEW
showing belting techniques
for 2 and 3

IONIC & GATHERED CHITON   (2 & 3)

(1/16 scale)

fold

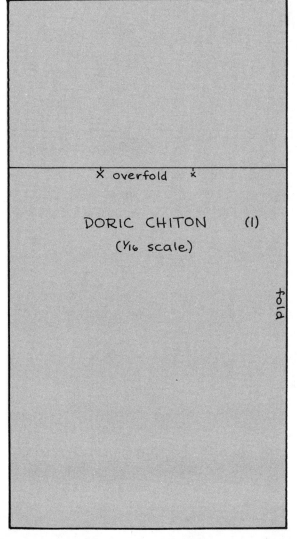

x overfold   x

DORIC CHITON   (1)

(1/16 scale)

fold

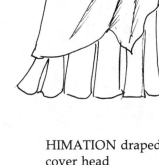

HIMATION

NARROW HIMATION

HIMATION draped to cover head

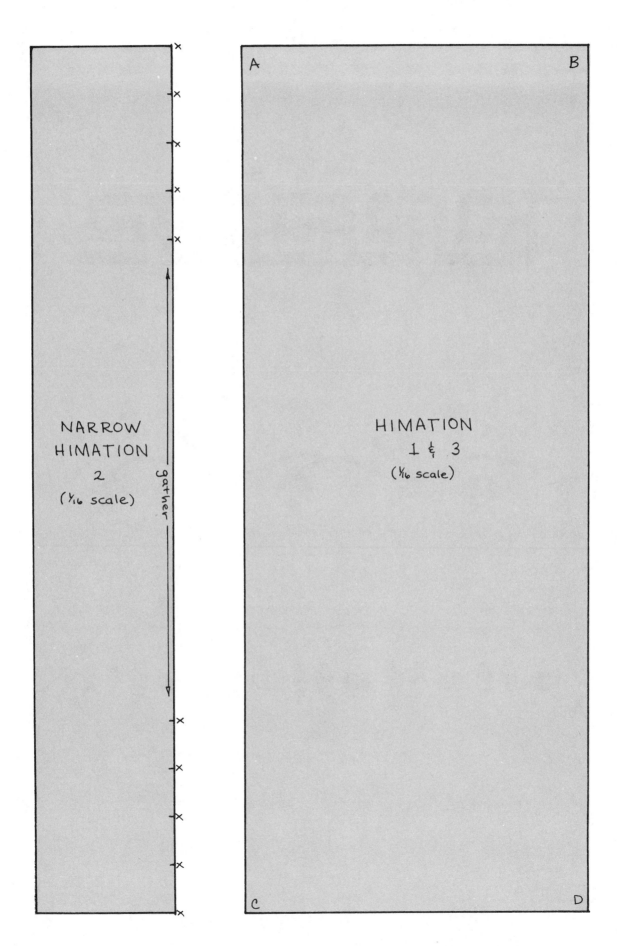

NARROW
HIMATION
2
(¹⁄₁₆ scale)

gather

HIMATION
1 & 3
(¹⁄₁₆ scale)

A

B

C

D

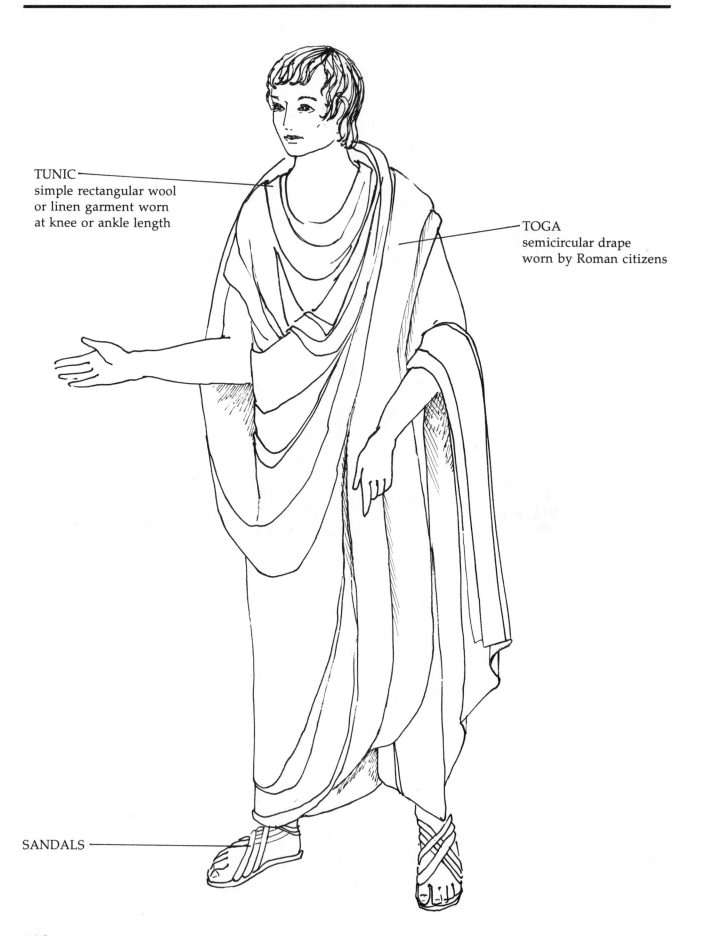

TUNIC
simple rectangular wool
or linen garment worn
at knee or ankle length

TOGA
semicircular drape
worn by Roman citizens

SANDALS

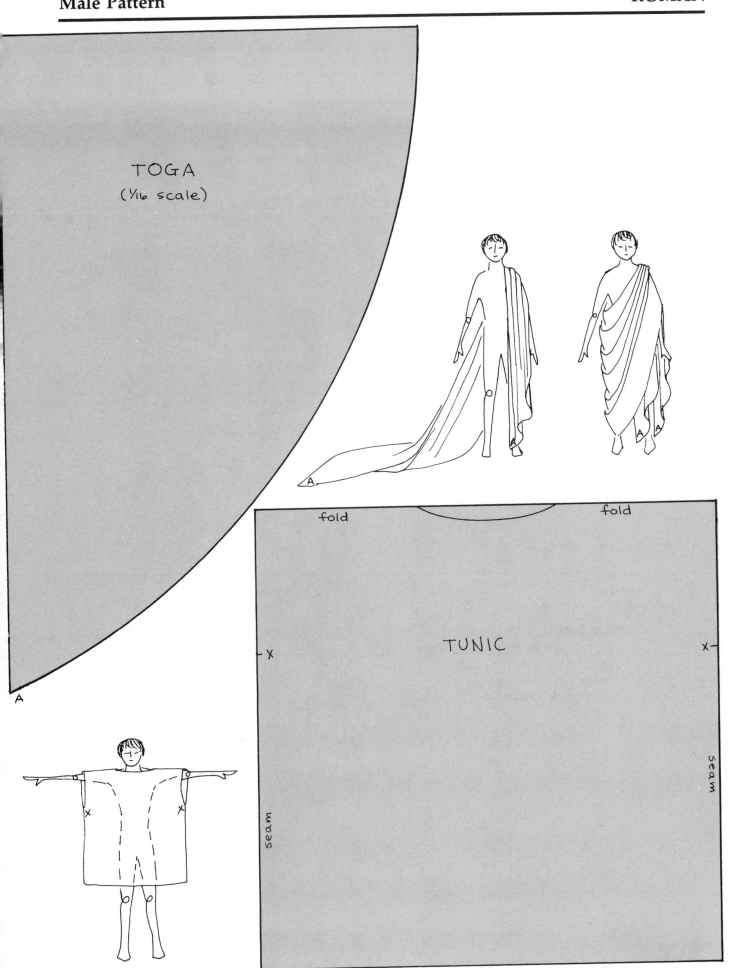

TOGA
(1/16 scale)

A

TUNIC

fold   fold

x   x

seam   seam

A

x   x

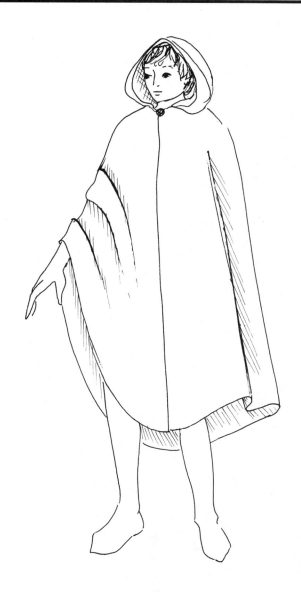

PAENULA
hooded rainproof cape made
of wool or leather, fastened
in front

LACERNA
lightweight woolen cloak clasped
at the right shoulder or in
front; similar to Greek
chlamys, but rounded at two
corners

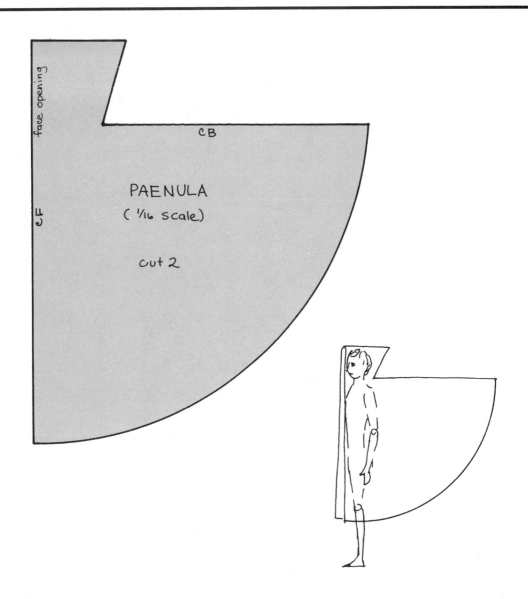

PAENULA

(1/16 scale)

cut 2

face opening

cF

cB

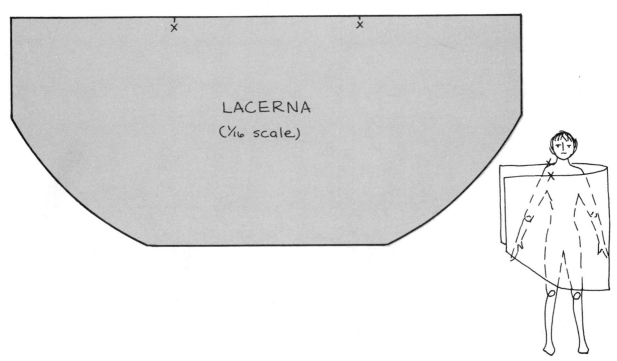

LACERNA

(1/16 scale)

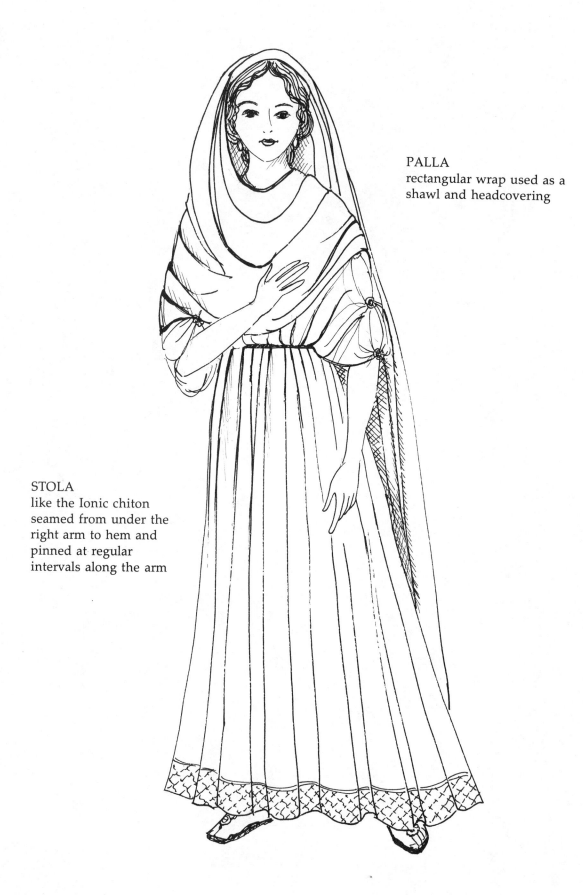

PALLA
rectangular wrap used as a
shawl and headcovering

STOLA
like the Ionic chiton
seamed from under the
right arm to hem and
pinned at regular
intervals along the arm

STOLA
(1/16 scale)

seam

fold

PALLA
(1/16 scale)

fold

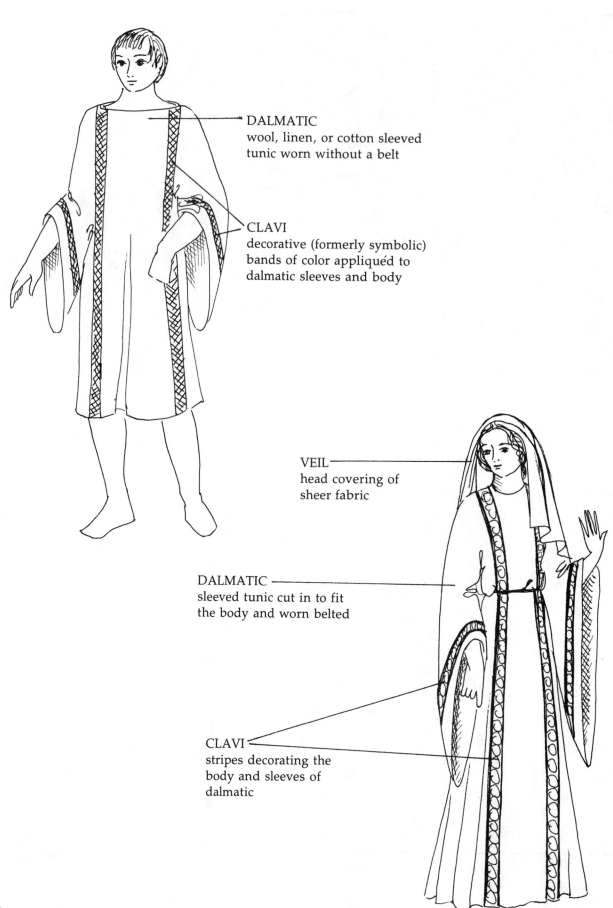

DALMATIC
wool, linen, or cotton sleeved
tunic worn without a belt

CLAVI
decorative (formerly symbolic)
bands of color appliquéd to
dalmatic sleeves and body

VEIL
head covering of
sheer fabric

DALMATIC
sleeved tunic cut in to fit
the body and worn belted

CLAVI
stripes decorating the
body and sleeves of
dalmatic

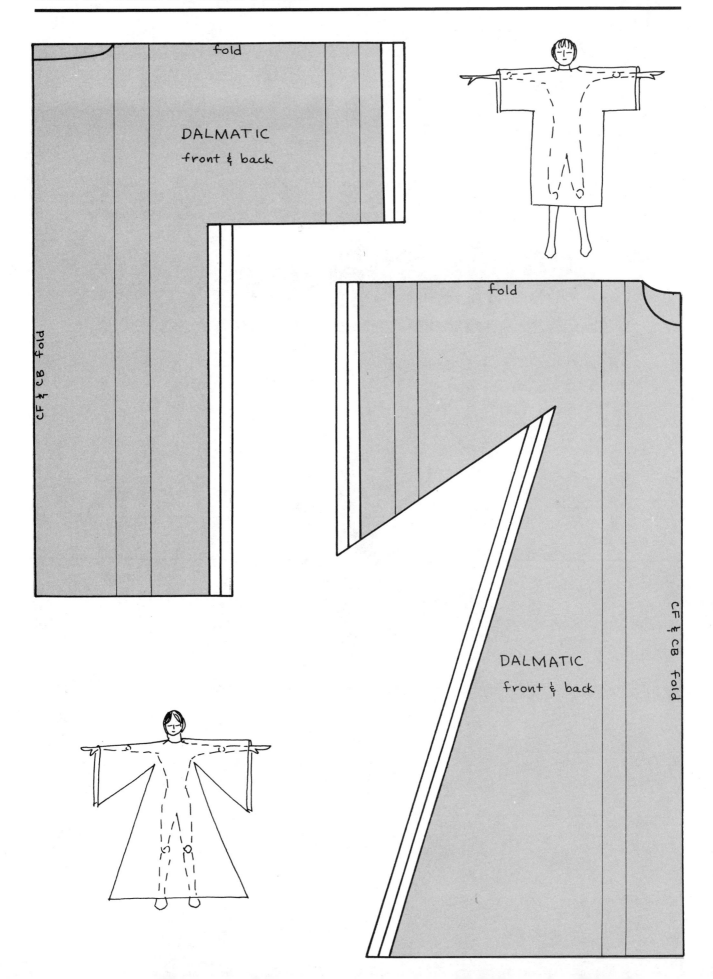

fold

DALMATIC
front & back

CF & CB fold

fold

DALMATIC
front & back

CF & CB fold

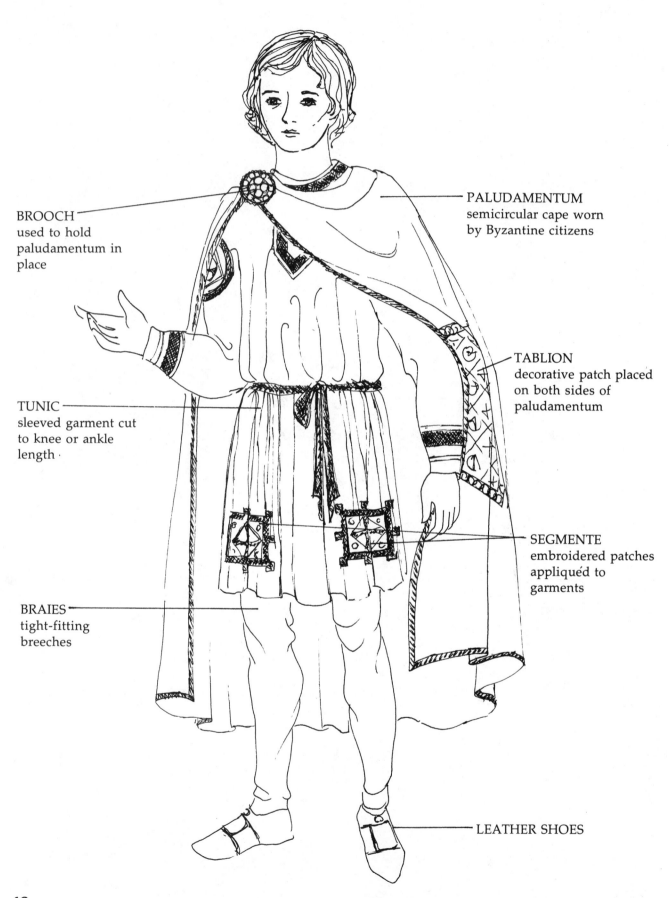

BROOCH
used to hold
paludamentum in
place

PALUDAMENTUM
semicircular cape worn
by Byzantine citizens

TABLION
decorative patch placed
on both sides of
paludamentum

TUNIC
sleeved garment cut
to knee or ankle
length ·

SEGMENTE
embroidered patches
appliquéd to
garments

BRAIES
tight-fitting
breeches

LEATHER SHOES

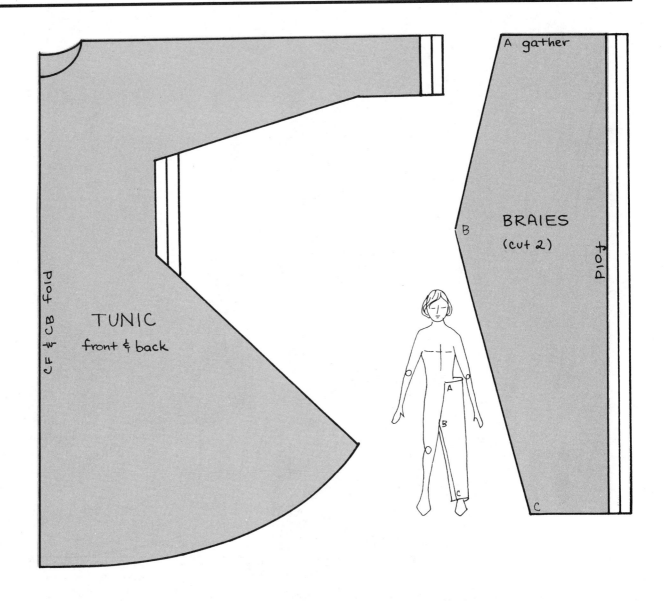

A gather

BRAIES
(cut 2)

fold

CF & CB fold

TUNIC
front & back

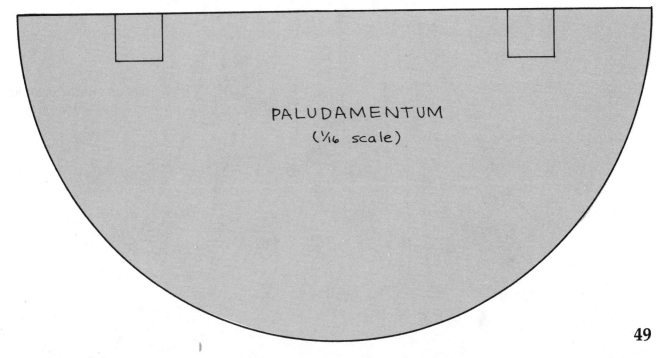

PALUDAMENTUM
(1/16 scale)

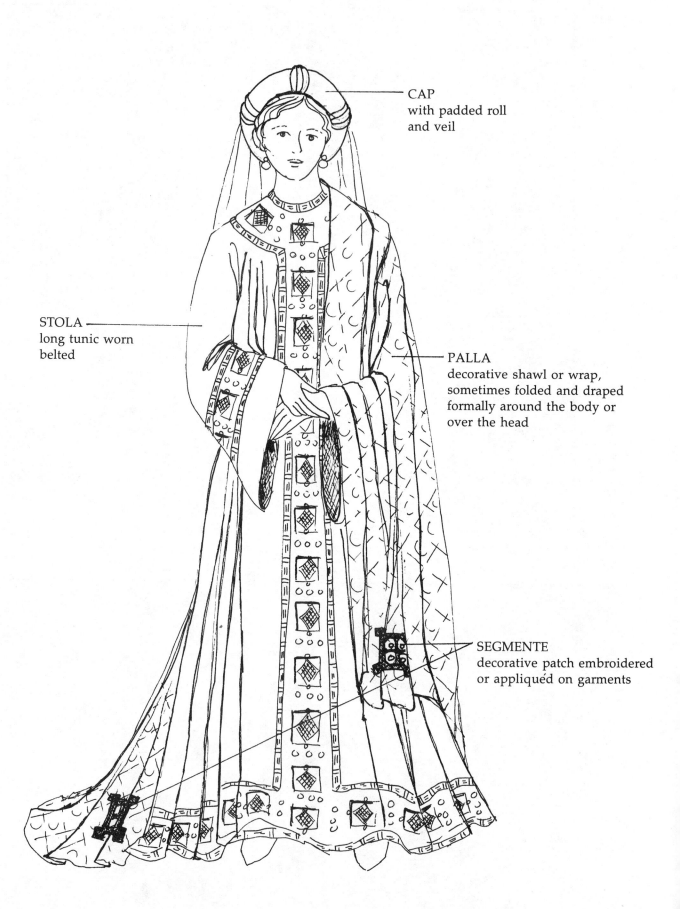

CAP
with padded roll
and veil

STOLA
long tunic worn
belted

PALLA
decorative shawl or wrap,
sometimes folded and draped
formally around the body or
over the head

SEGMENTE
decorative patch embroidered
or appliquéd on garments

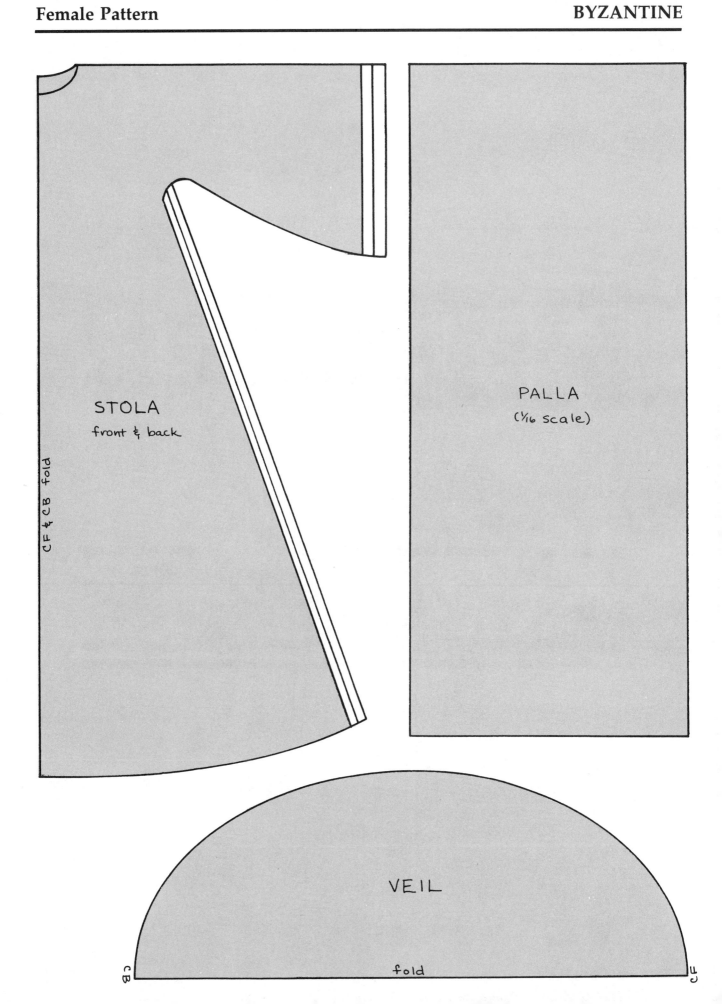

STOLA
front & back

CF & CB fold

PALLA
(1/16 scale)

VEIL

CB

fold

CF

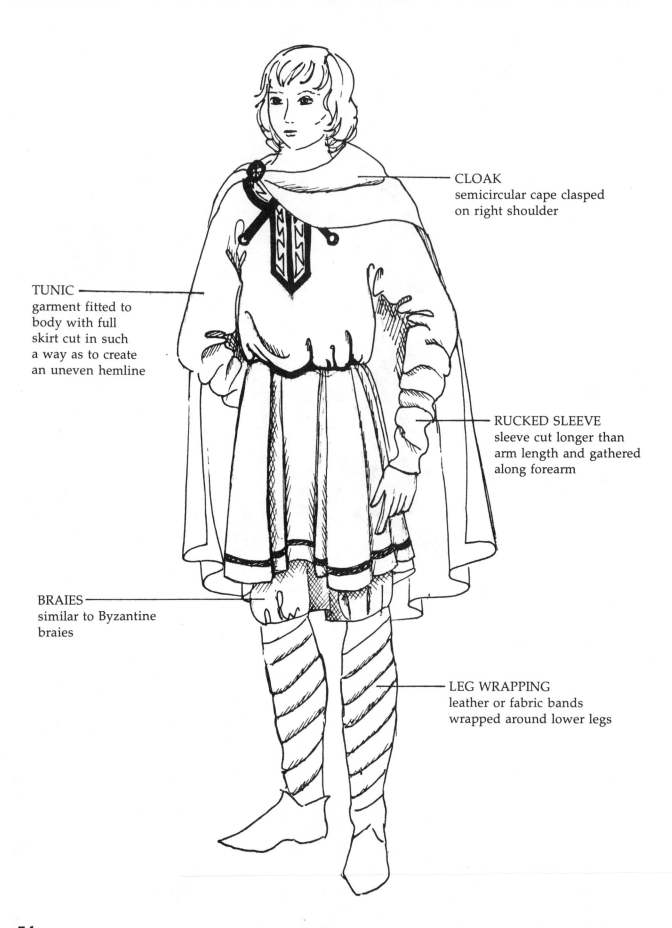

CLOAK
semicircular cape clasped
on right shoulder

TUNIC
garment fitted to
body with full
skirt cut in such
a way as to create
an uneven hemline

RUCKED SLEEVE
sleeve cut longer than
arm length and gathered
along forearm

BRAIES
similar to Byzantine
braies

LEG WRAPPING
leather or fabric bands
wrapped around lower legs

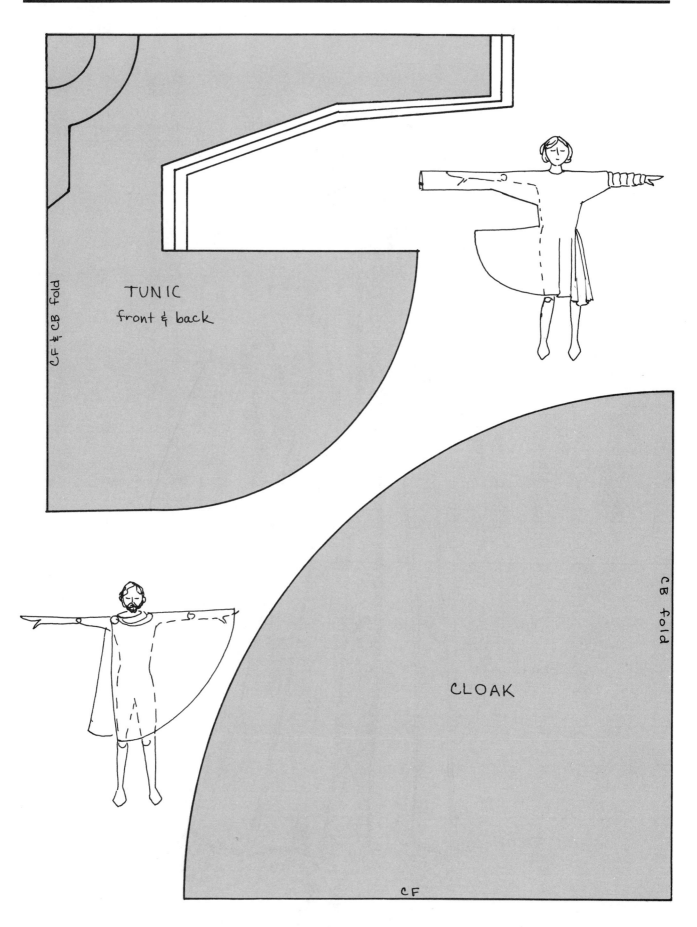

TUNIC
front & back

CF & CB fold

CLOAK

CB fold

CF

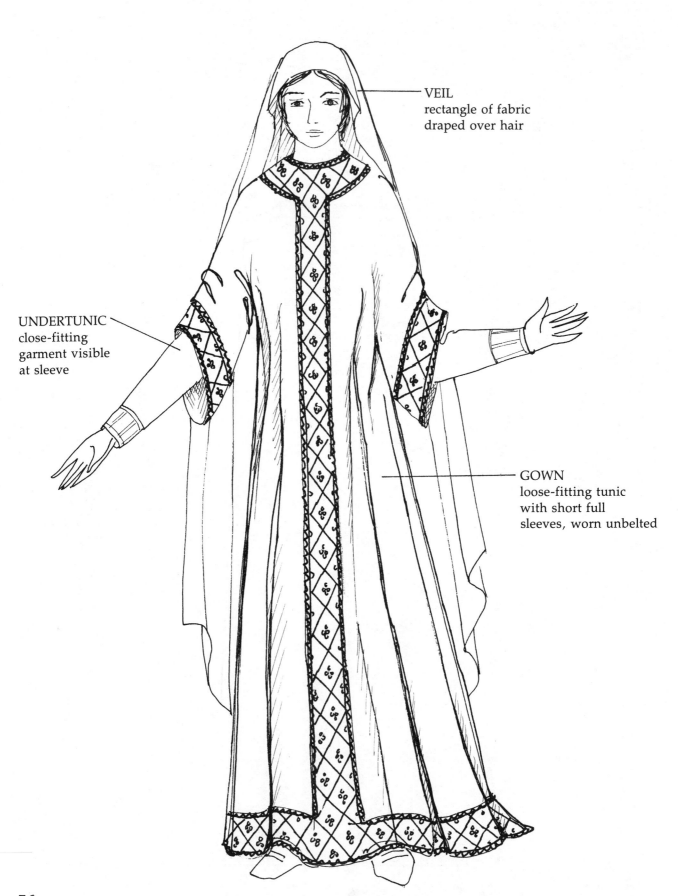

VEIL
rectangle of fabric
draped over hair

UNDERTUNIC
close-fitting
garment visible
at sleeve

GOWN
loose-fitting tunic
with short full
sleeves, worn unbelted

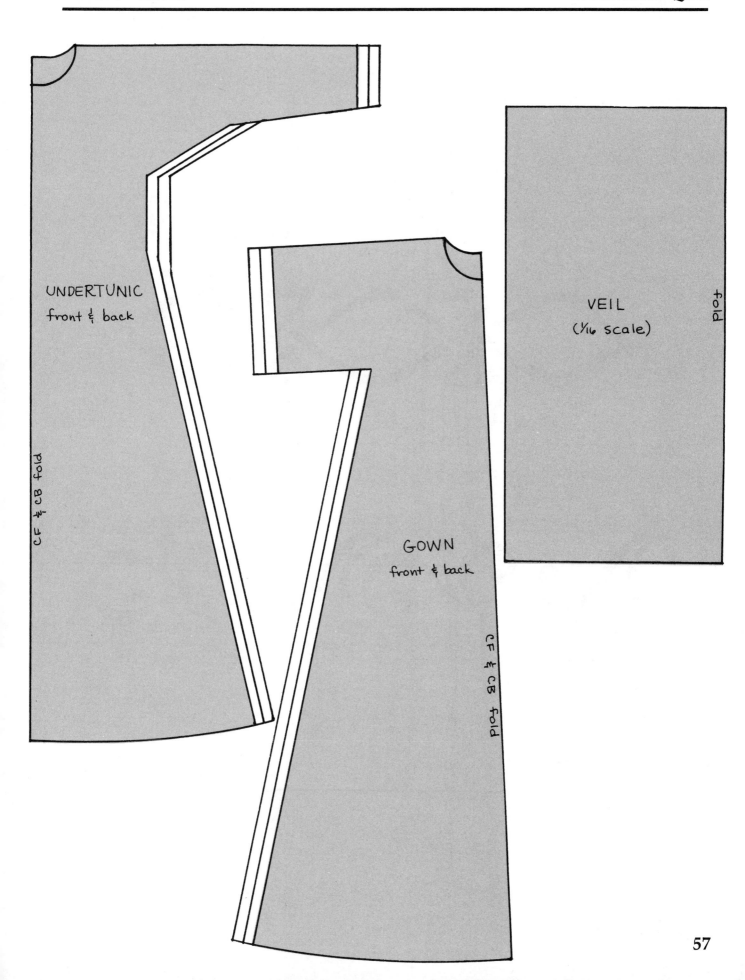

UNDERTUNIC
front & back

CF & CB fold

GOWN
front & back

CF & CB fold

VEIL
(¹⁄₁₆ scale)

fold

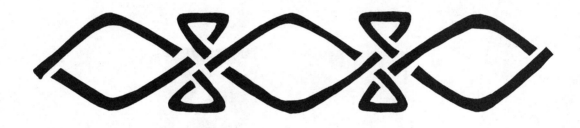

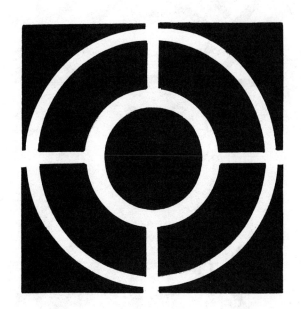

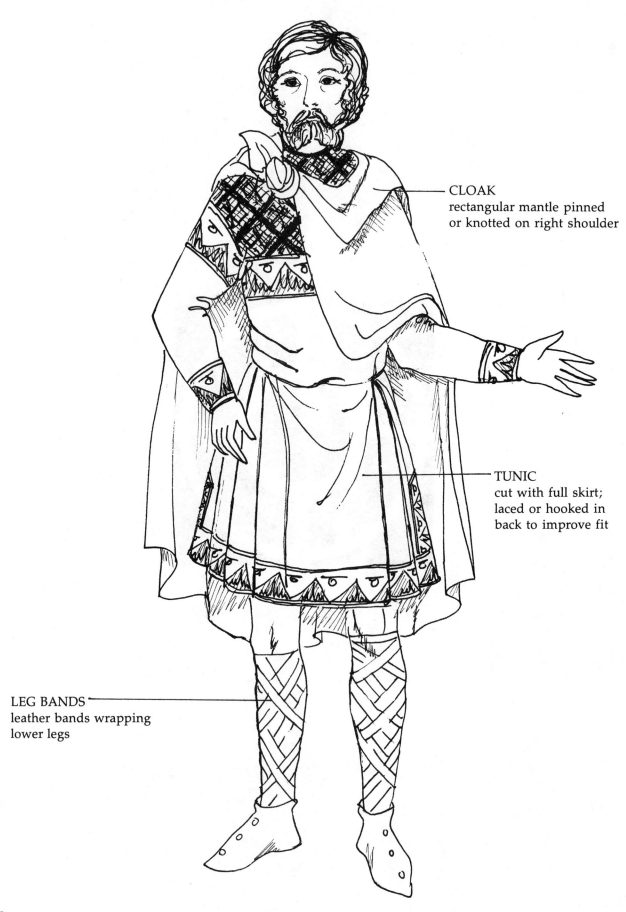

CLOAK
rectangular mantle pinned
or knotted on right shoulder

TUNIC
cut with full skirt;
laced or hooked in
back to improve fit

LEG BANDS
leather bands wrapping
lower legs

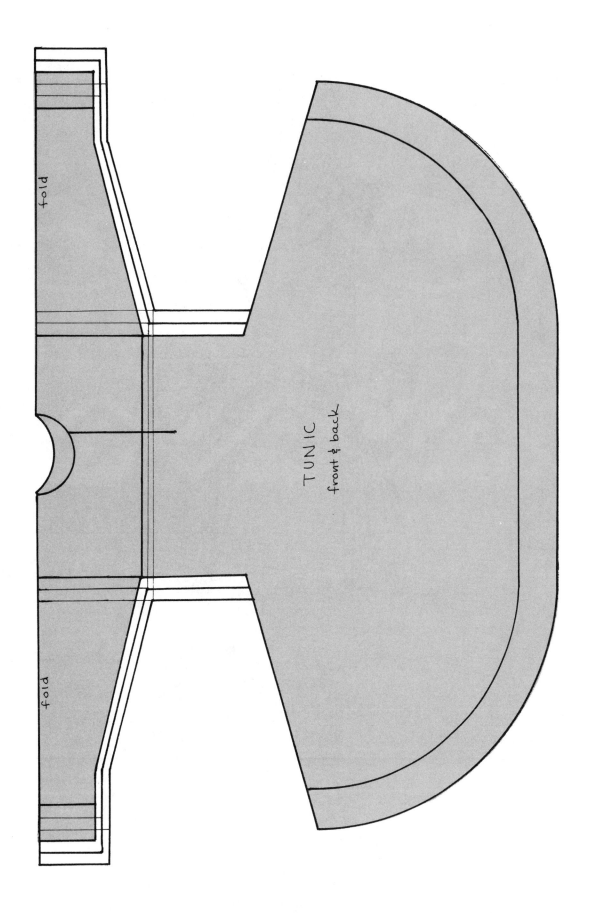

fold

fold

TUNIC
front & back

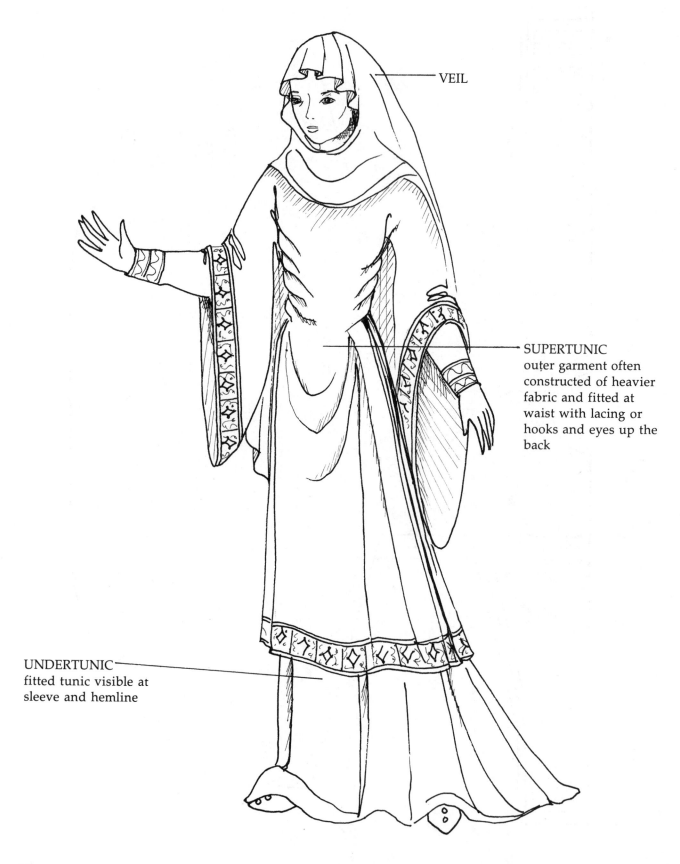

VEIL

SUPERTUNIC
outer garment often
constructed of heavier
fabric and fitted at
waist with lacing or
hooks and eyes up the
back

UNDERTUNIC
fitted tunic visible at
sleeve and hemline

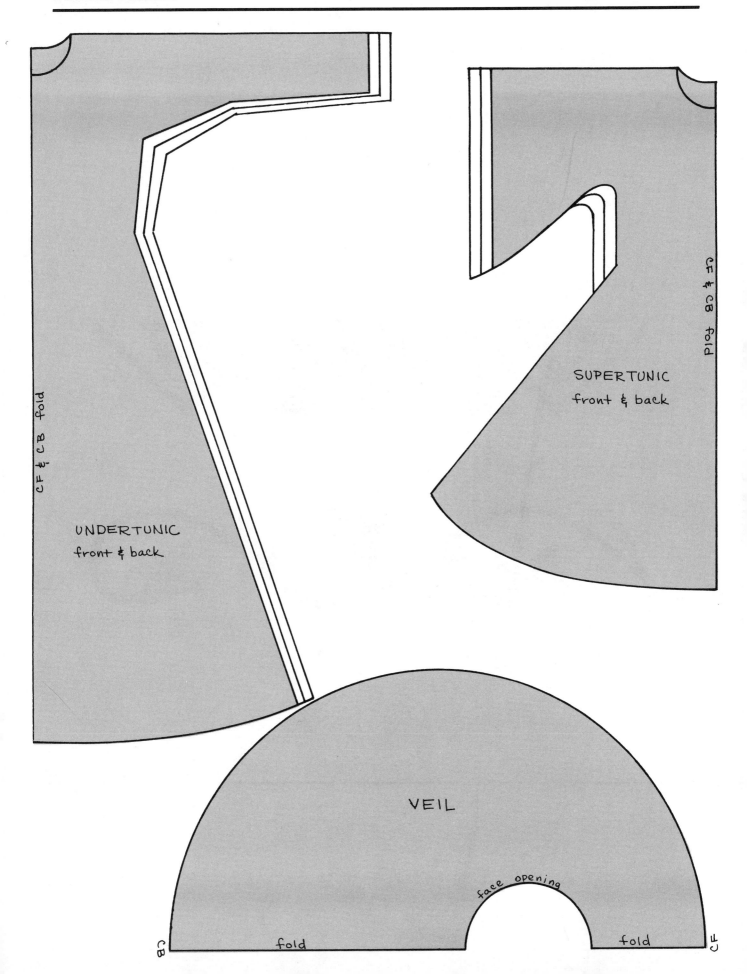

UNDERTUNIC
front & back

CF & CB fold

SUPERTUNIC
front & back

CF & CB fold

VEIL

face opening

CB   fold   fold   CF

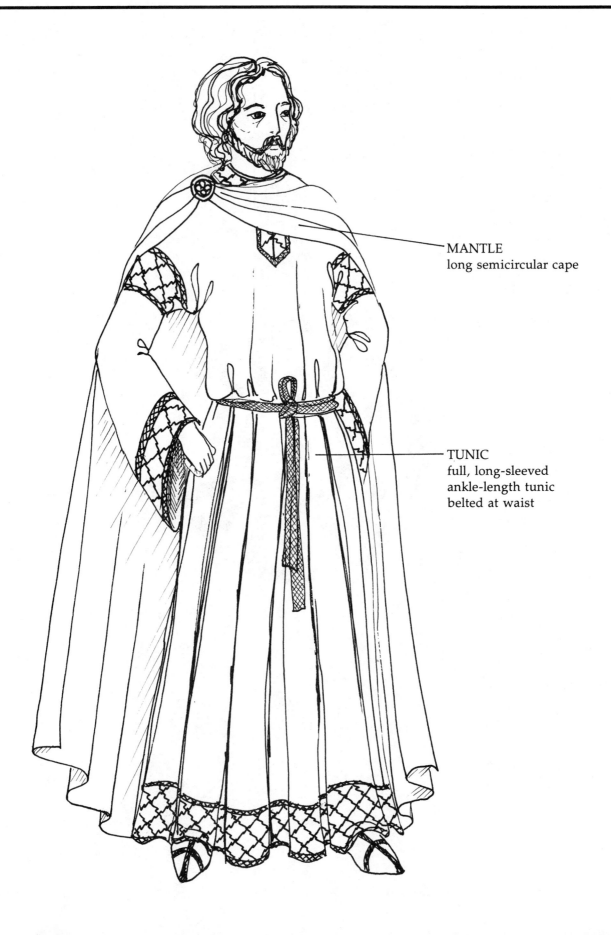

MANTLE
long semicircular cape

TUNIC
full, long-sleeved
ankle-length tunic
belted at waist

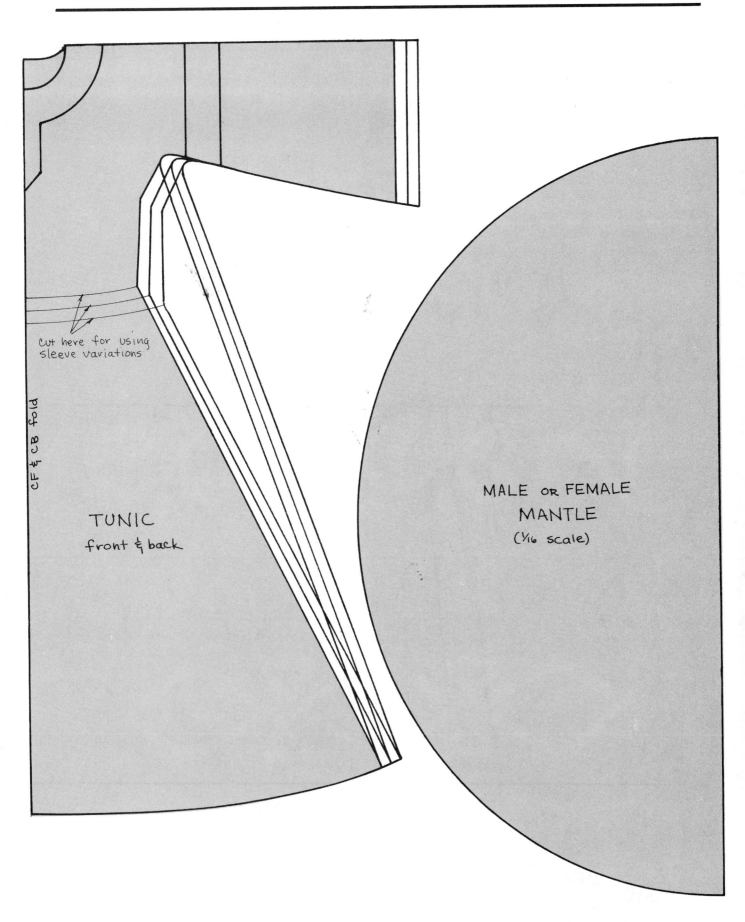

Cut here for using
sleeve variations

CF & CB fold

TUNIC
front & back

MALE OR FEMALE
MANTLE
(1/16 scale)

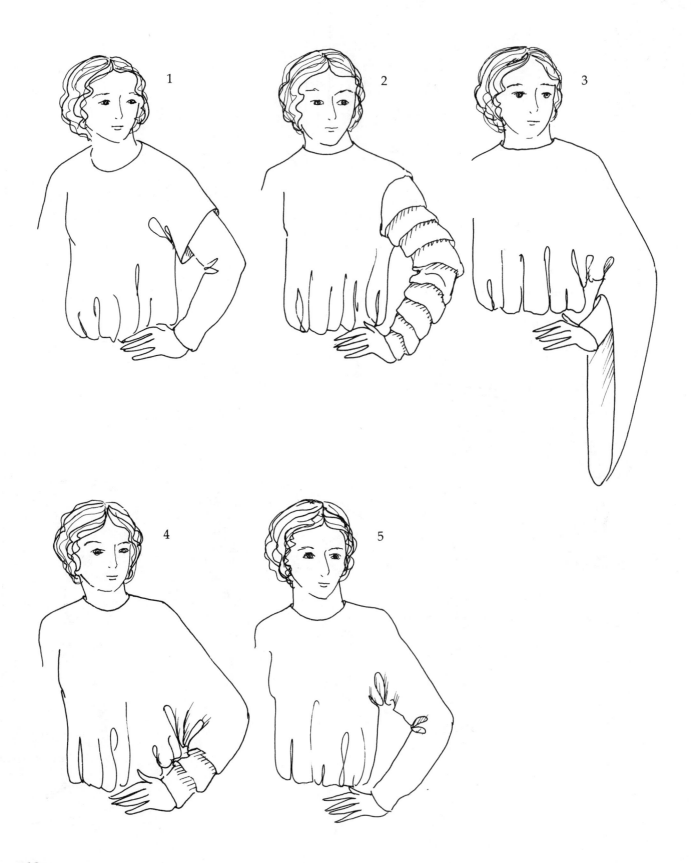

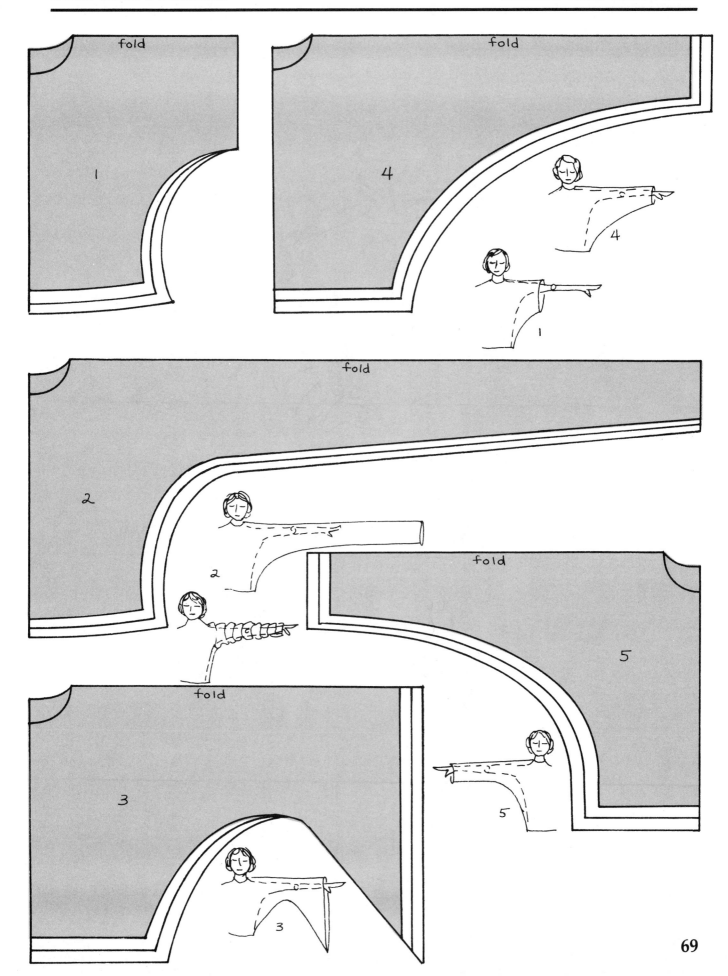

VEIL
long oval head covering,
sometimes wrapped around
neck and knotted to
control fullness and
for style

GOWN
cut long at hem and sleeve
length; sleeves sometimes
knotted to keep them from
dragging on the ground and
for style

MANTLE
semicircular
cape

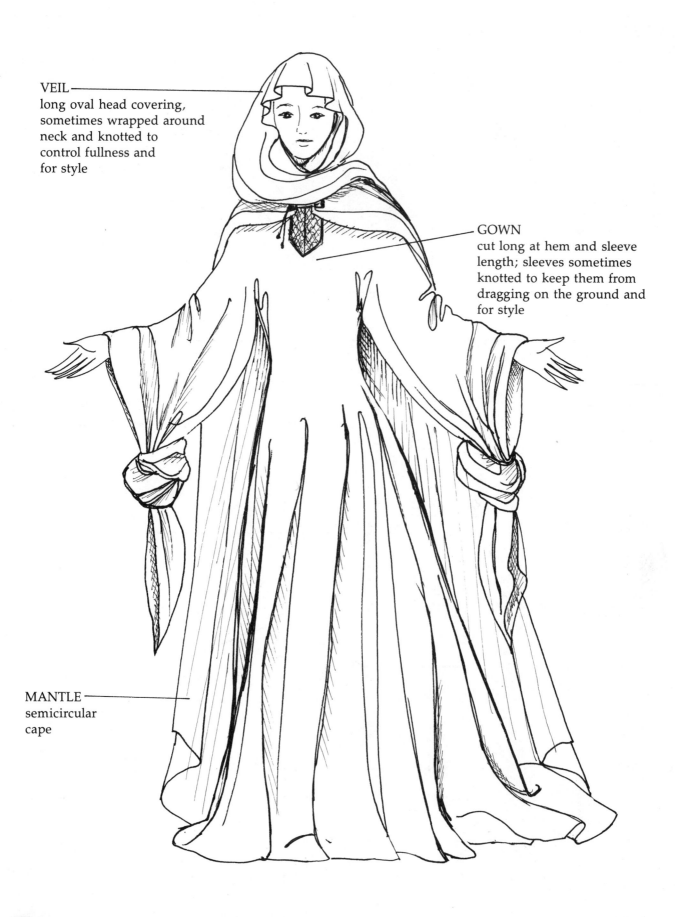

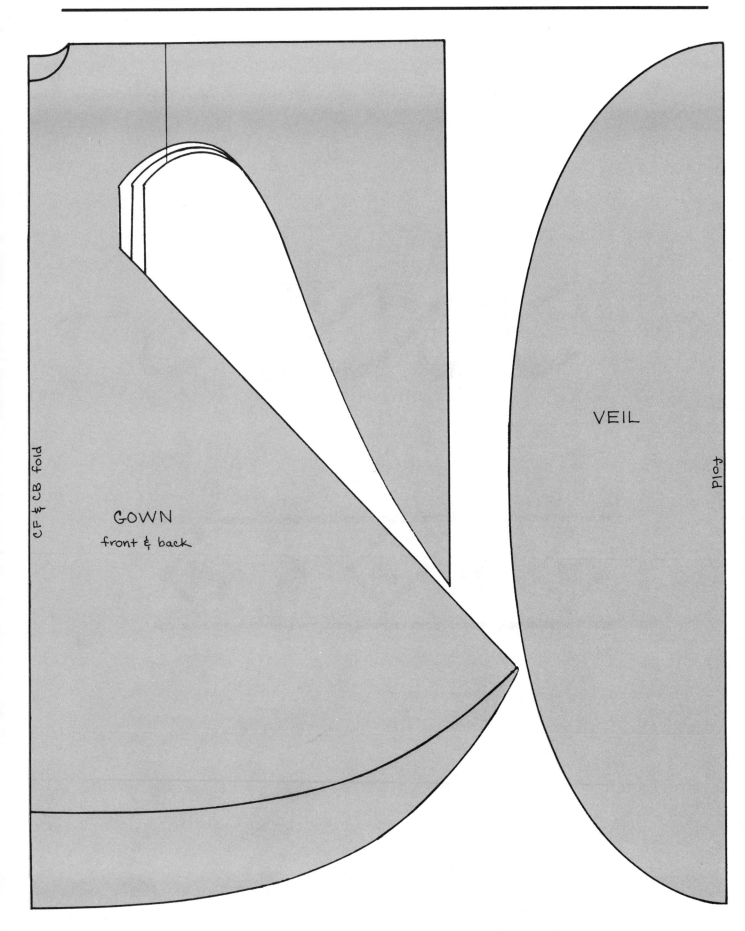

CF & CB fold

GOWN
front & back

VEIL

fold

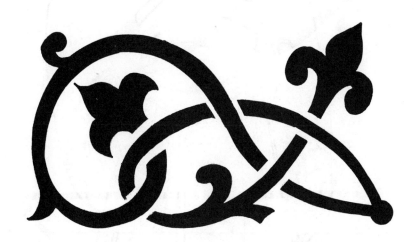

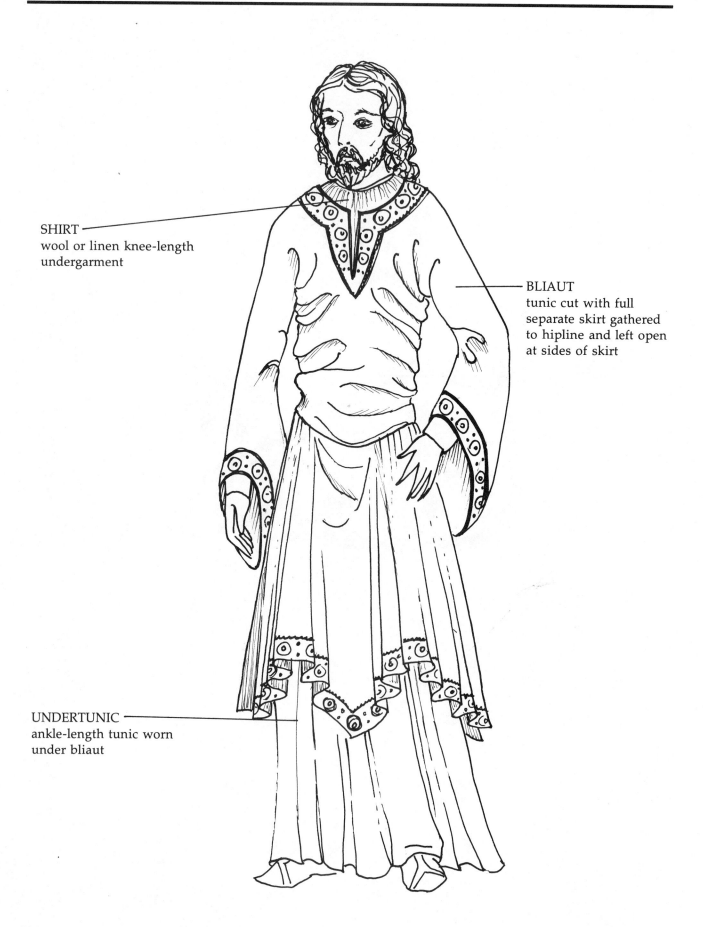

SHIRT
wool or linen knee-length
undergarment

BLIAUT
tunic cut with full
separate skirt gathered
to hipline and left open
at sides of skirt

UNDERTUNIC
ankle-length tunic worn
under bliaut

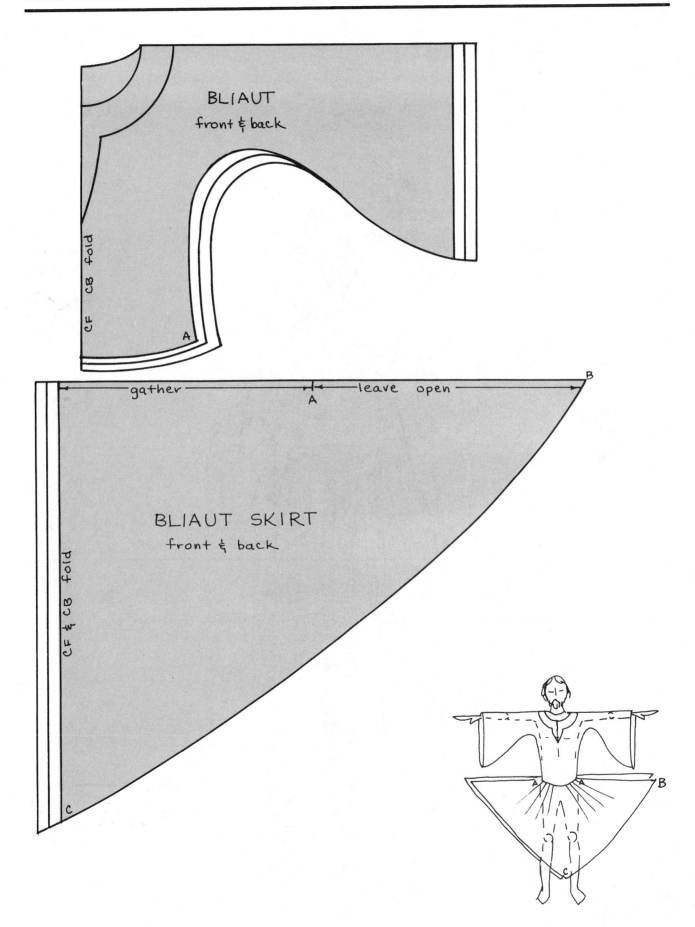

BLIAUT
front & back

CF CB fold

A

gather   A   leave open   B

BLIAUT SKIRT
front & back

CF & CB fold

C

A   A   B

C

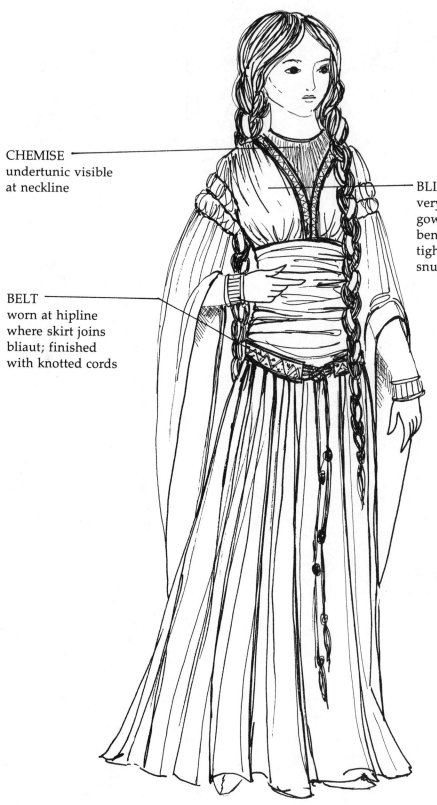

CHEMISE
undertunic visible
at neckline

BLIAUT
very full, intricately pleated
gown constructed with a corset
beneath or girdle above to
tighten midriff area into a
snug fit

BELT
worn at hipline
where skirt joins
bliaut; finished
with knotted cords

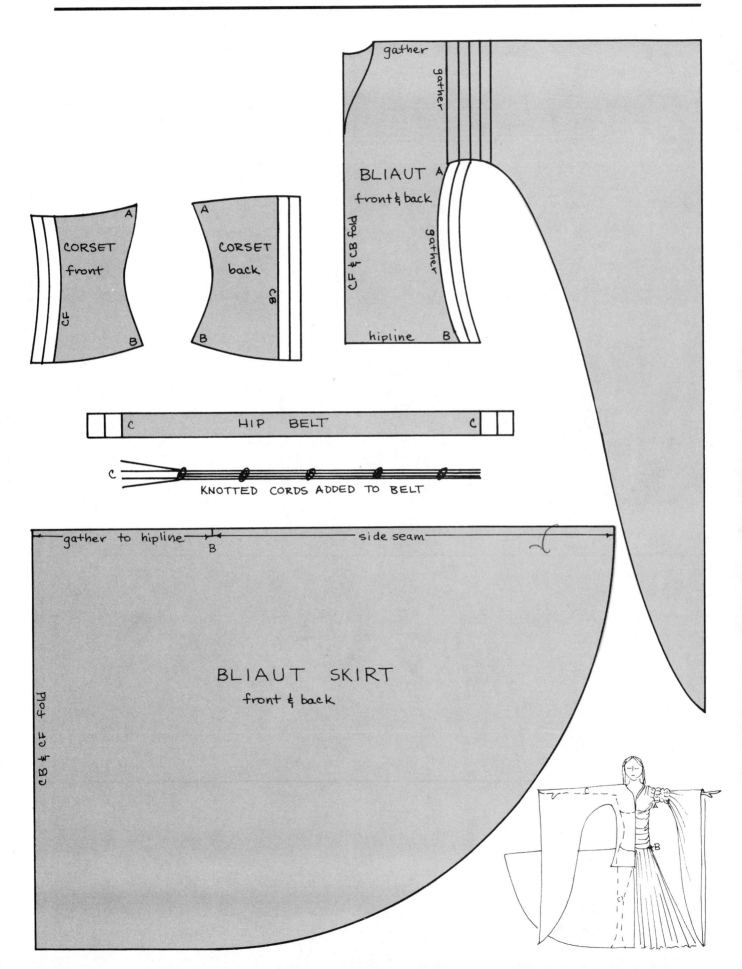

gather

gather

BLIAUT A

front & back

CF & CB fold

gather

hipline

B

A

CORSET

front

CF

B

A

CORSET

back

CB

B

C   HIP   BELT   C

C

KNOTTED CORDS ADDED TO BELT

gather to hipline   B   side seam

CB & CF fold

BLIAUT   SKIRT

front & back

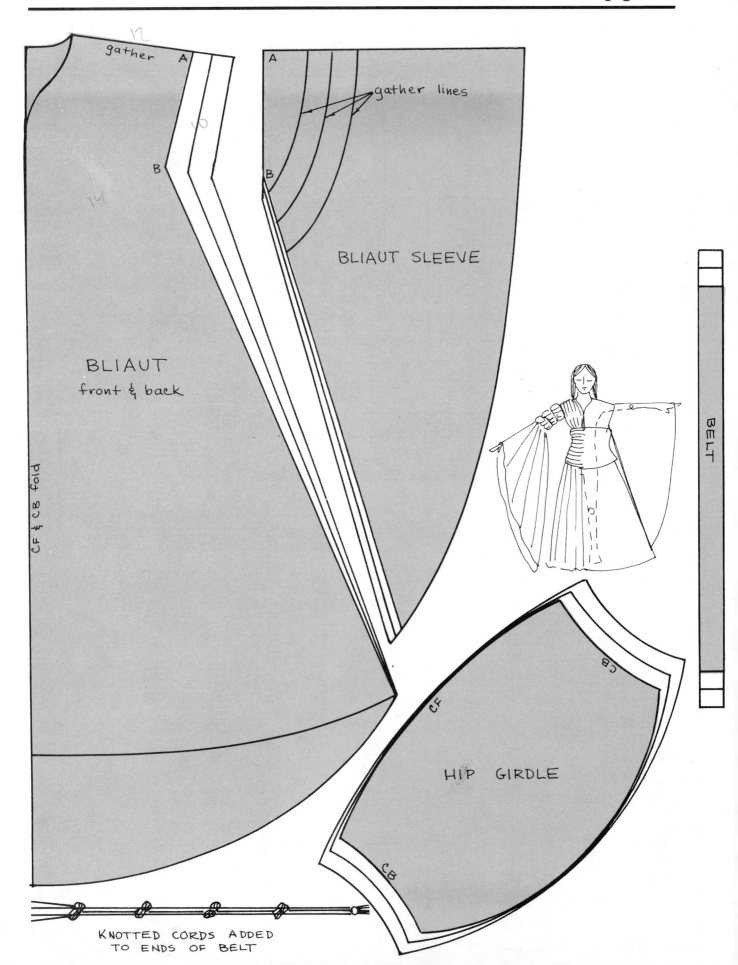

gather

A

B

BLIAUT
front & back

CF & CB fold

A

B

gather lines

BLIAUT SLEEVE

BELT

CF

CB

HIP GIRDLE

KNOTTED CORDS ADDED
TO ENDS OF BELT

ORIENTAL SURCOAT
Persian coat made of light
material; worn over bliaut
as an outer wrap

FULL DRESS BLIAUT
including double wrapped
belt, veil, and headband

CORSAGE
tight-fitting vest laced
up the back; worn over
bliaut

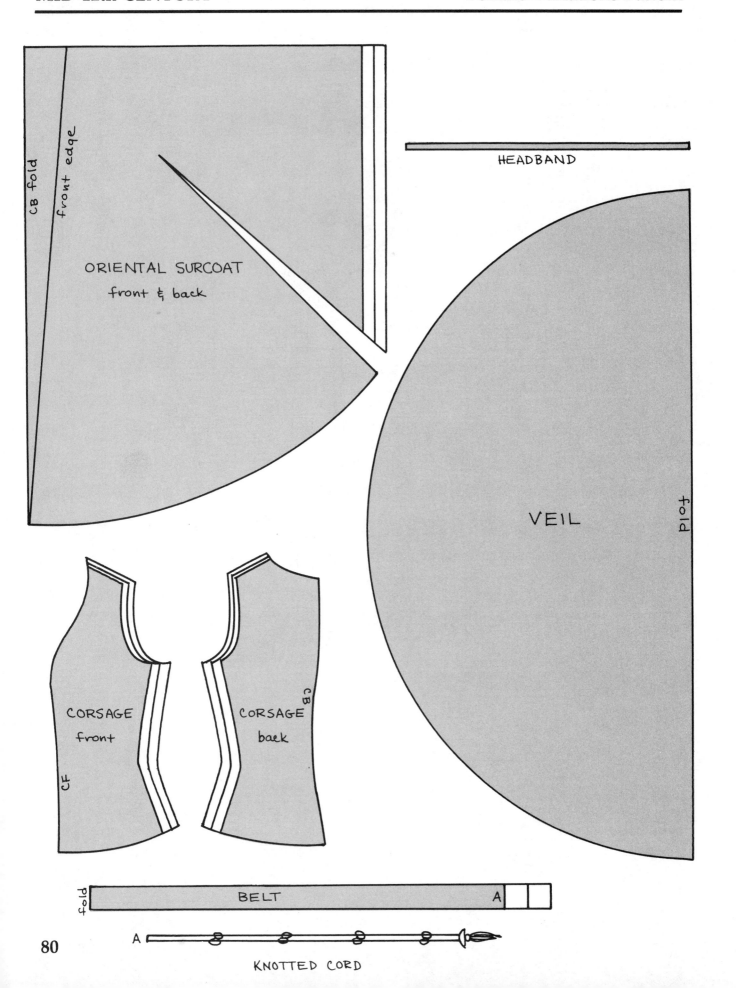

HEADBAND

CB fold

front edge

ORIENTAL SURCOAT
front & back

VEIL

fold

CORSAGE
front

CF

CORSAGE
back

CB

fold

BELT

A

A

KNOTTED CORD

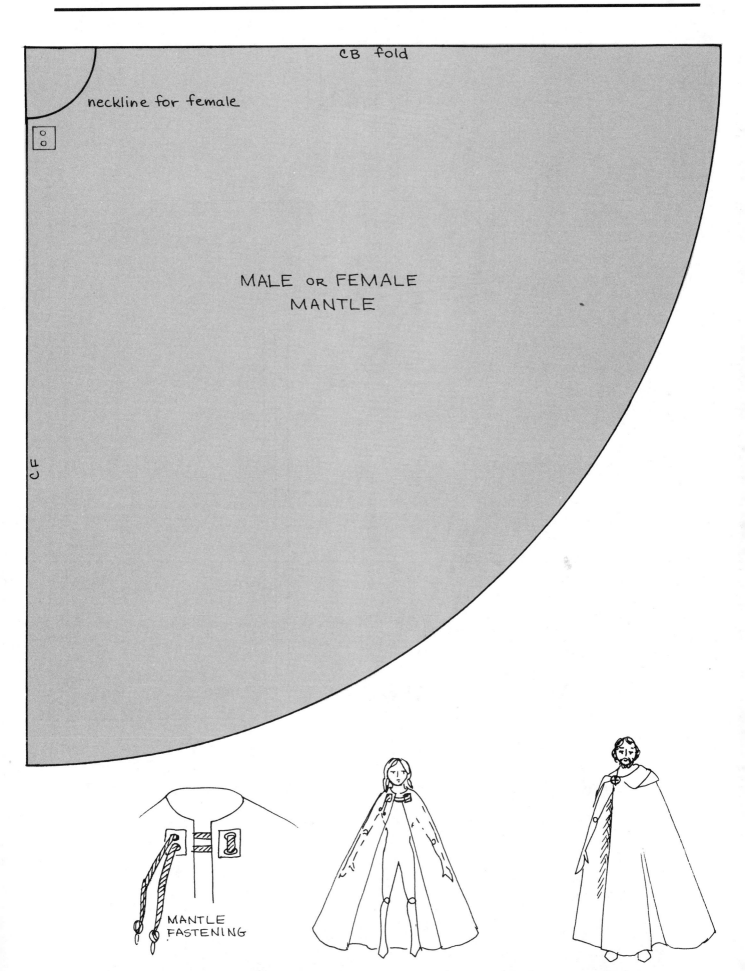

CB fold

neckline for female

CF

MALE or FEMALE MANTLE

MANTLE FASTENING

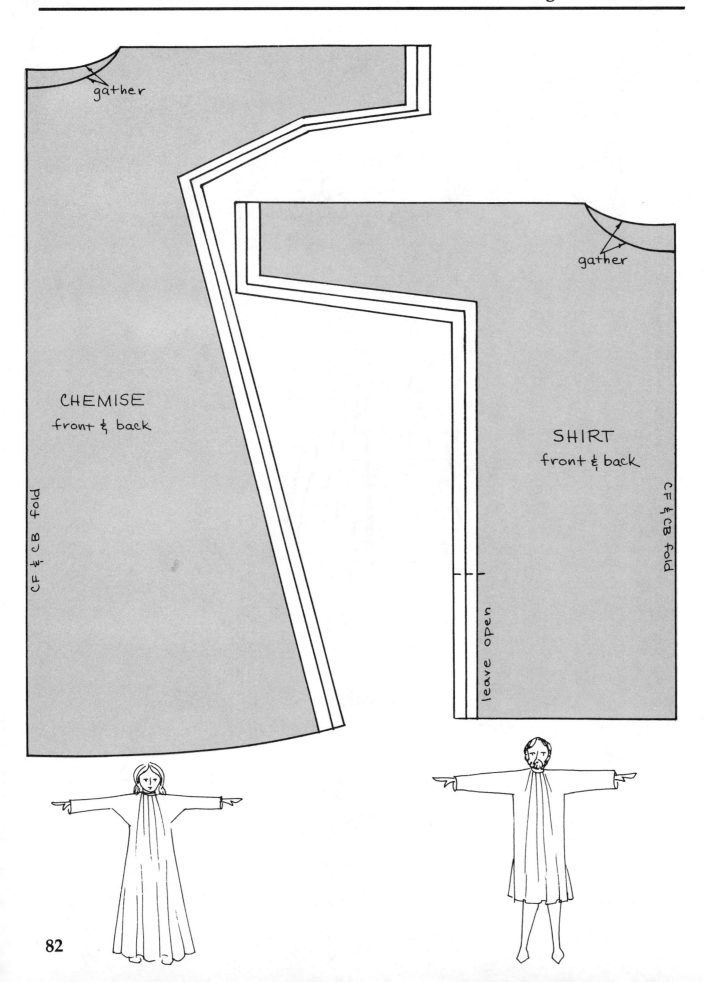

gather

CHEMISE
front & back

CF & CB fold

SHIRT
front & back

gather

CF & CB fold

leave open

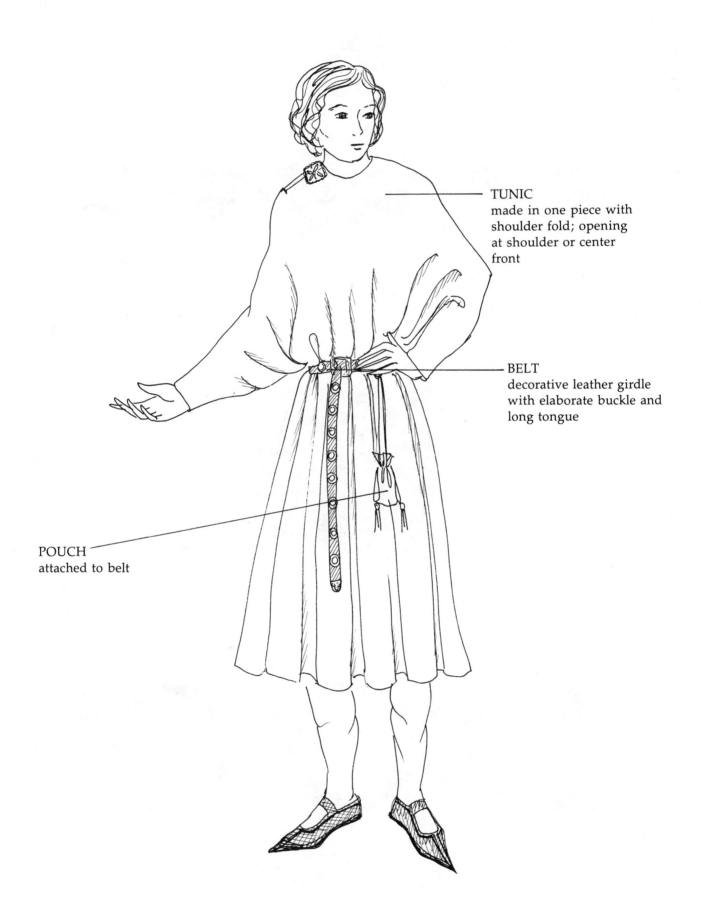

TUNIC
made in one piece with
shoulder fold; opening
at shoulder or center
front

BELT
decorative leather girdle
with elaborate buckle and
long tongue

POUCH
attached to belt

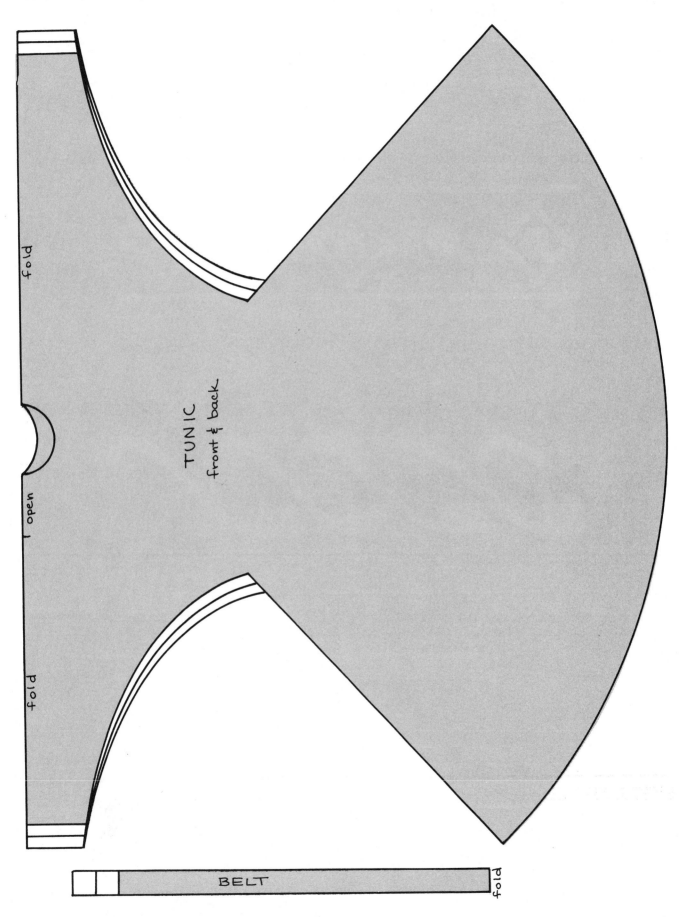

fold

fold

open

TUNIC
front & back

fold

fold

BELT

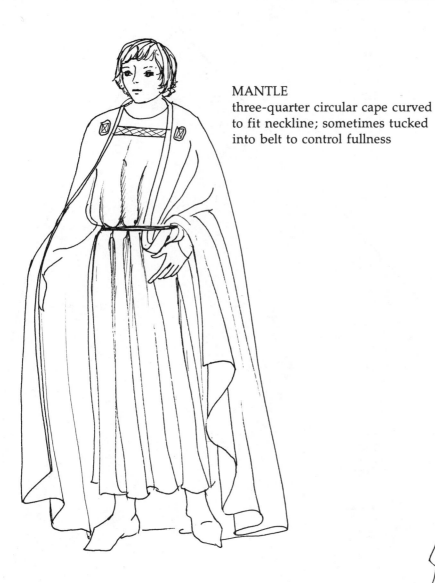

MANTLE
three-quarter circular cape curved
to fit neckline; sometimes tucked
into belt to control fullness

HOOD
with attached cape collar
fastened under the chin

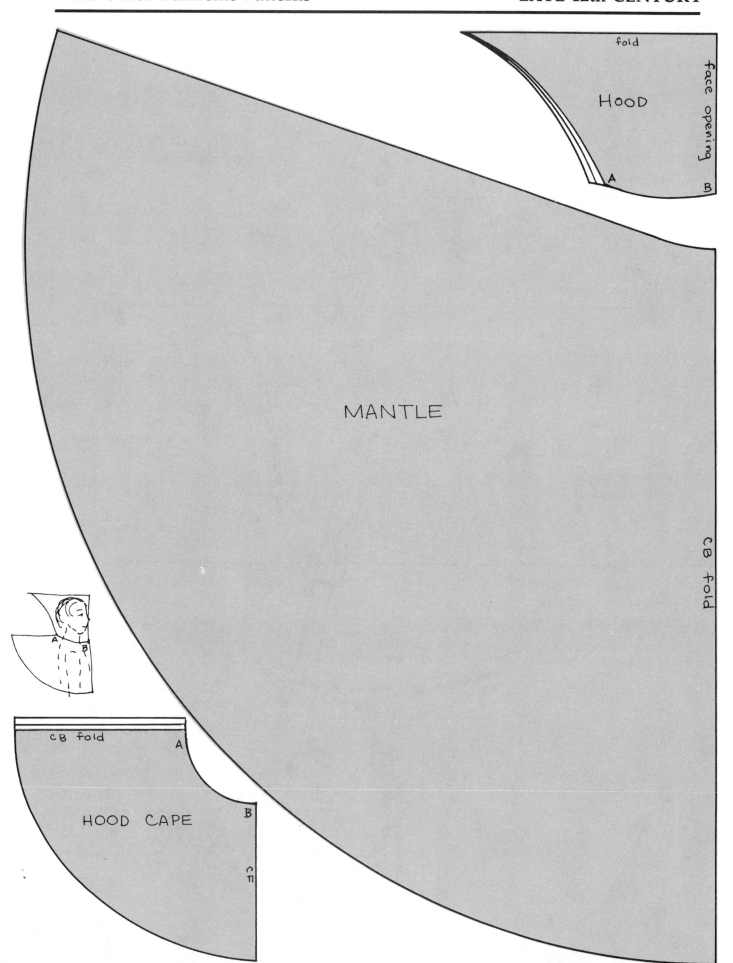

HOOD

fold

face opening

A

B

MANTLE

CB fold

CB fold

A

B

HOOD CAPE

C

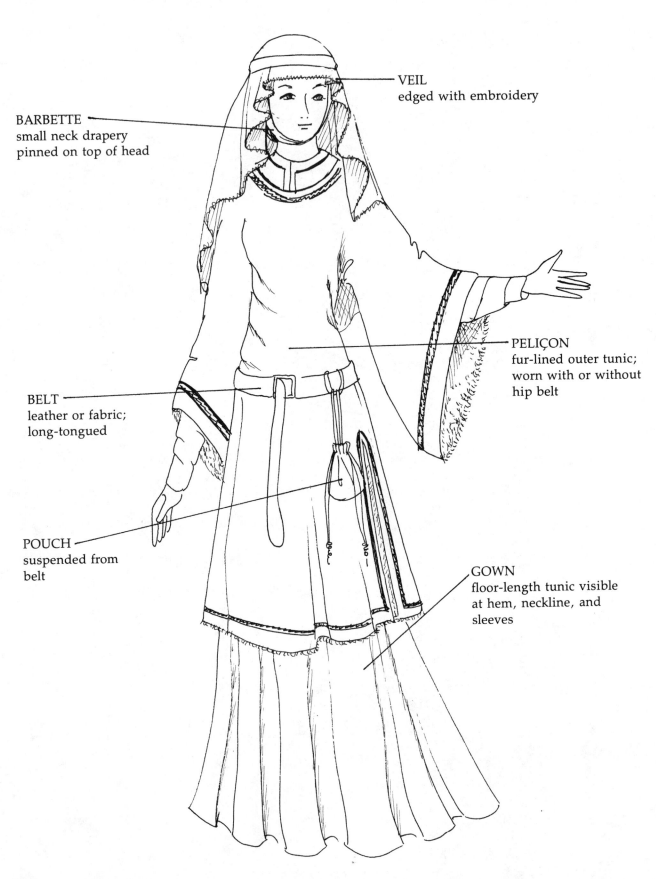

BARBETTE
small neck drapery
pinned on top of head

VEIL
edged with embroidery

PELIÇON
fur-lined outer tunic;
worn with or without
hip belt

BELT
leather or fabric;
long-tongued

POUCH
suspended from
belt

GOWN
floor-length tunic visible
at hem, neckline, and
sleeves

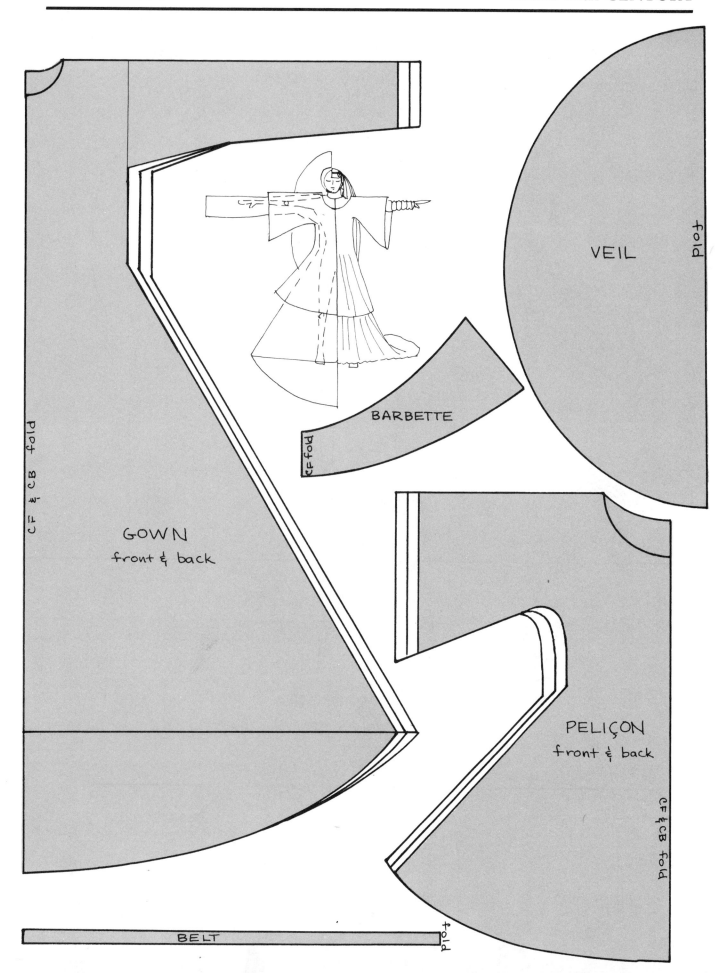

VEIL

fold

BARBETTE

CF fold

GOWN
front & back

CF & CB fold

PELIÇON
front & back

CF & CB fold

BELT

fold

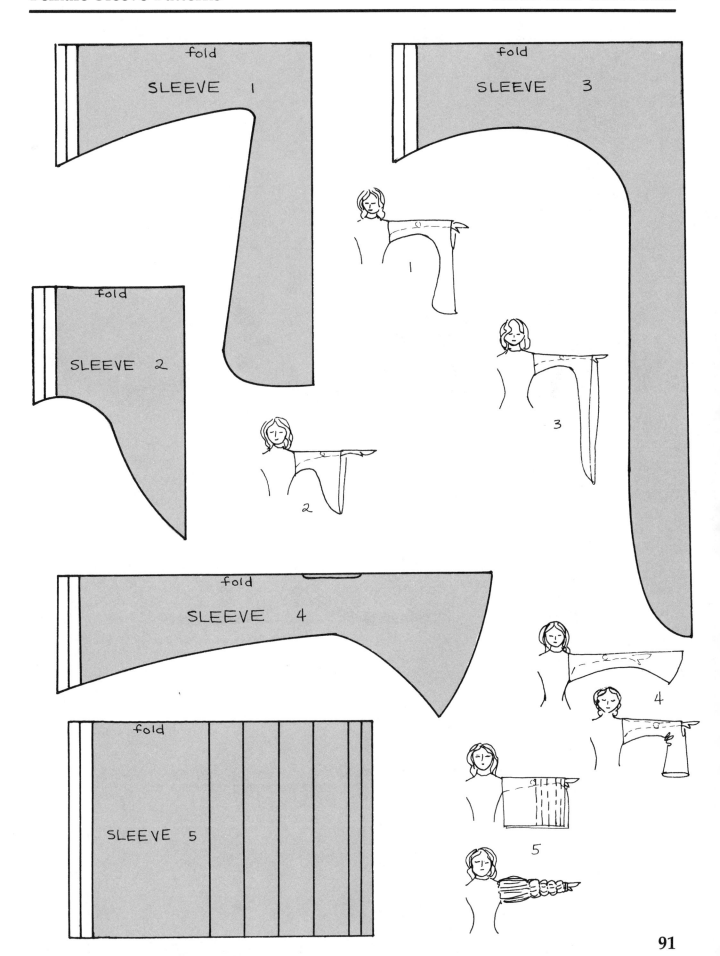

fold

SLEEVE 1

fold

SLEEVE 3

fold

SLEEVE 2

fold

SLEEVE 4

fold

SLEEVE 5

1

2

3

4

5

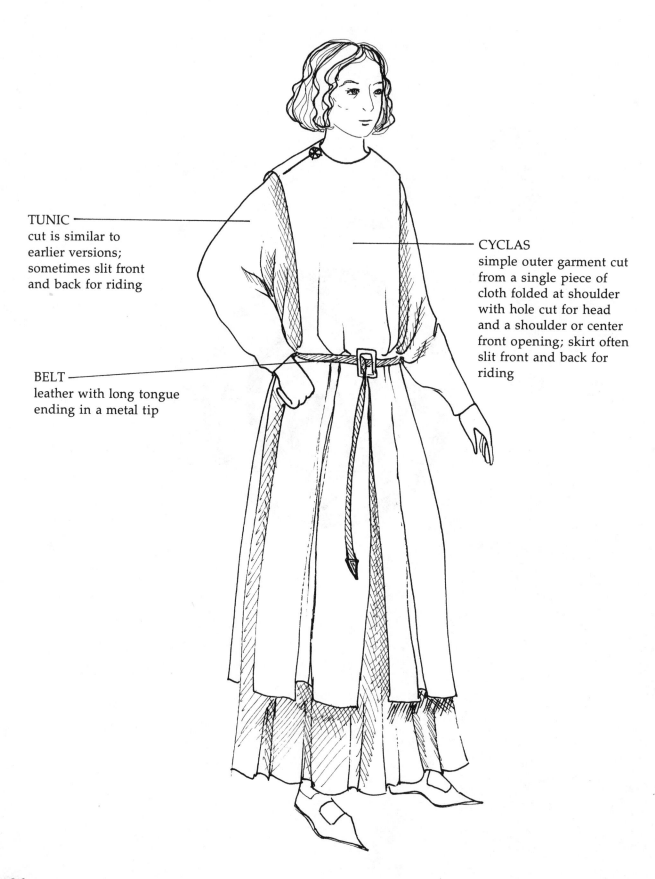

TUNIC
cut is similar to
earlier versions;
sometimes slit front
and back for riding

BELT
leather with long tongue
ending in a metal tip

CYCLAS
simple outer garment cut
from a single piece of
cloth folded at shoulder
with hole cut for head
and a shoulder or center
front opening; skirt often
slit front and back for
riding

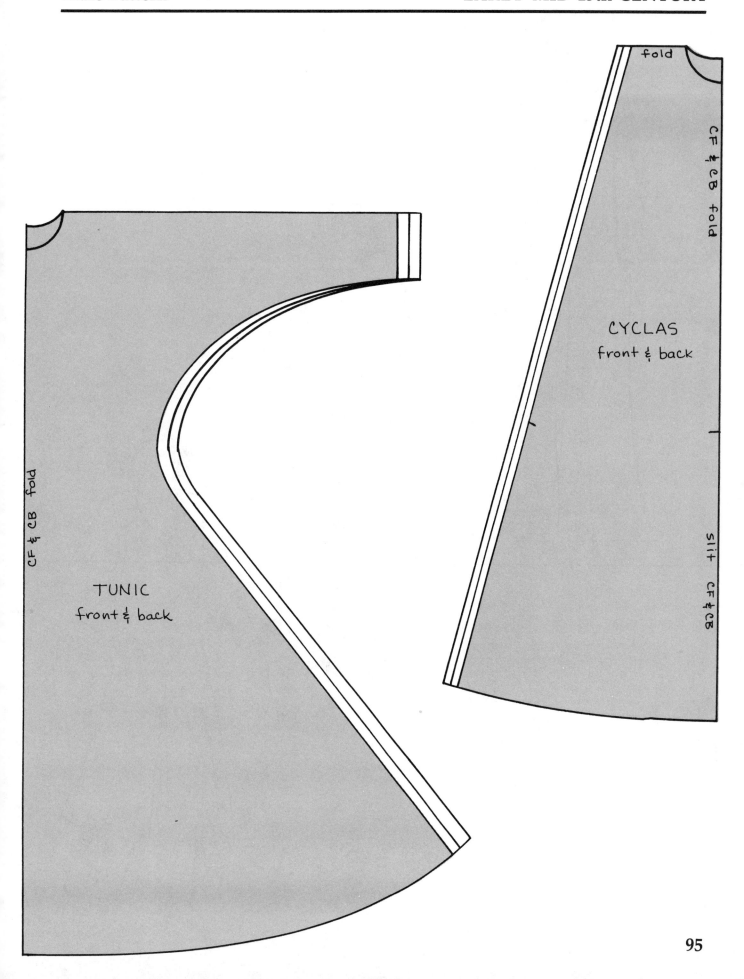

fold

CF & CB fold

CYCLAS
front & back

slit CF & CB

CF & CB fold

TUNIC
front & back

1

2

3

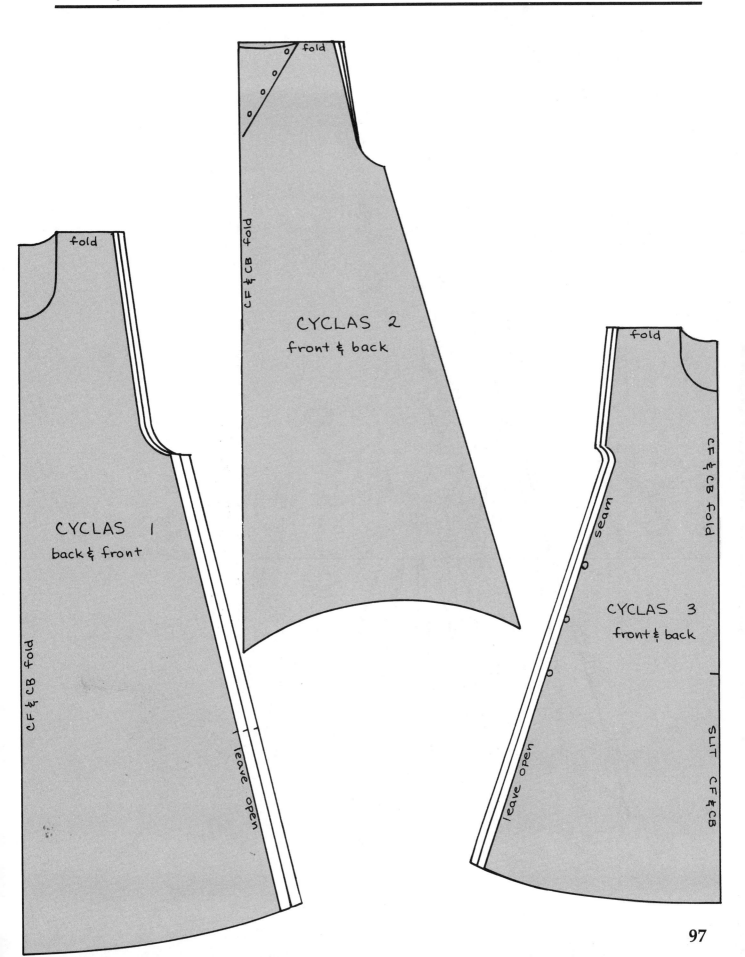

CYCLAS 2
front & back

CF & CB fold

fold

CYCLAS 1
back & front

CF & CB fold

fold

leave open

CYCLAS 3
front & back

fold

CF & CB fold

seam

leave open

SLIT CF & CB

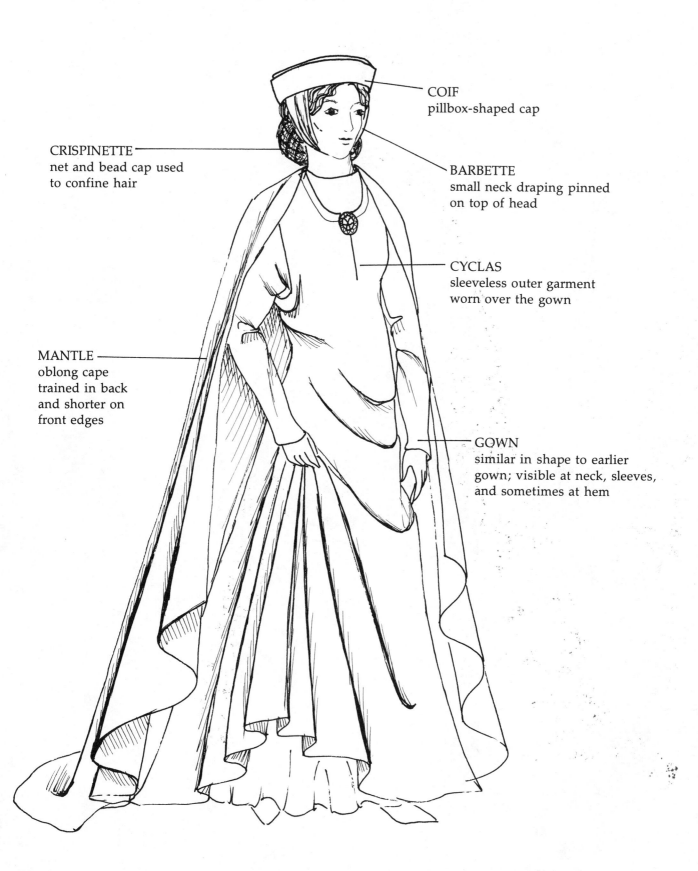

CRISPINETTE
net and bead cap used
to confine hair

MANTLE
oblong cape
trained in back
and shorter on
front edges

COIF
pillbox-shaped cap

BARBETTE
small neck draping pinned
on top of head

CYCLAS
sleeveless outer garment
worn over the gown

GOWN
similar in shape to earlier
gown; visible at neck, sleeves,
and sometimes at hem

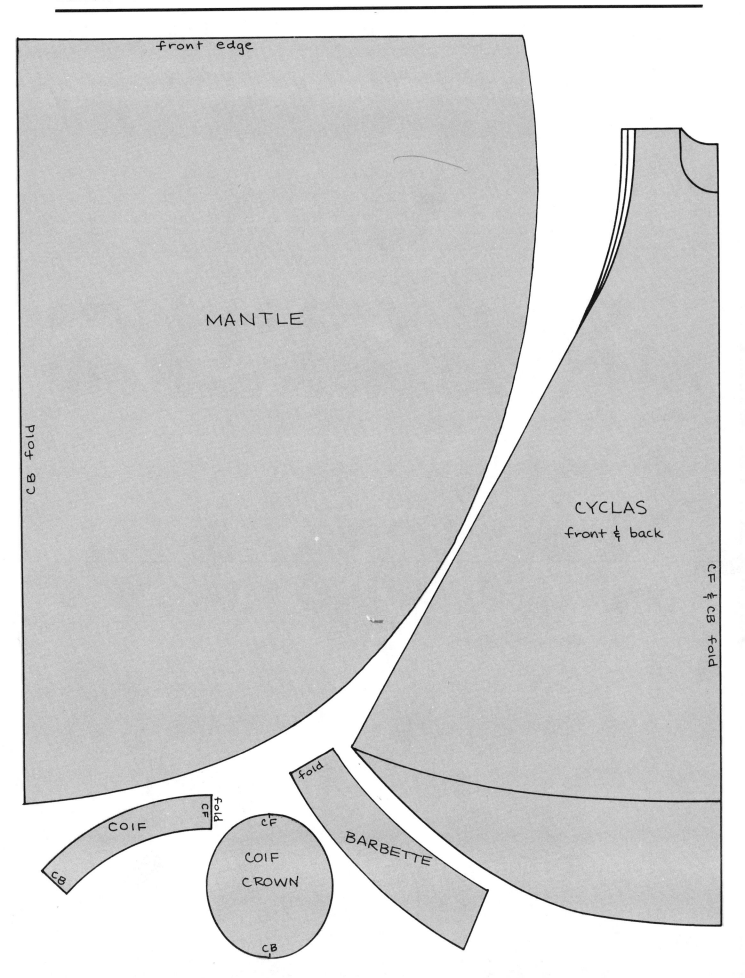

front edge

MANTLE

CB fold

CYCLAS

front & back

CF & CB fold

COIF

fold

CF

CB

COIF CROWN

CF

CB

fold

BARBETTE

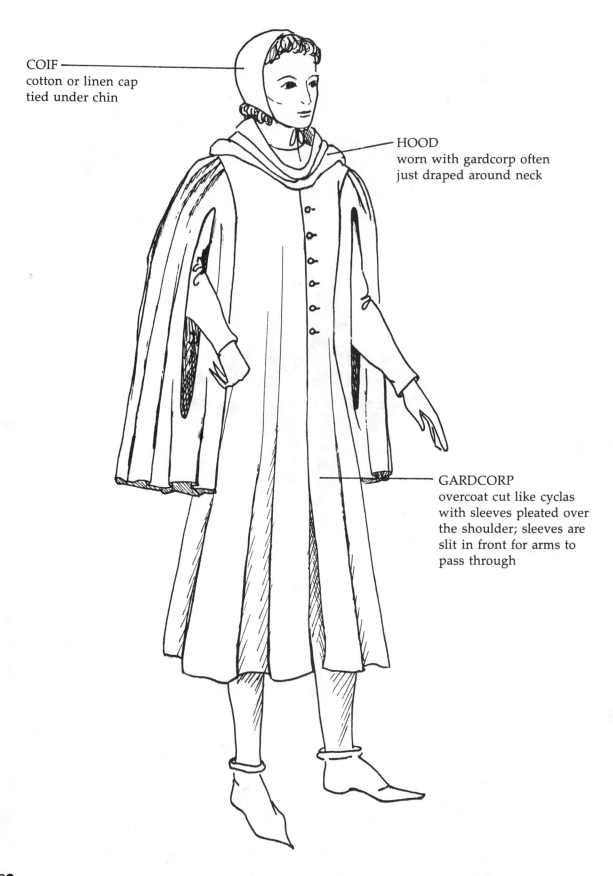

COIF
cotton or linen cap
tied under chin

HOOD
worn with gardcorp often
just draped around neck

GARDCORP
overcoat cut like cyclas
with sleeves pleated over
the shoulder; sleeves are
slit in front for arms to
pass through

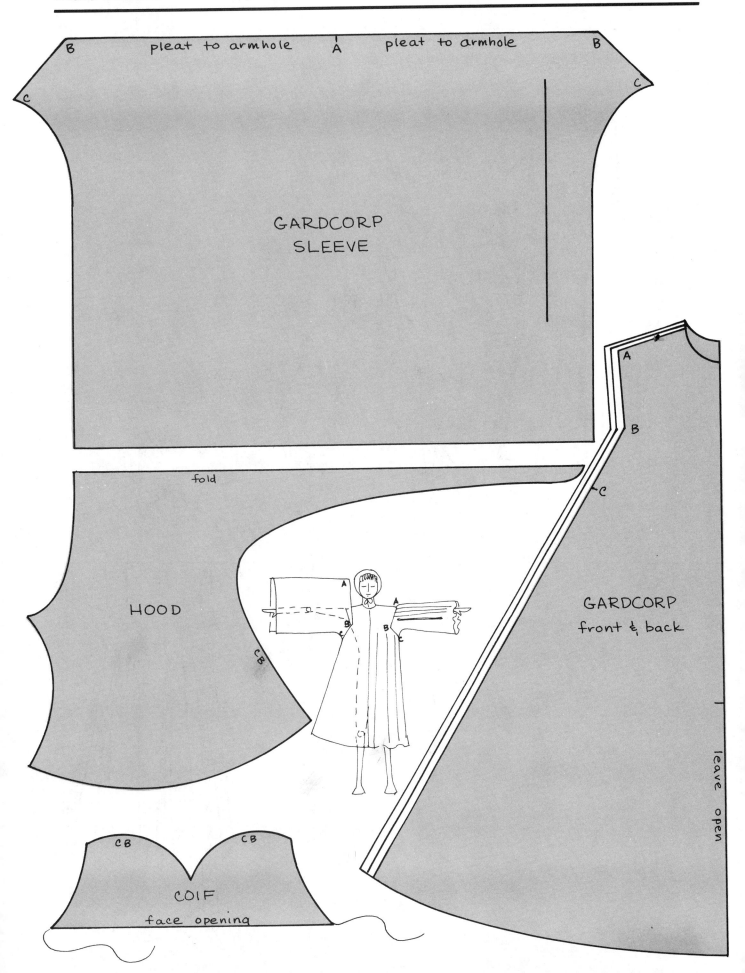

B   pleat to armhole   A   pleat to armhole   B

C

C

GARDCORP
SLEEVE

A

B

C

fold

HOOD

GARDCORP
front & back

A

B

C

CB

leave open

CB   CB

COIF

face opening

1

SURCOAT

2

SURCOAT

3

GANACHE
overcoat with
attached hood

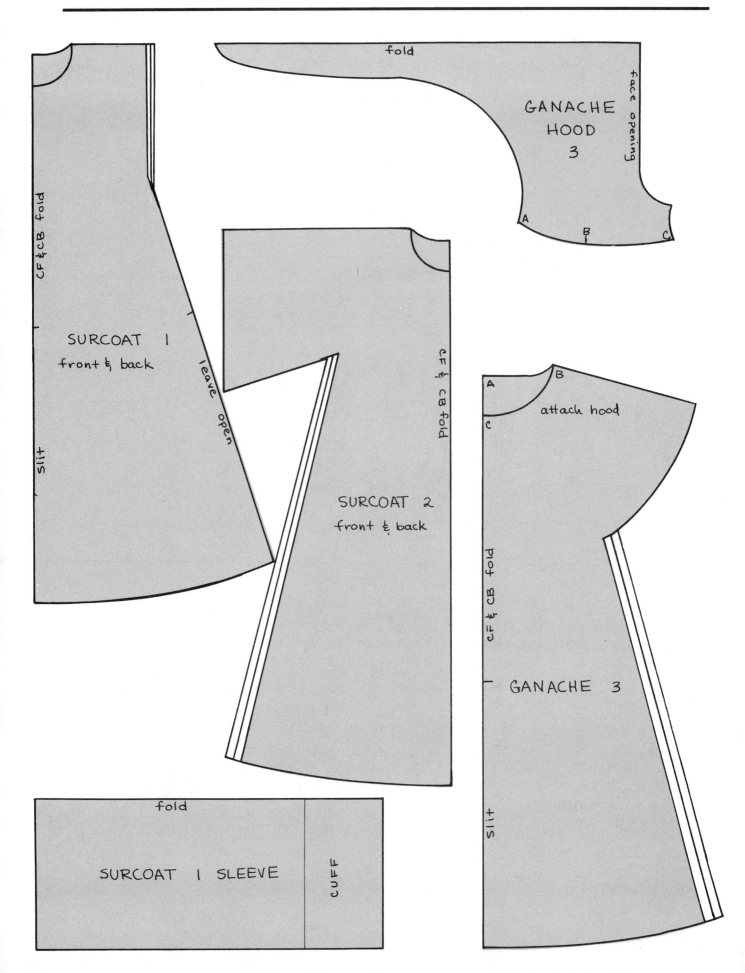

fold

GANACHE
HOOD
3

face opening

A　　B　　C

CF & CB fold

SURCOAT 1
front & back

slit

leave open

SURCOAT 2
front & back

CF & CB fold

A　　B
c
attach hood

CF & CB fold

GANACHE 3

slit

fold

SURCOAT 1 SLEEVE

CUFF

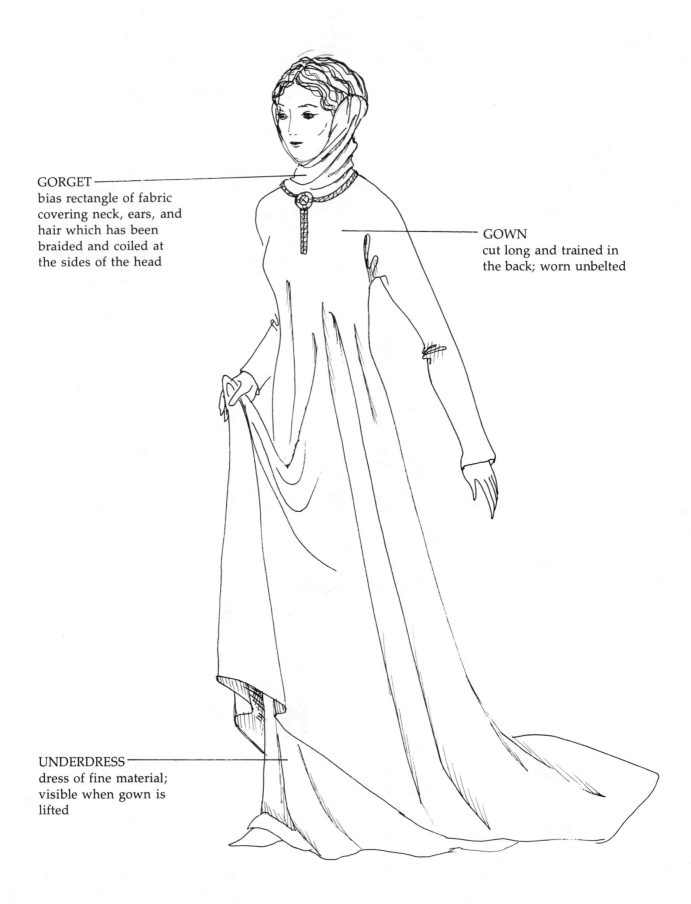

GORGET
bias rectangle of fabric
covering neck, ears, and
hair which has been
braided and coiled at
the sides of the head

GOWN
cut long and trained in
the back; worn unbelted

UNDERDRESS
dress of fine material;
visible when gown is
lifted

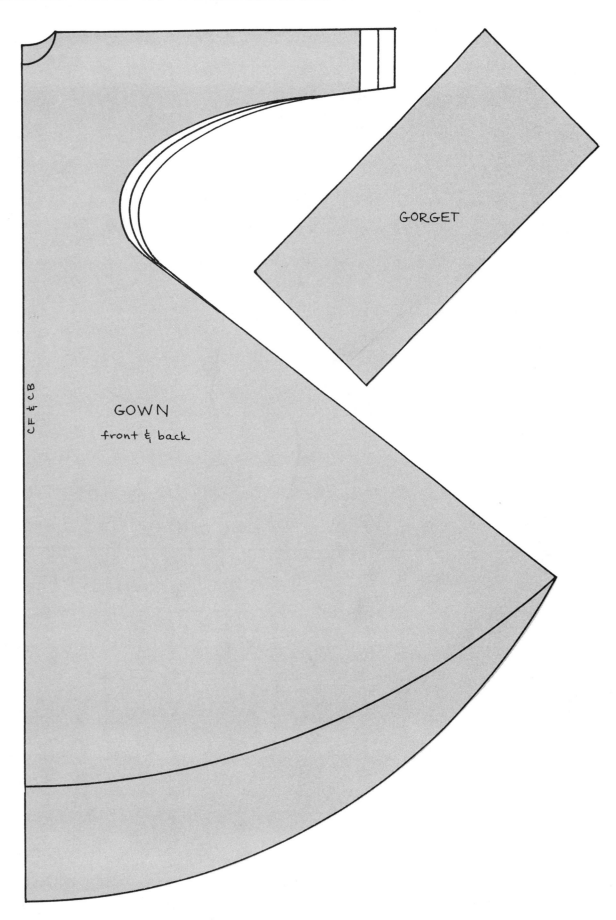

GORGET

GOWN
front & back

CF & CB

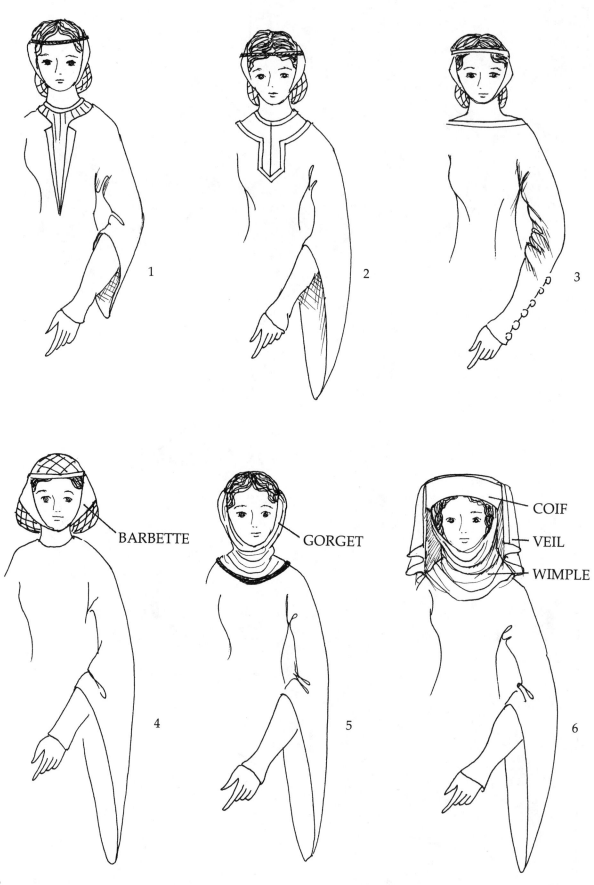

1

2

3

BARBETTE

GORGET

COIF

VEIL

WIMPLE

4

5

6

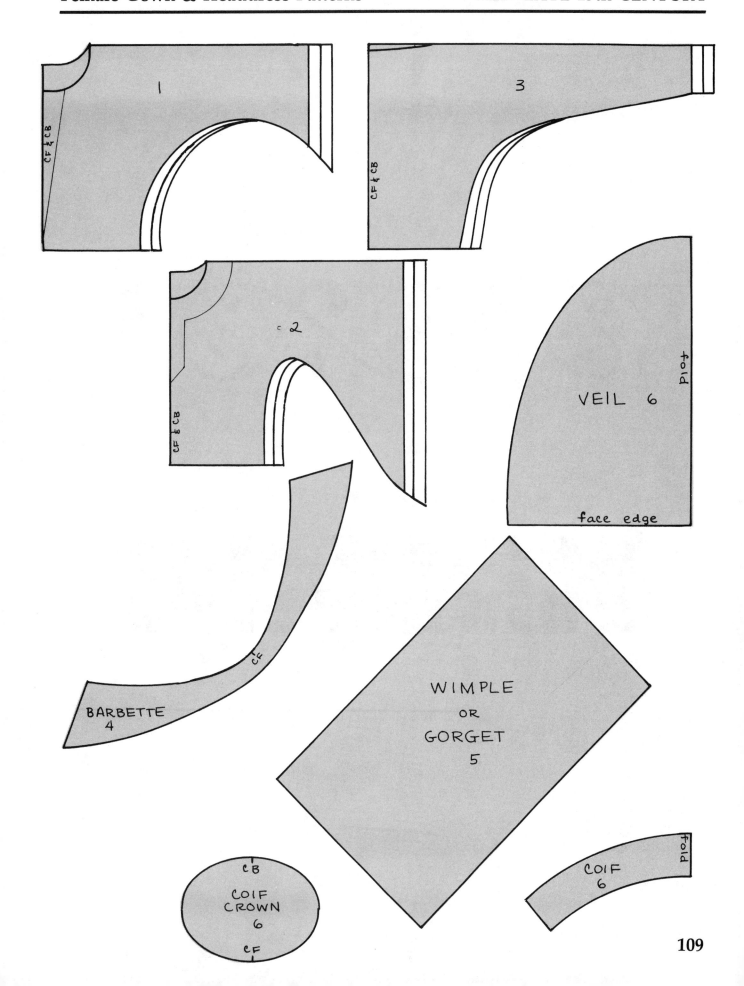

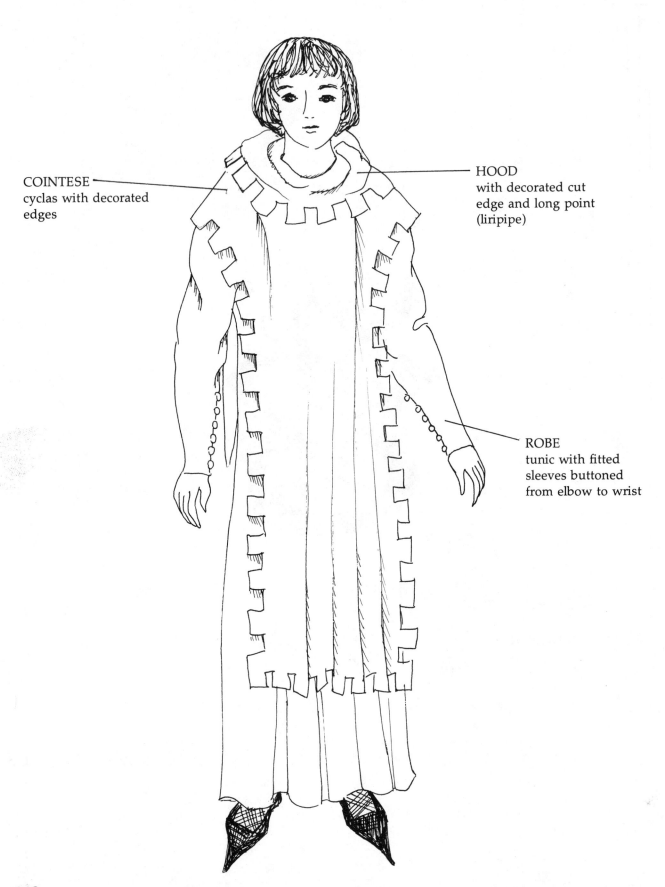

COINTESE
cyclas with decorated
edges

HOOD
with decorated cut
edge and long point
(liripipe)

ROBE
tunic with fitted
sleeves buttoned
from elbow to wrist

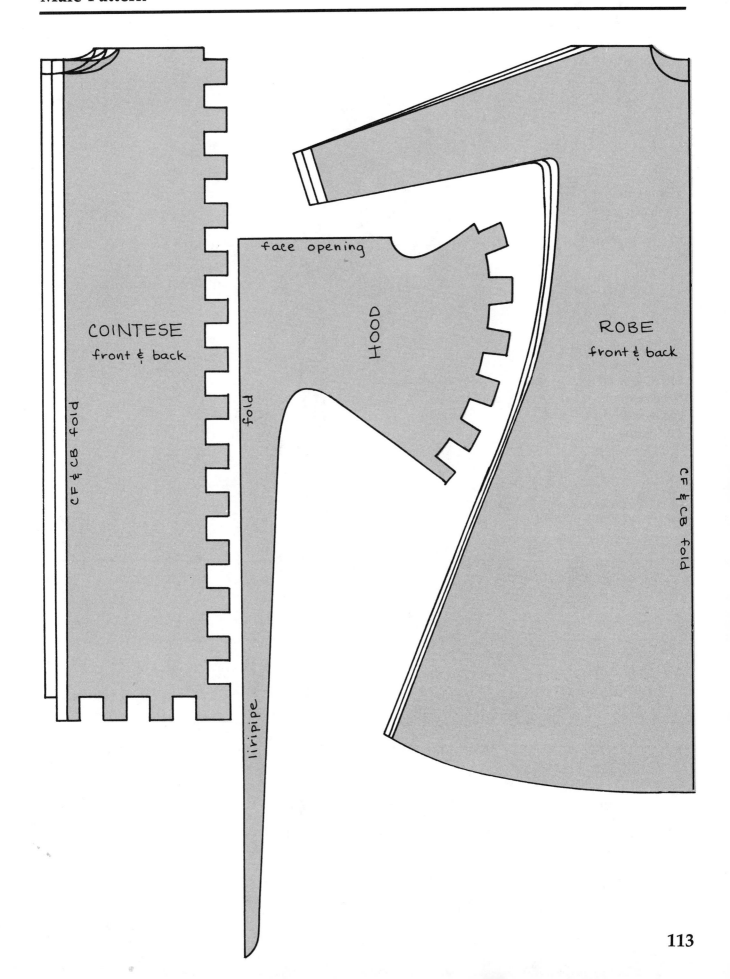

COINTESE
front & back

CF & CB fold

HOOD

face opening

fold

liripipe

ROBE
front & back

CF & CB fold

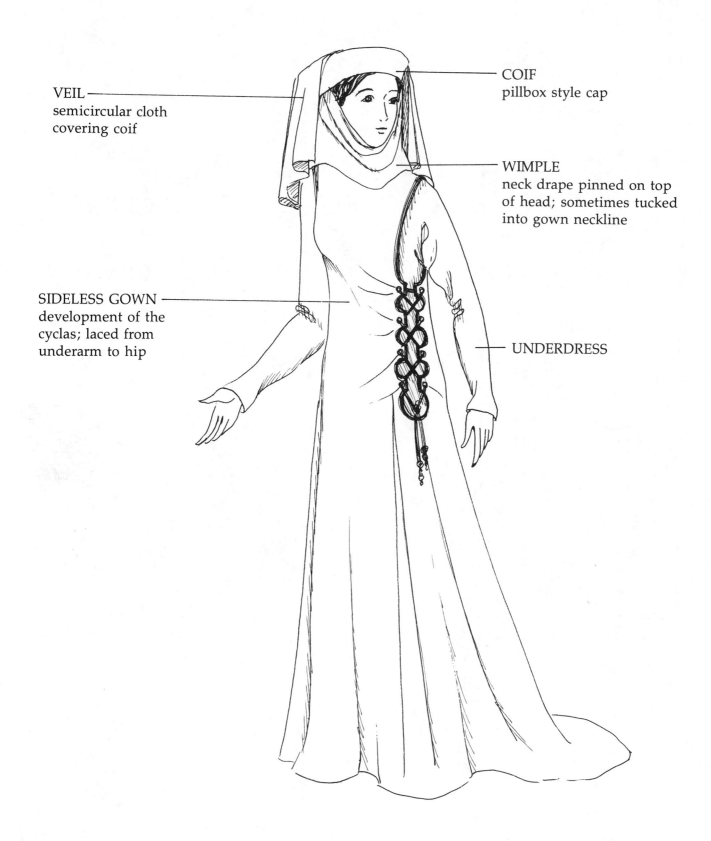

VEIL
semicircular cloth
covering coif

COIF
pillbox style cap

WIMPLE
neck drape pinned on top
of head; sometimes tucked
into gown neckline

SIDELESS GOWN
development of the
cyclas; laced from
underarm to hip

UNDERDRESS

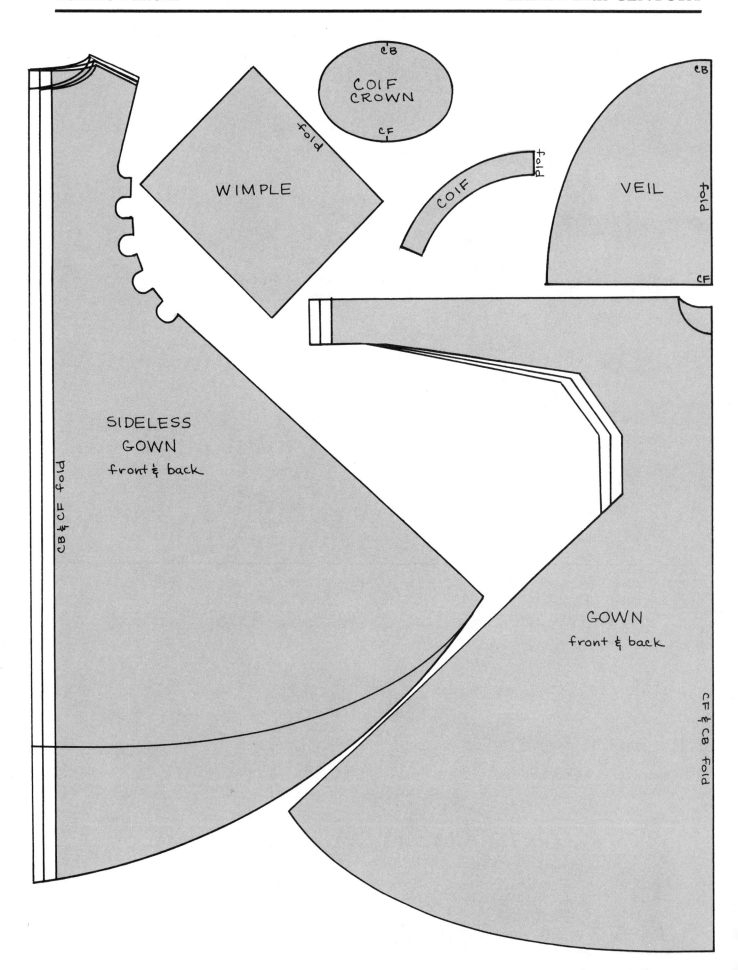

COIF
CROWN

CB

CF

WIMPLE

fold

COIF

fold

VEIL

CB

CF

fold

SIDELESS
GOWN
front & back

CB & CF fold

GOWN
front & back

CF & CB
fold

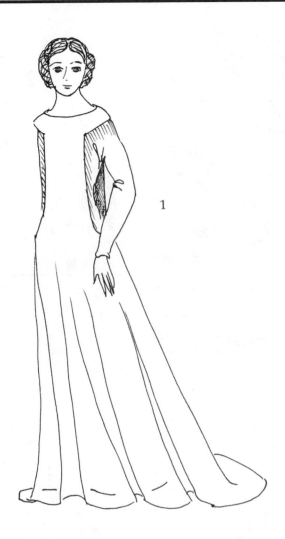

1

2

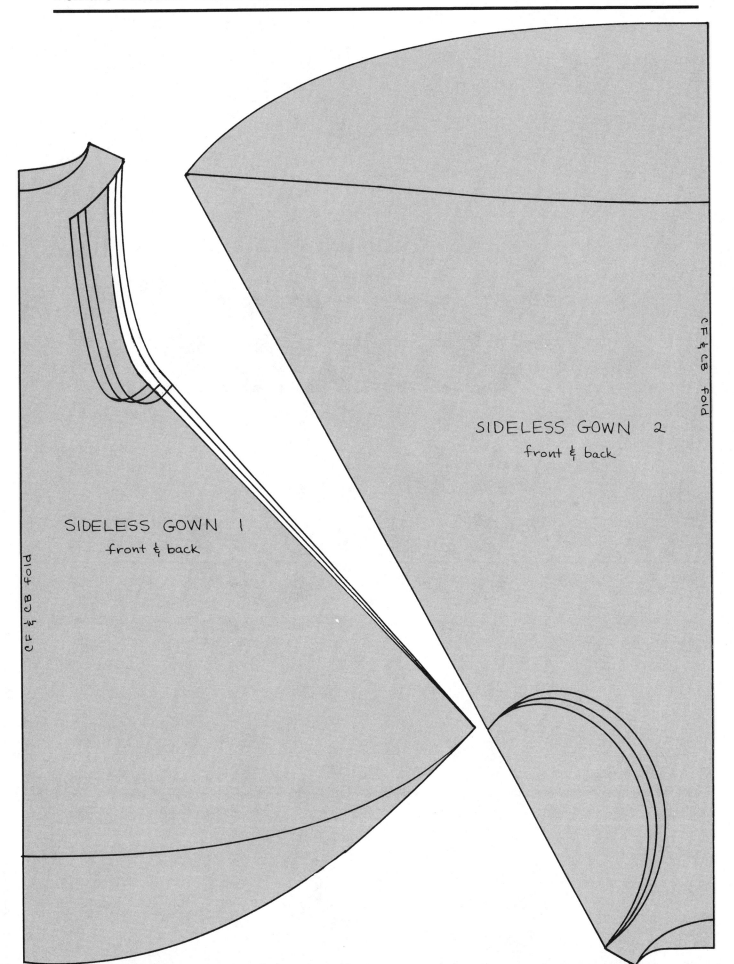

SIDELESS GOWN 1
front & back

SIDELESS GOWN 2
front & back

CF & CB fold

CF & CB fold

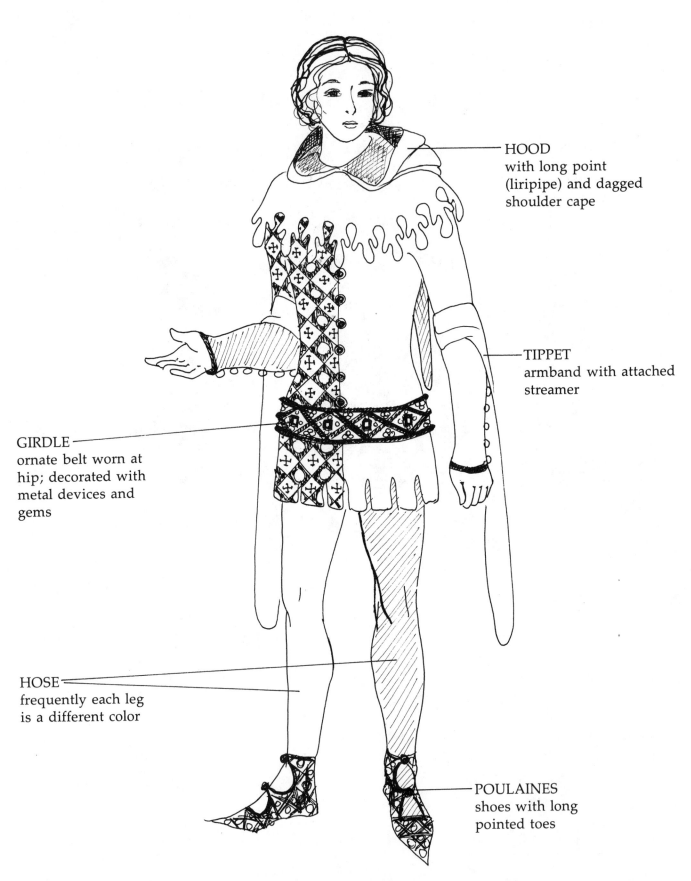

HOOD
with long point
(liripipe) and dagged
shoulder cape

TIPPET
armband with attached
streamer

GIRDLE
ornate belt worn at
hip; decorated with
metal devices and
gems

HOSE
frequently each leg
is a different color

POULAINES
shoes with long
pointed toes

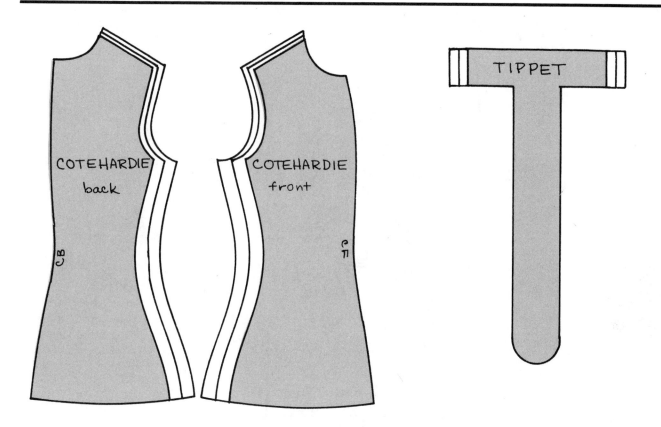

TIPPET

COTEHARDIE back

CB

COTEHARDIE front

CF

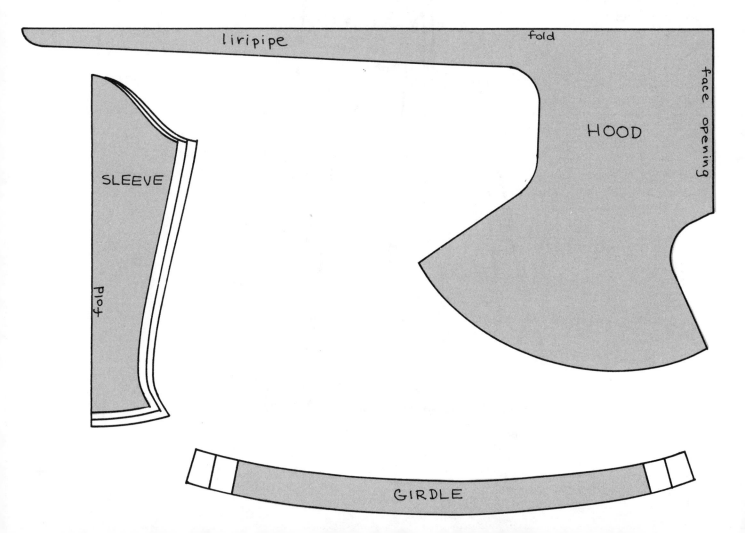

liripipe

fold

HOOD

face opening

SLEEVE

fold

GIRDLE

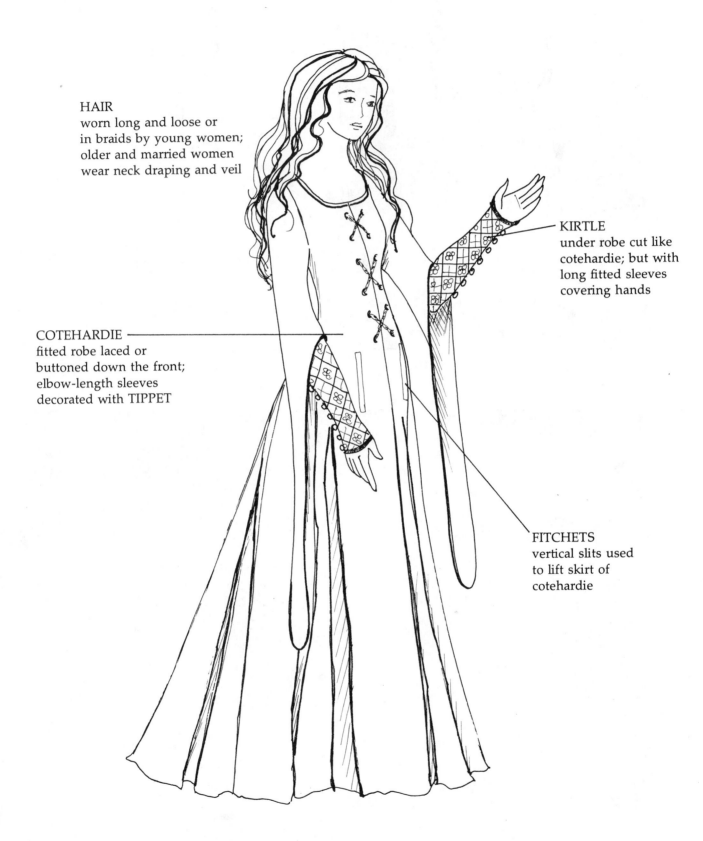

HAIR
worn long and loose or
in braids by young women;
older and married women
wear neck draping and veil

KIRTLE
under robe cut like
cotehardie; but with
long fitted sleeves
covering hands

COTEHARDIE
fitted robe laced or
buttoned down the front;
elbow-length sleeves
decorated with TIPPET

FITCHETS
vertical slits used
to lift skirt of
cotehardie

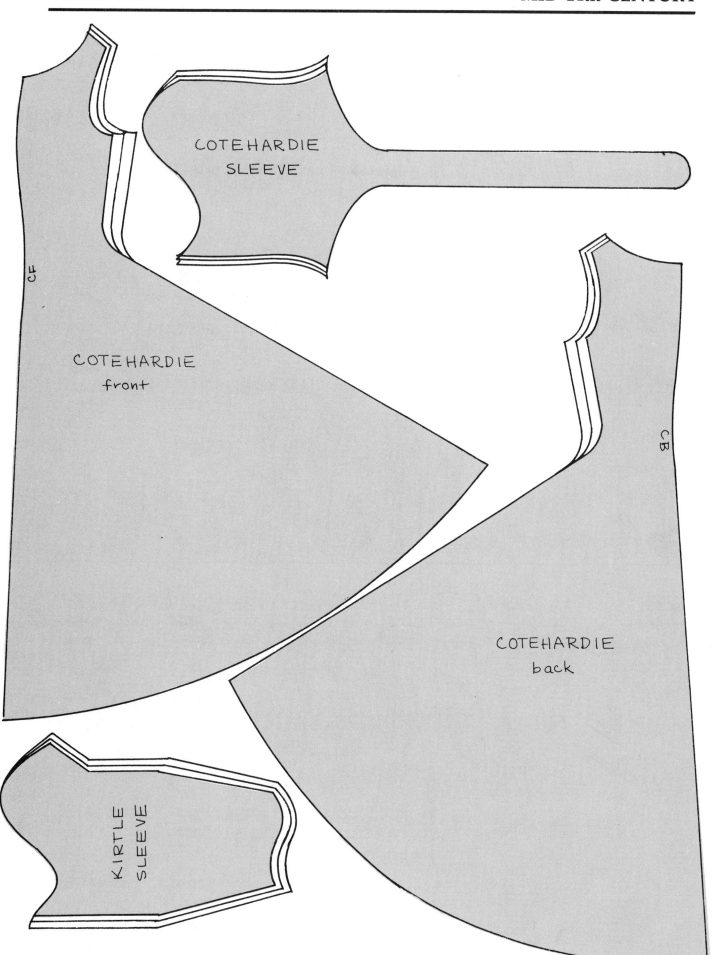

COTEHARDIE
SLEEVE

CF

COTEHARDIE
front

CB

COTEHARDIE
back

KIRTLE
SLEEVE

1

CLOAK
semicircular cape gathered at neck

2

PELICON
furlined outer tunic

3

SURCOAT
loose coat with sleeves
worn buttoned or unbuttoned
from shoulder to wrist

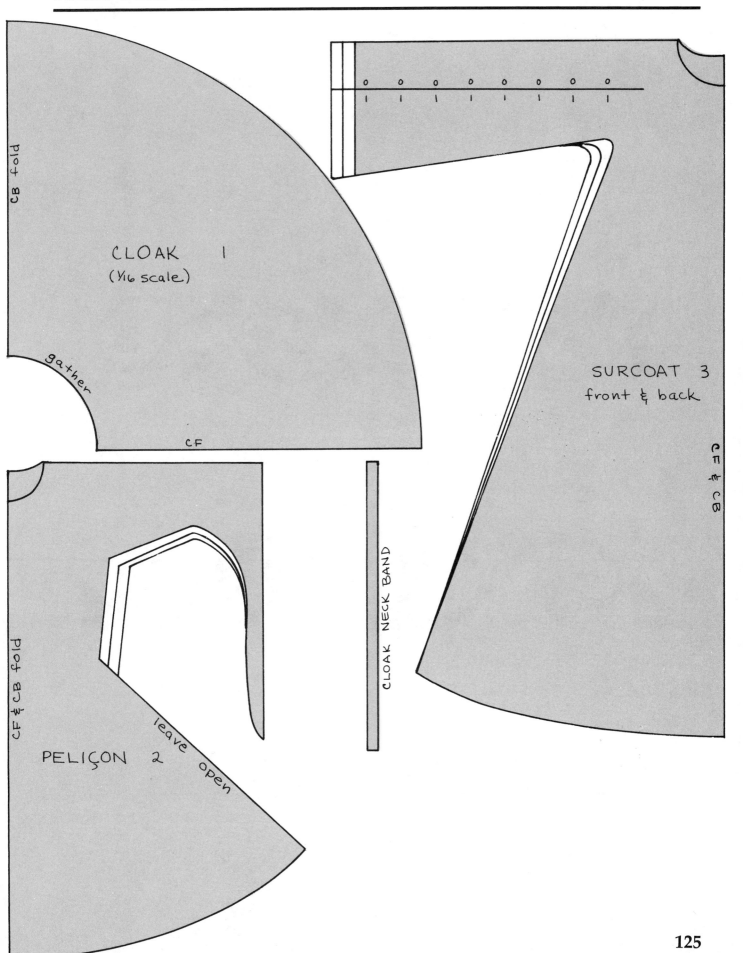

CB fold

CLOAK　　1
(1/16 scale)

gather

CF

PELIÇON　2

CF & CB fold

leave open

CLOAK NECK BAND

SURCOAT 3
front & back

CF & CB

HOOD
worn with face opening
around head, hood cape
draped to one side, and
liripipe wrapped
around head

HOUPPELANDE
long full robe often
lined in fur with
wide dagged funnel
sleeves and standing
collar

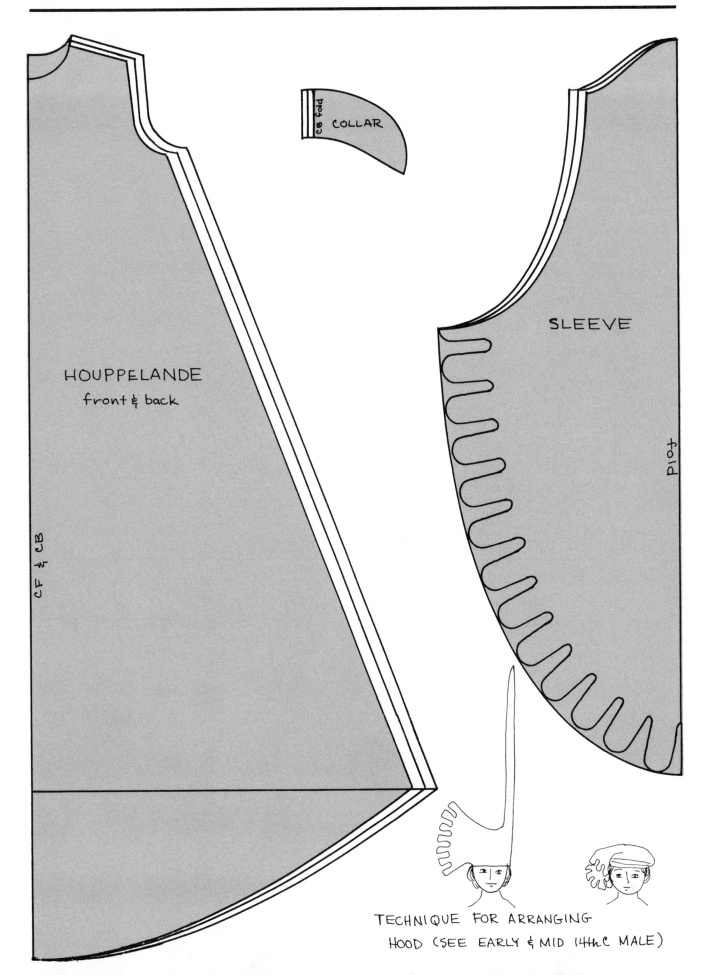

COLLAR

cB fold

HOUPPELANDE
front & back

CF & CB

SLEEVE

fold

TECHNIQUE FOR ARRANGING
HOOD (SEE EARLY & MID 14thC MALE)

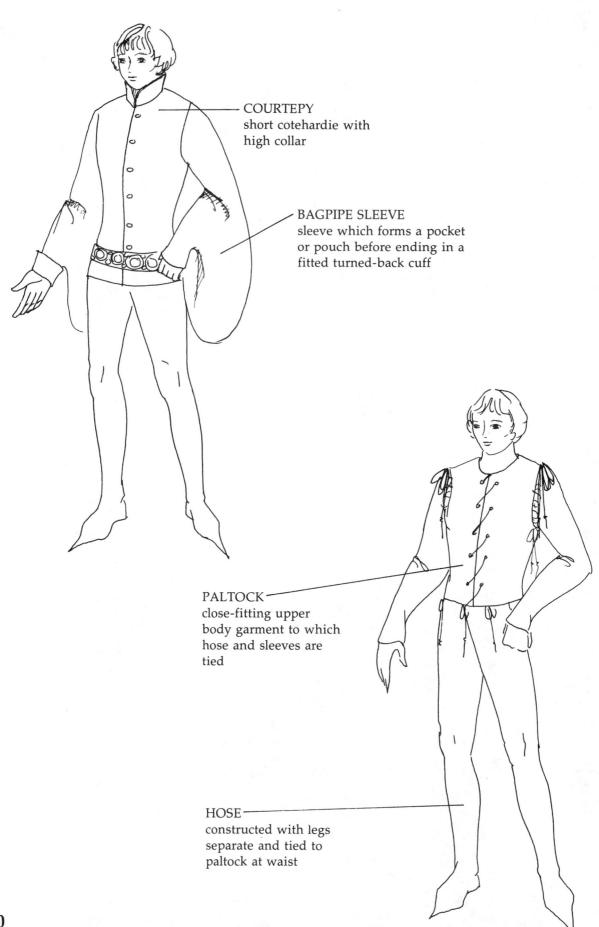

COURTEPY
short cotehardie with
high collar

BAGPIPE SLEEVE
sleeve which forms a pocket
or pouch before ending in a
fitted turned-back cuff

PALTOCK
close-fitting upper
body garment to which
hose and sleeves are
tied

HOSE
constructed with legs
separate and tied to
paltock at waist

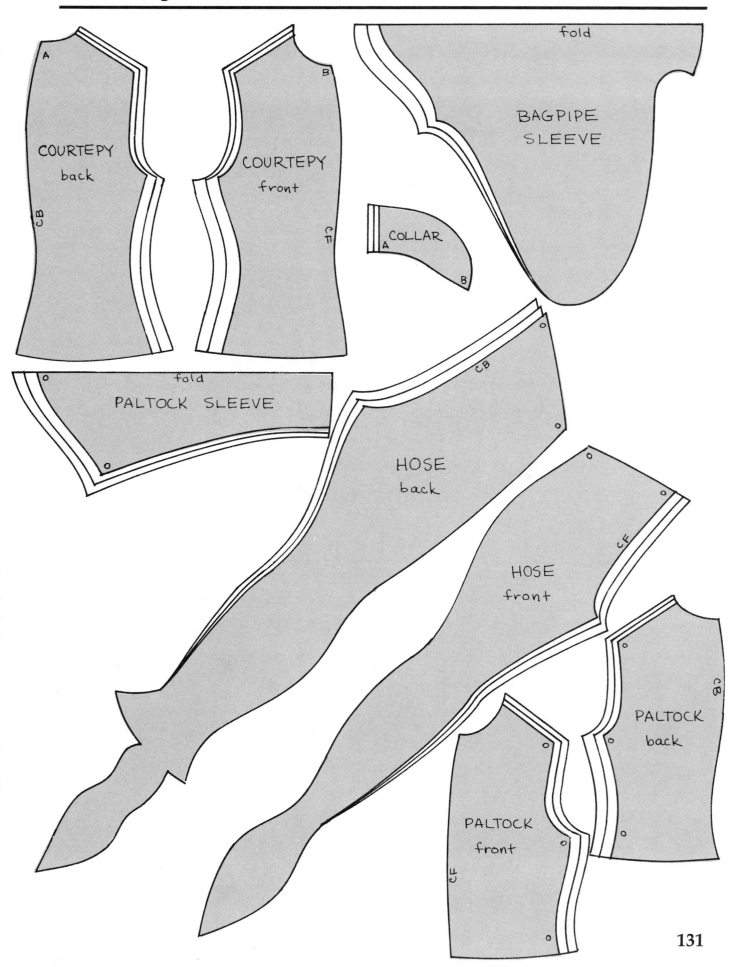

VEIL AND BAND

RAMSHORN HAIRDRESS
style of wearing hair with
a braid coiled over each ear

KIRTLE
dress worn under sideless
gown with buttoned sleeves
from elbow to wrist; often
buttoned through plastron
to hold gown in position

SIDELESS GOWN
constructed with very
full skirt and deep
armhole openings;
often lined in fur

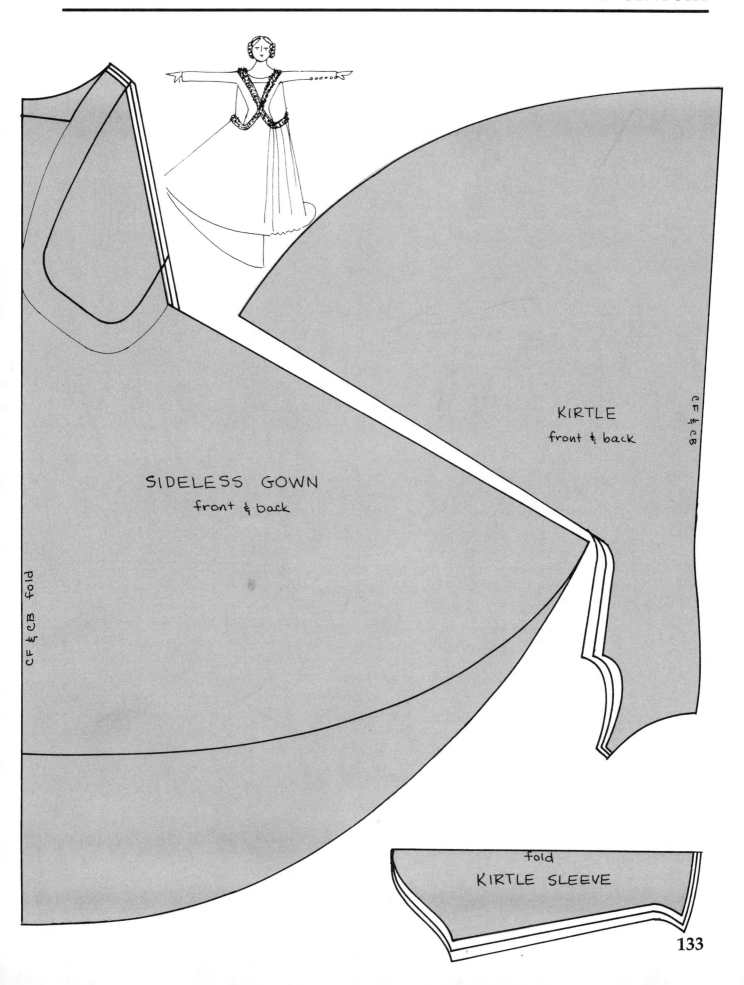

SIDELESS GOWN
front & back

KIRTLE
front & back

CF & CB fold

CF & CB

CF & CB

fold
KIRTLE SLEEVE

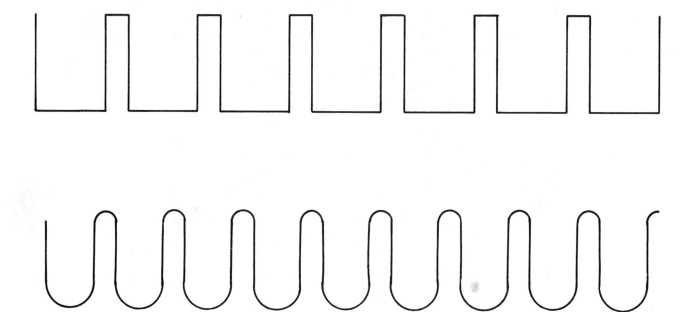

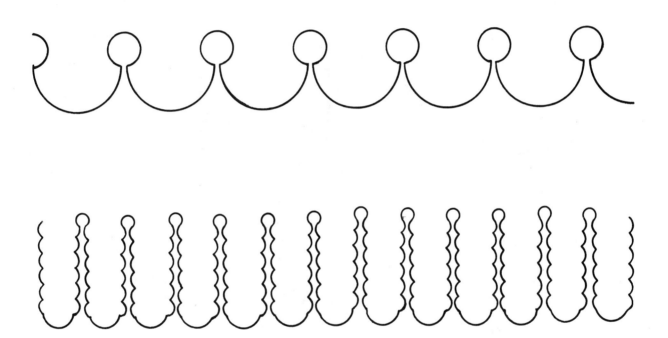

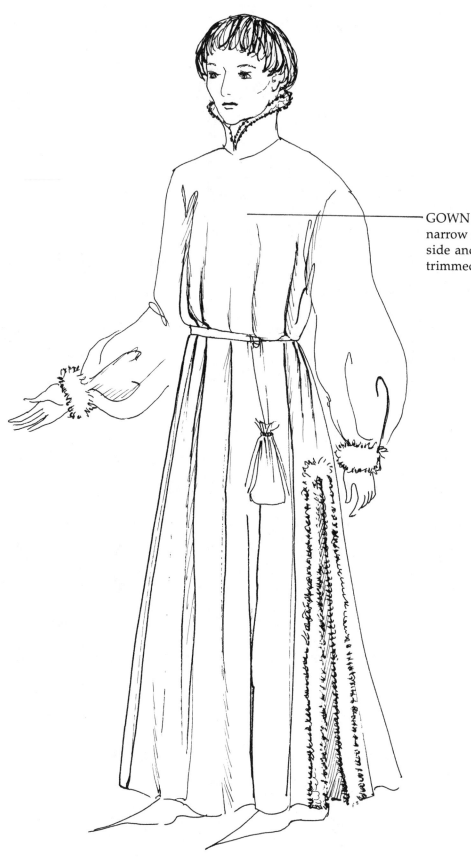

GOWN
narrow robe with slit at
side and standing collar
trimmed in fur

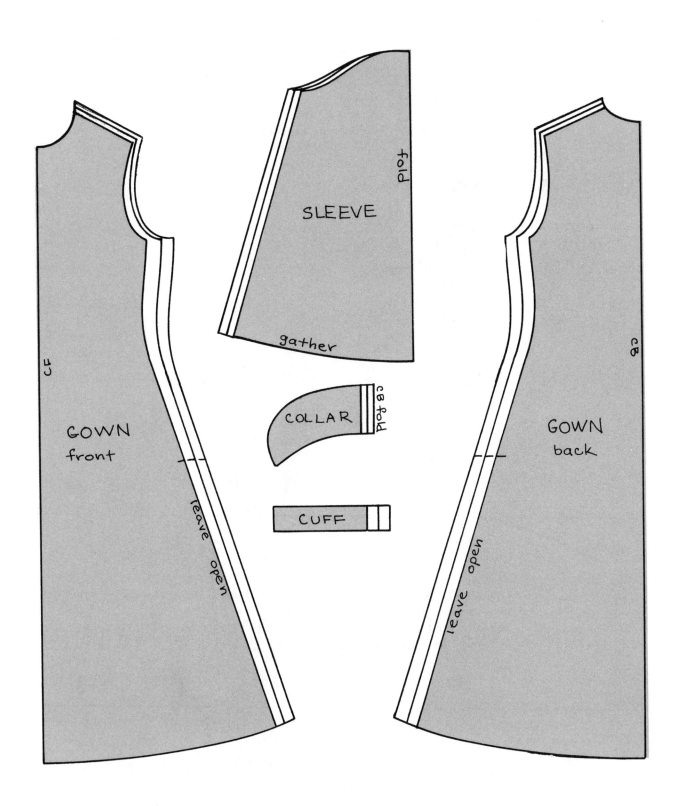

1

TUNIC
short full tunic with
split funnel, fur lined
sleeves; belted at waist
to form skirt pleating

2

CLOAK TUNIC
three-quarters of a circle;
belted in front and
allowed to hang free in
the back

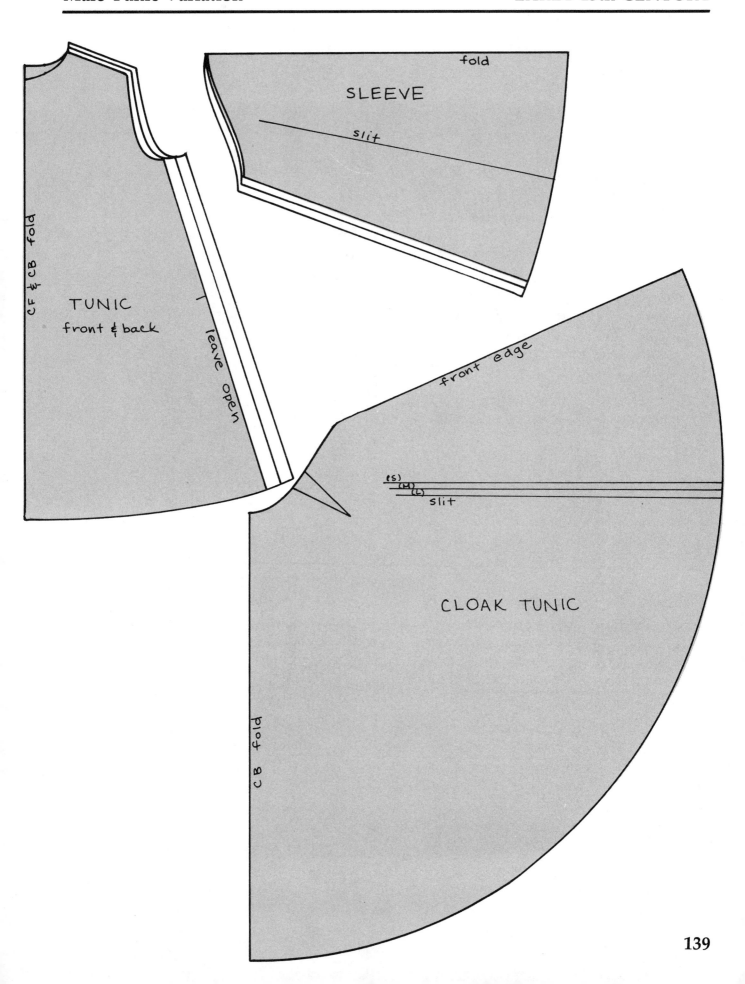

SLEEVE

fold

slit

CF & CB fold

TUNIC
front & back

leave open

front edge

(S)
(M)
(L)
slit

CLOAK TUNIC

CB fold

HEADDRESS
elaborate arrangement
of netting, padded
roll, and veil with
pinked edge

HOUPPELANDE
very full gown with long
flowing sleeves; belted high
with long girdle buckled in
the back; edges may be dagged

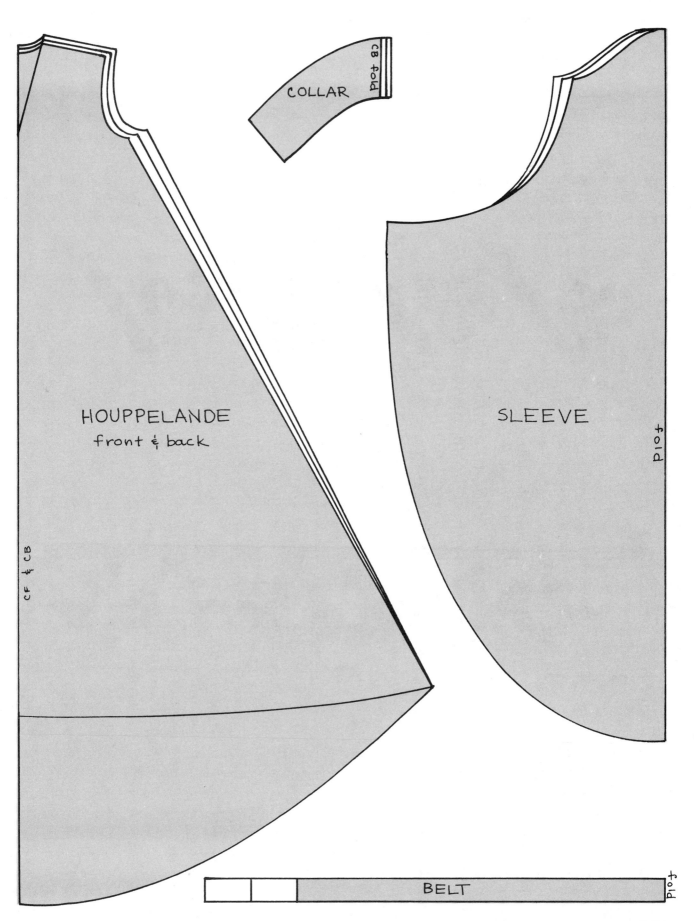

COLLAR

CB fold

HOUPPELANDE
front & back

CF & CB

SLEEVE

fold

BELT

fold

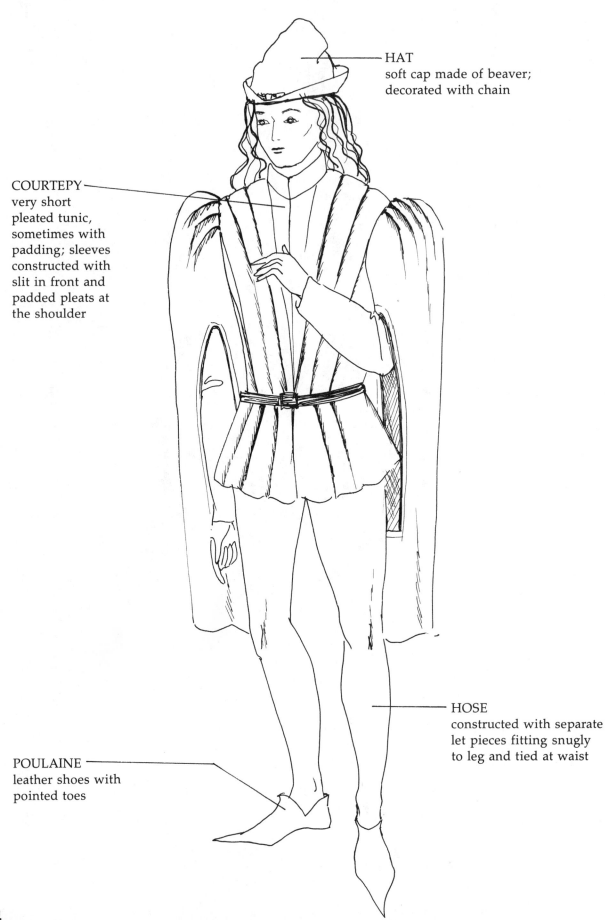

HAT
soft cap made of beaver;
decorated with chain

COURTEPY
very short
pleated tunic,
sometimes with
padding; sleeves
constructed with
slit in front and
padded pleats at
the shoulder

HOSE
constructed with separate
let pieces fitting snugly
to leg and tied at waist

POULAINE
leather shoes with
pointed toes

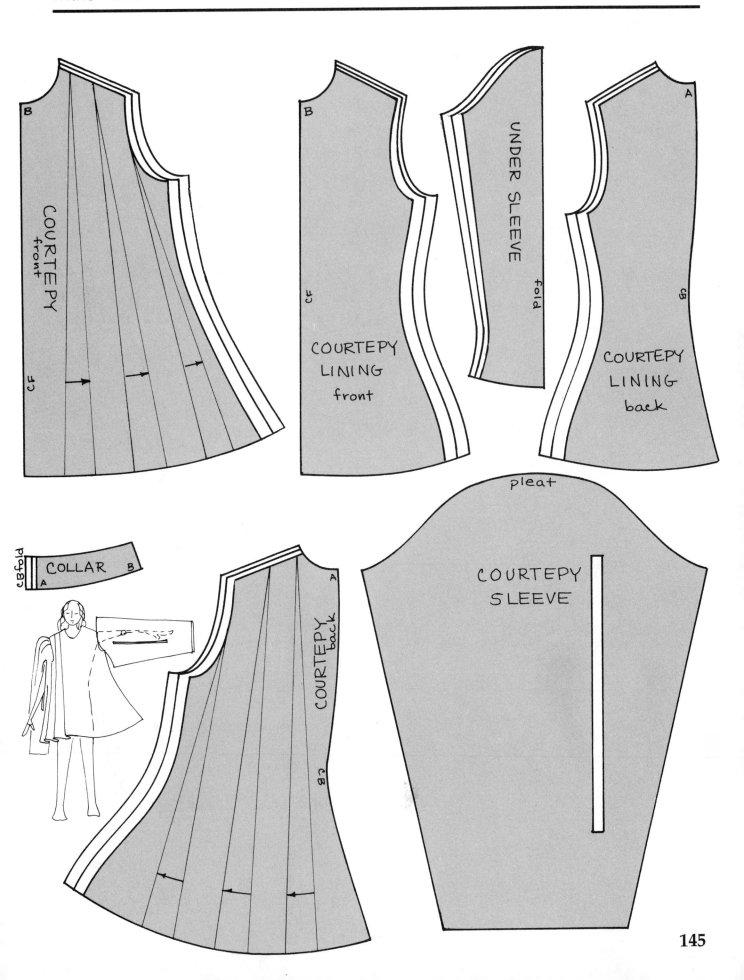

COURTEPY
front

COURTEPY
LINING
front

UNDER SLEEVE

fold

COURTEPY
LINING
back

pleat

COURTEPY
SLEEVE

COLLAR

COURTEPY
back

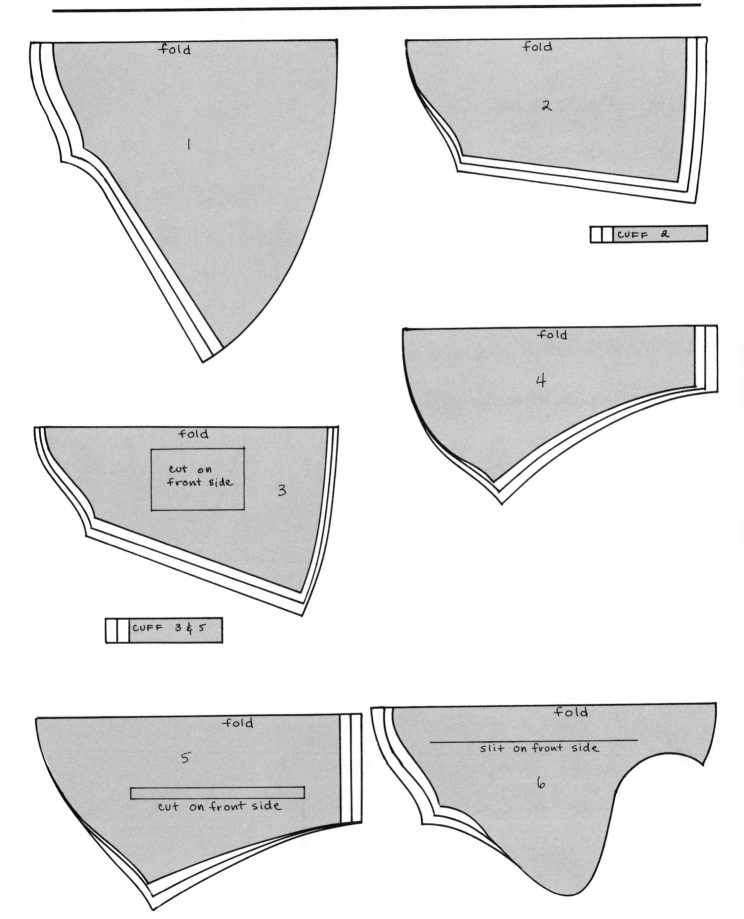

fold

1

fold

2

CUFF 2

fold

cut on
front side

3

fold

4

CUFF 3 & 5

fold

5

cut on front side

fold

slit on front side

6

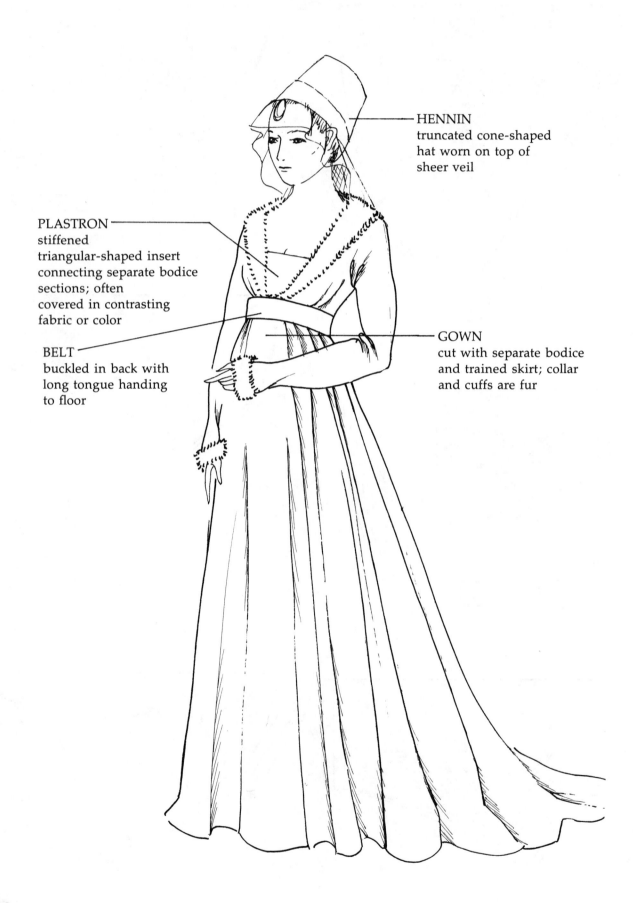

HENNIN
truncated cone-shaped
hat worn on top of
sheer veil

PLASTRON
stiffened
triangular-shaped insert
connecting separate bodice
sections; often
covered in contrasting
fabric or color

BELT
buckled in back with
long tongue handing
to floor

GOWN
cut with separate bodice
and trained skirt; collar
and cuffs are fur

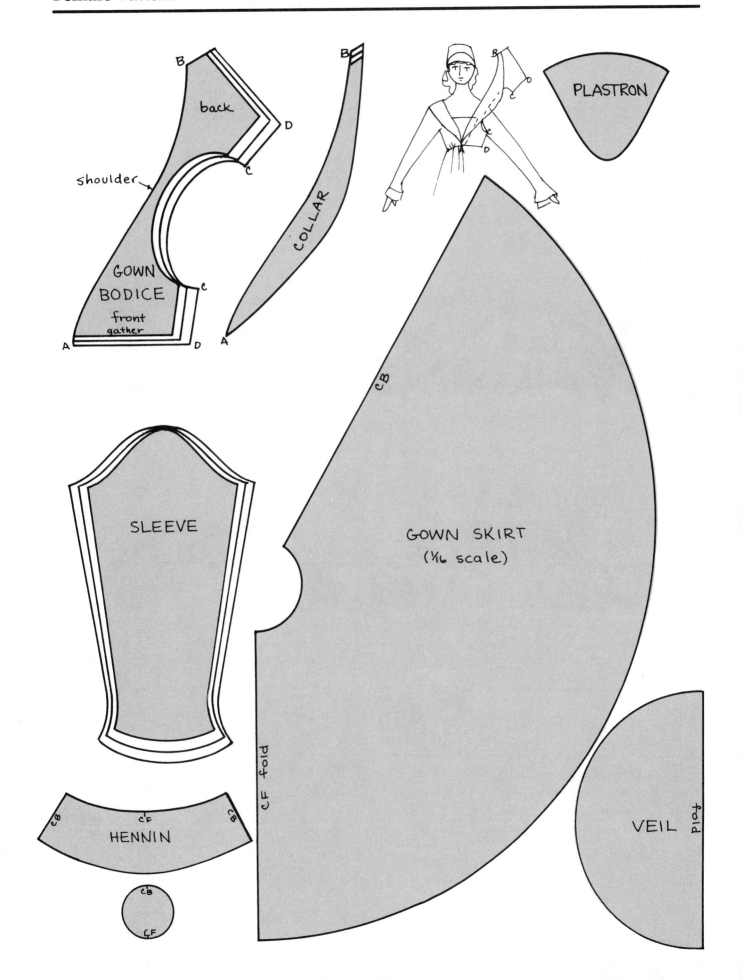

GOWN
BODICE

back

shoulder

front gather

COLLAR

PLASTRON

SLEEVE

GOWN SKIRT
(1/16 scale)

CF fold

CB

HENNIN

VEIL

fold

HAT
small, soft crown gathered
into a stiffened turned-up
brim; decorated with
brooch

DOUBLET
waist-length,
snug-fitting garment,
often padded

SIMAR
loose robe folded
back at neck to
reveal lining and
held closed by a silk
sash tied in the front

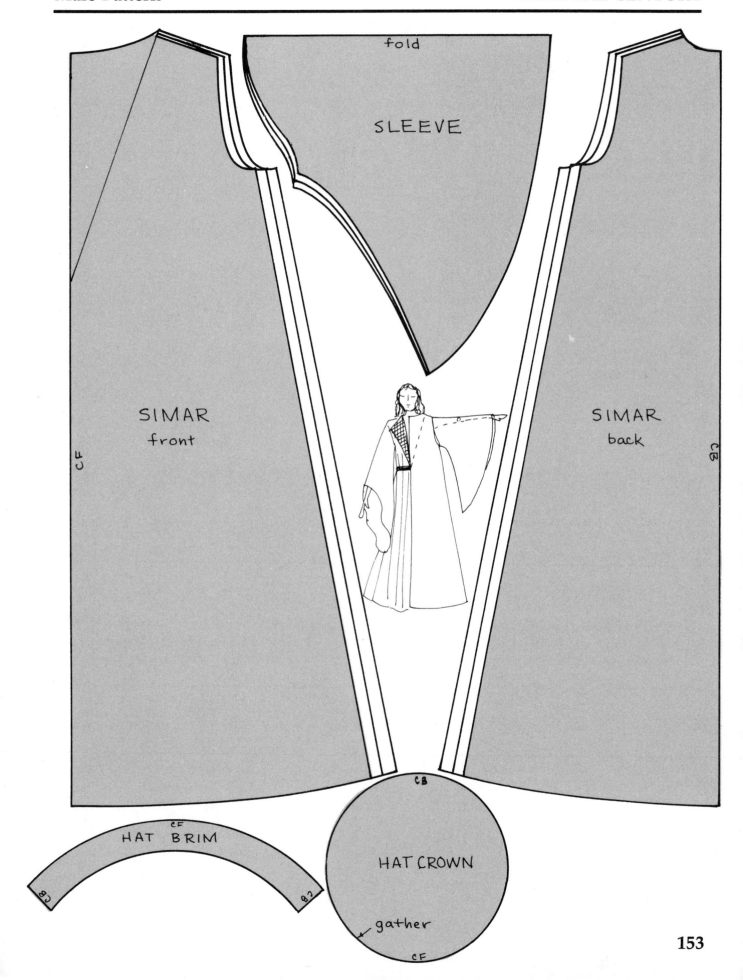

fold

SLEEVE

SIMAR
front

SIMAR
back

CF

CB

HAT BRIM

CF

CB

CB

CB

HAT CROWN

CB

CF

gather

JOURNADE
very short, circular-cut
garment worn for
riding; often edged
in fur

SURCOAT
semicircular coat lined
in fur, with turn-back
collar (revere) and
hanging sleeves

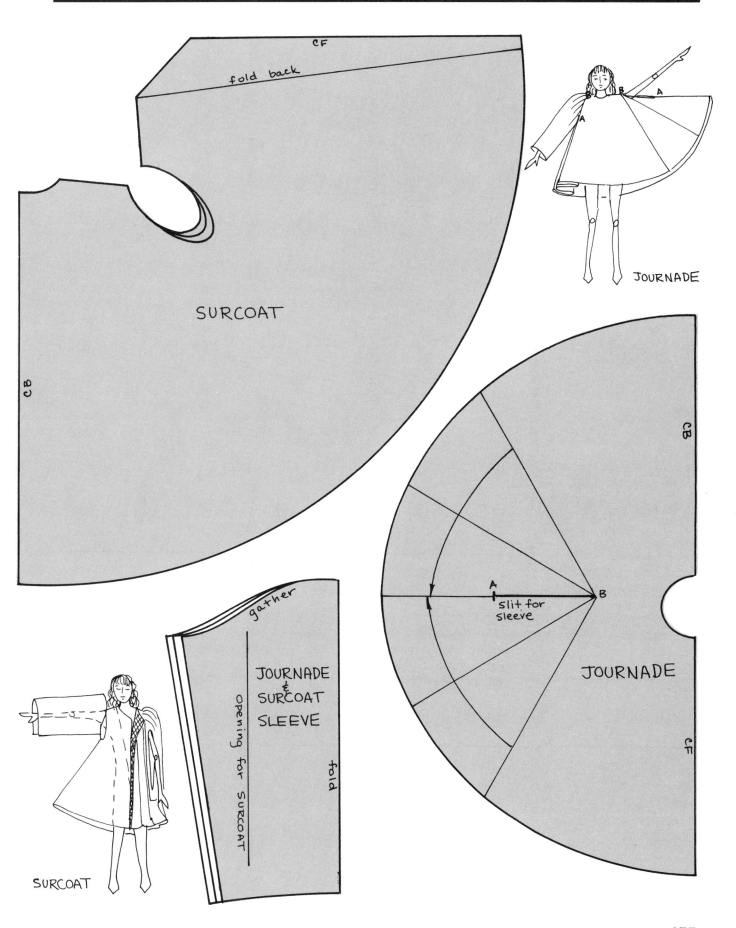

CF

fold back

SURCOAT

CB

JOURNADE

CB

A
slit for
sleeve
B

JOURNADE

CF

gather

JOURNADE
&
SURCOAT
SLEEVE

opening for SURCOAT

fold

SURCOAT

KIRTLE
Low-necked, fitted,
informal dress

BELT
long tongued with
metal tip; buckled
on hip and hanging
down front

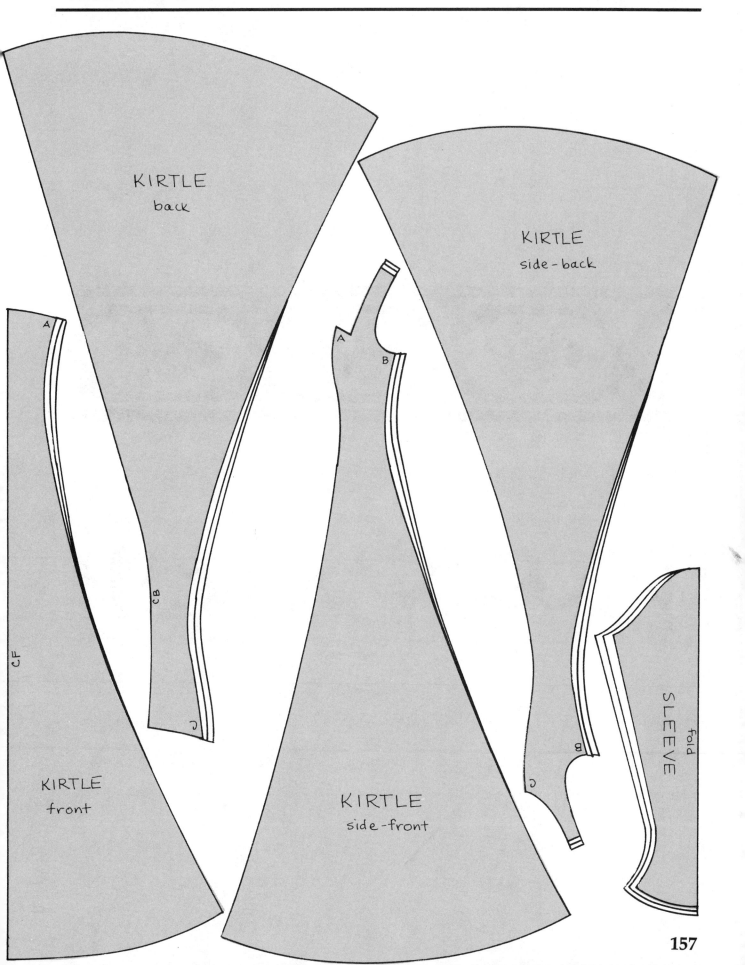

KIRTLE
back

KIRTLE
side-back

KIRTLE
front

KIRTLE
side-front

SLEEVE
fold

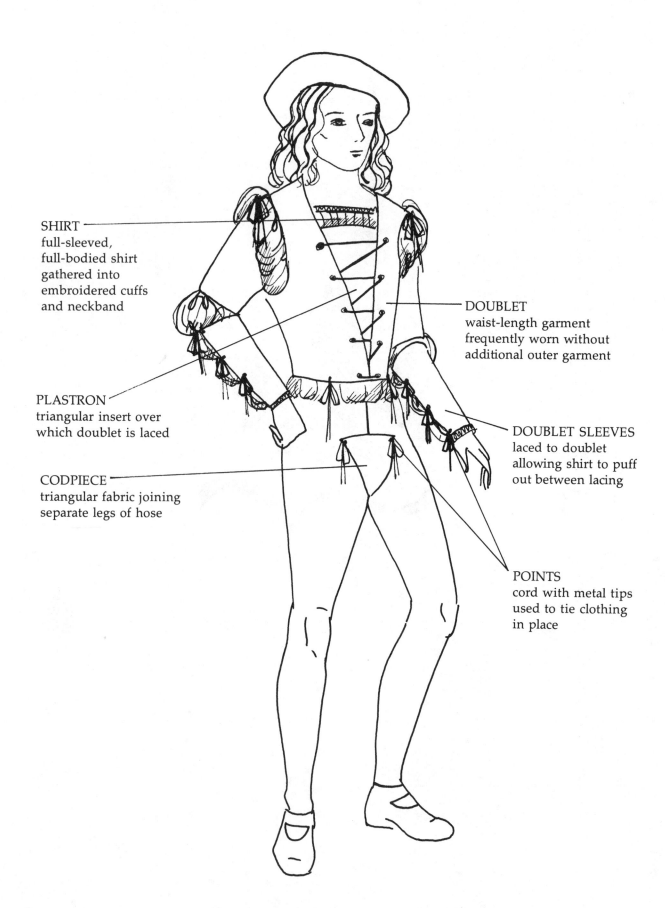

SHIRT
full-sleeved,
full-bodied shirt
gathered into
embroidered cuffs
and neckband

PLASTRON
triangular insert over
which doublet is laced

CODPIECE
triangular fabric joining
separate legs of hose

DOUBLET
waist-length garment
frequently worn without
additional outer garment

DOUBLET SLEEVES
laced to doublet
allowing shirt to puff
out between lacing

POINTS
cord with metal tips
used to tie clothing
in place

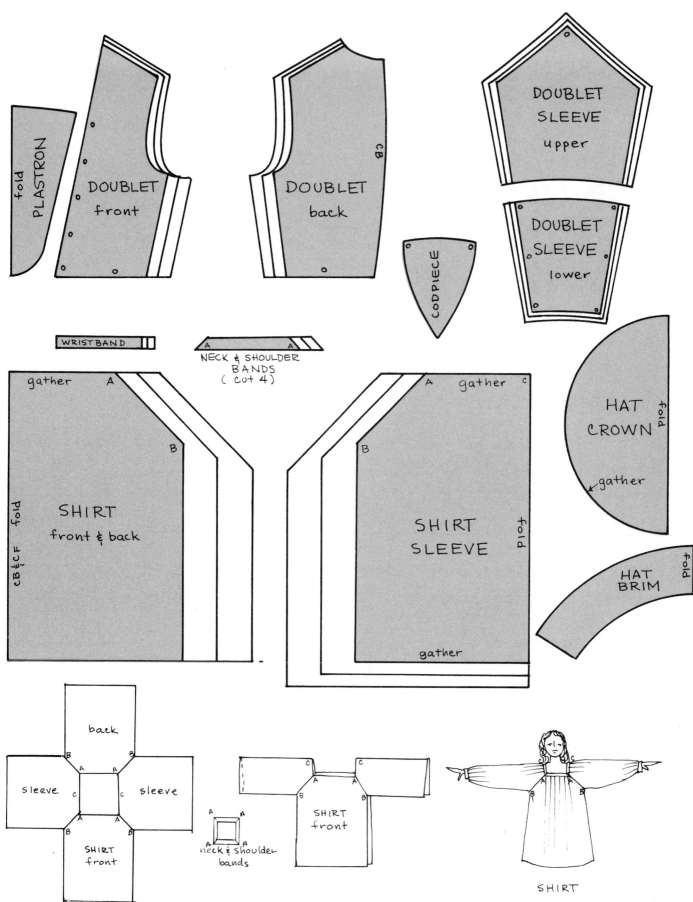

PLASTRON

fold

DOUBLET
front

DOUBLET
back

CB

DOUBLET
SLEEVE
upper

DOUBLET
SLEEVE
lower

CODPIECE

WRISTBAND

A   A
NECK & SHOULDER
BANDS
(cut 4)

gather   A

B

SHIRT
front & back

cB & cF   fold

A   gather   C

B

SHIRT
SLEEVE

fold

gather

HAT
CROWN

fold

gather

HAT
BRIM

fold

back

B   B
A   A
sleeve   C   C   sleeve
A   A
B   B

SHIRT
front

A   A

A   A
neck & shoulder
bands

C   C
A   A
B   B

SHIRT
front

B   B

SHIRT

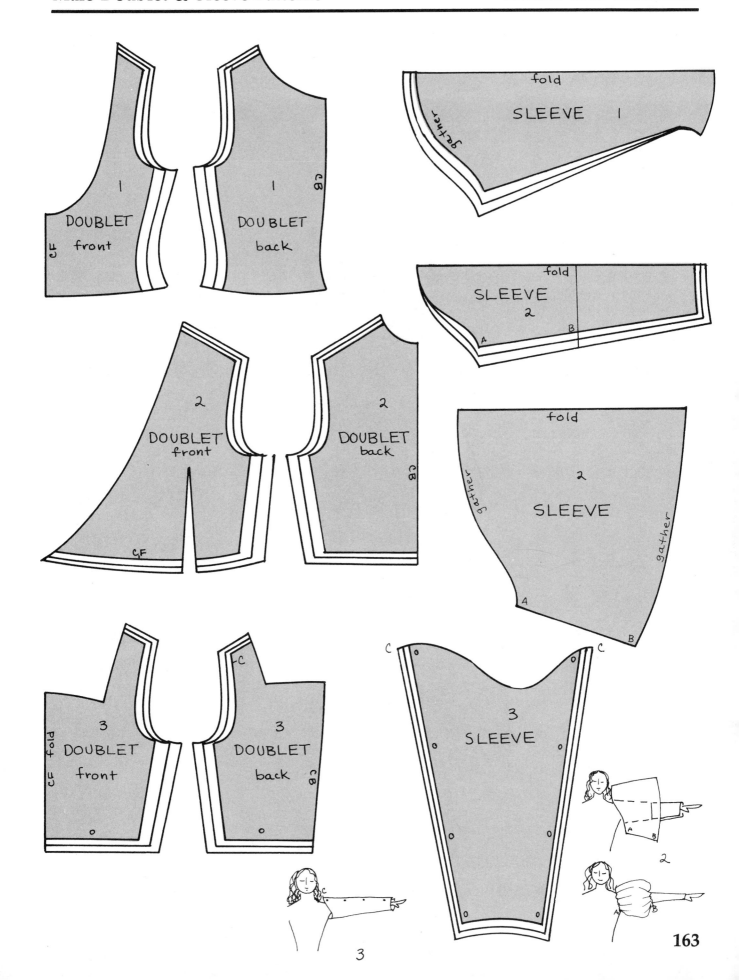

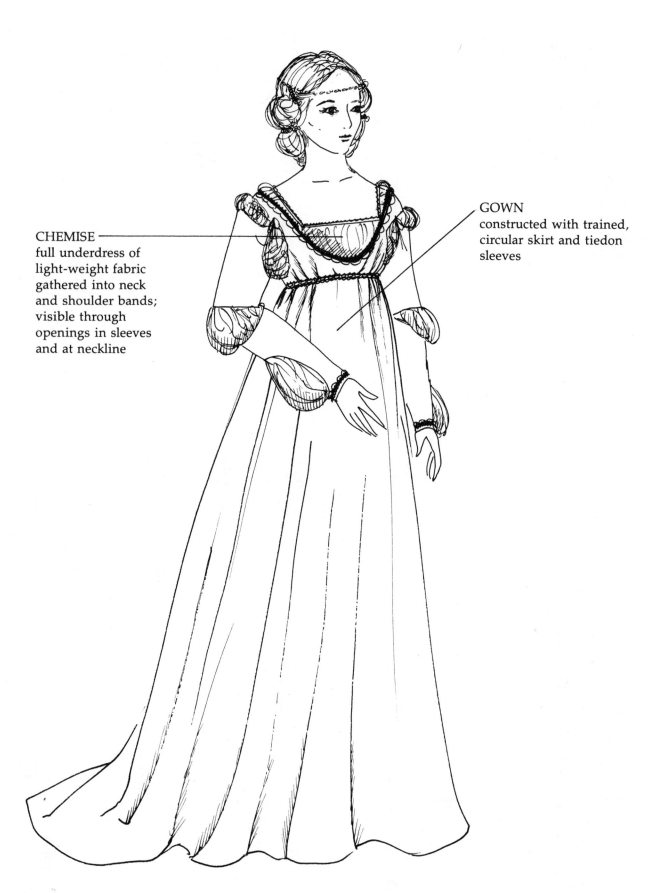

CHEMISE
full underdress of
light-weight fabric
gathered into neck
and shoulder bands;
visible through
openings in sleeves
and at neckline

GOWN
constructed with trained,
circular skirt and tiedon
sleeves

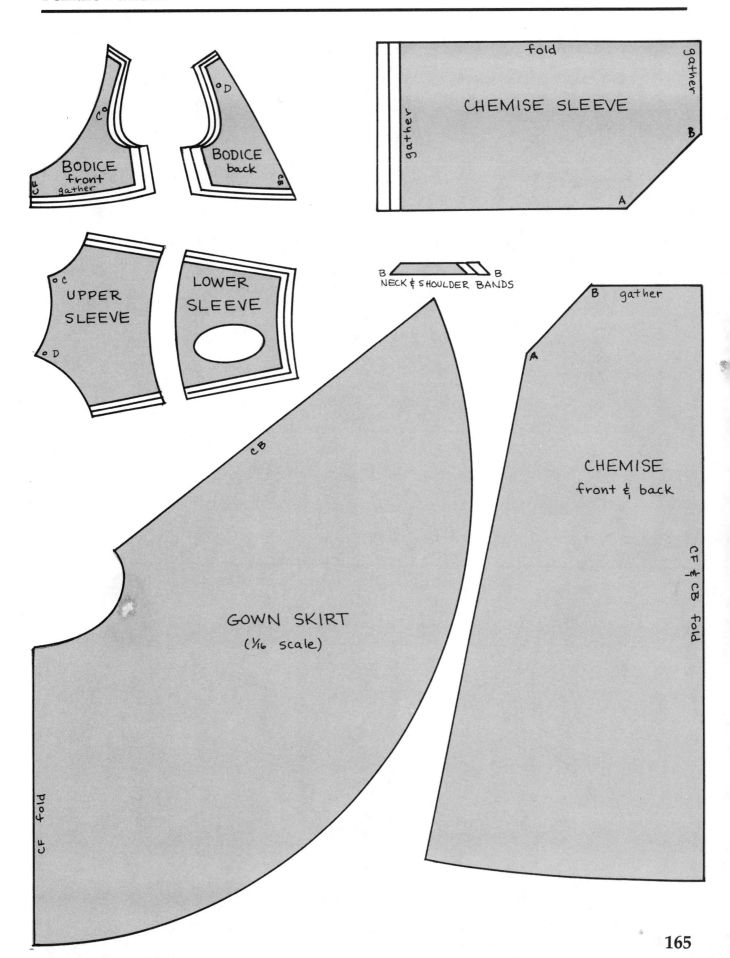

BODICE front gather

BODICE back

CHEMISE SLEEVE

fold

gather

gather

A

B

UPPER SLEEVE

LOWER SLEEVE

B B
NECK & SHOULDER BANDS

GOWN SKIRT
(1/16 scale)

CB

CF fold

CHEMISE
front & back

B gather

A

CF & CB fold

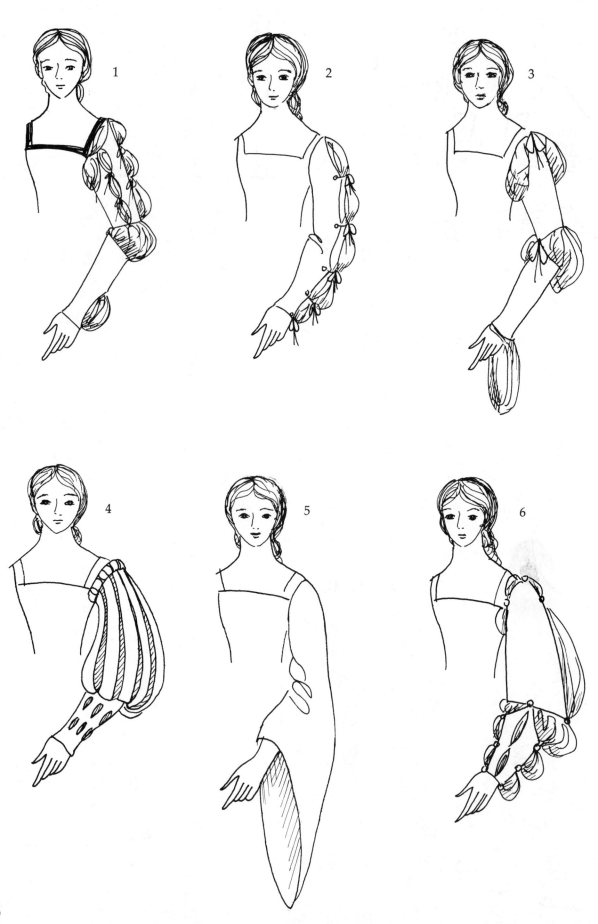

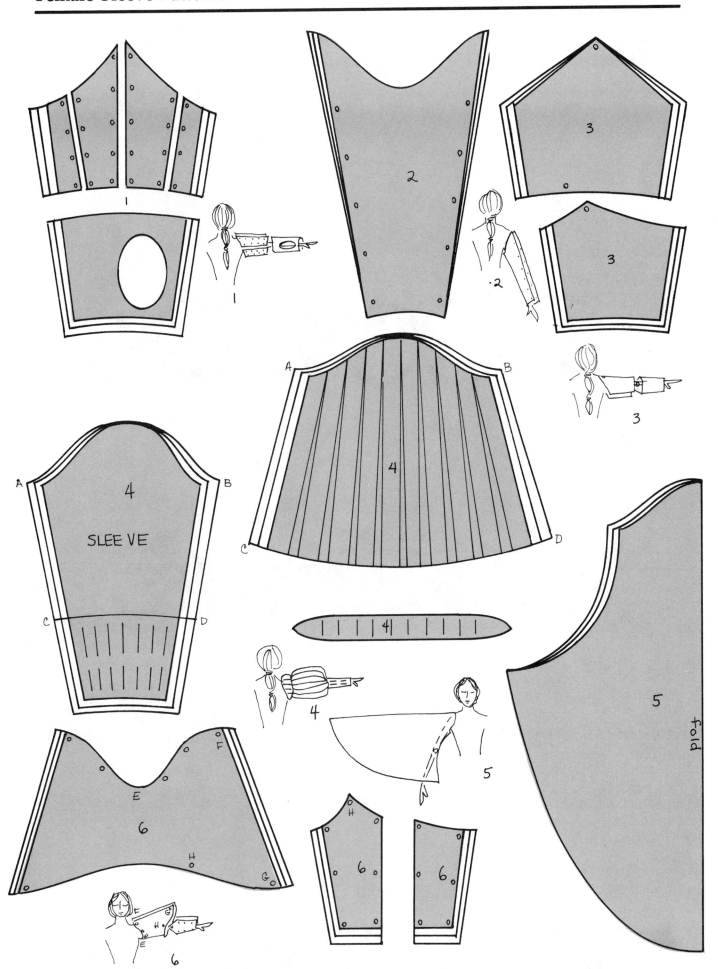

1

2

3

3

4

SLEEVE

A B

C D

A B

C D

4

4

5

fold

6

E

F

G

H

6

6

5

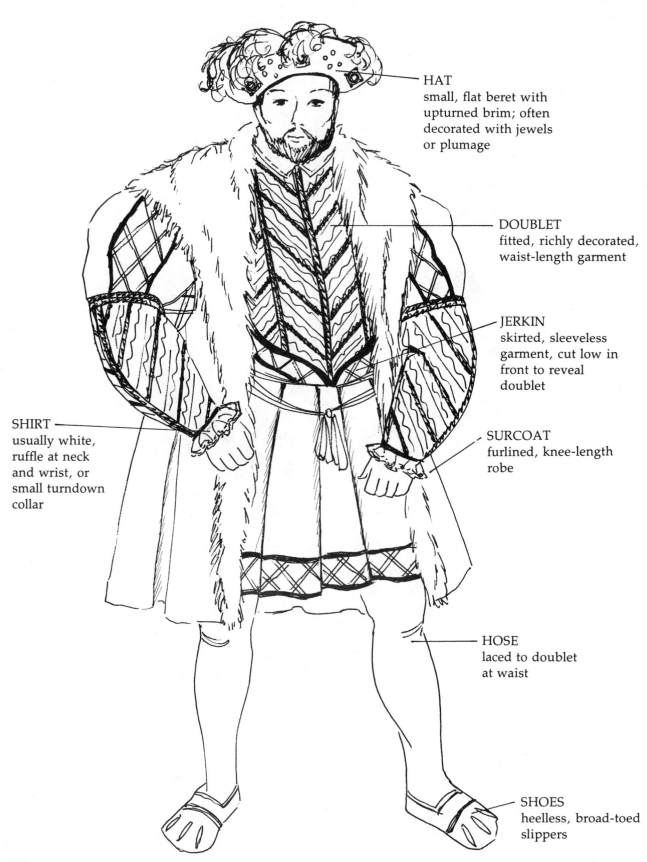

HAT
small, flat beret with upturned brim; often decorated with jewels or plumage

DOUBLET
fitted, richly decorated, waist-length garment

JERKIN
skirted, sleeveless garment, cut low in front to reveal doublet

SHIRT
usually white, ruffle at neck and wrist, or small turndown collar

SURCOAT
furlined, knee-length robe

HOSE
laced to doublet at waist

SHOES
heelless, broad-toed slippers

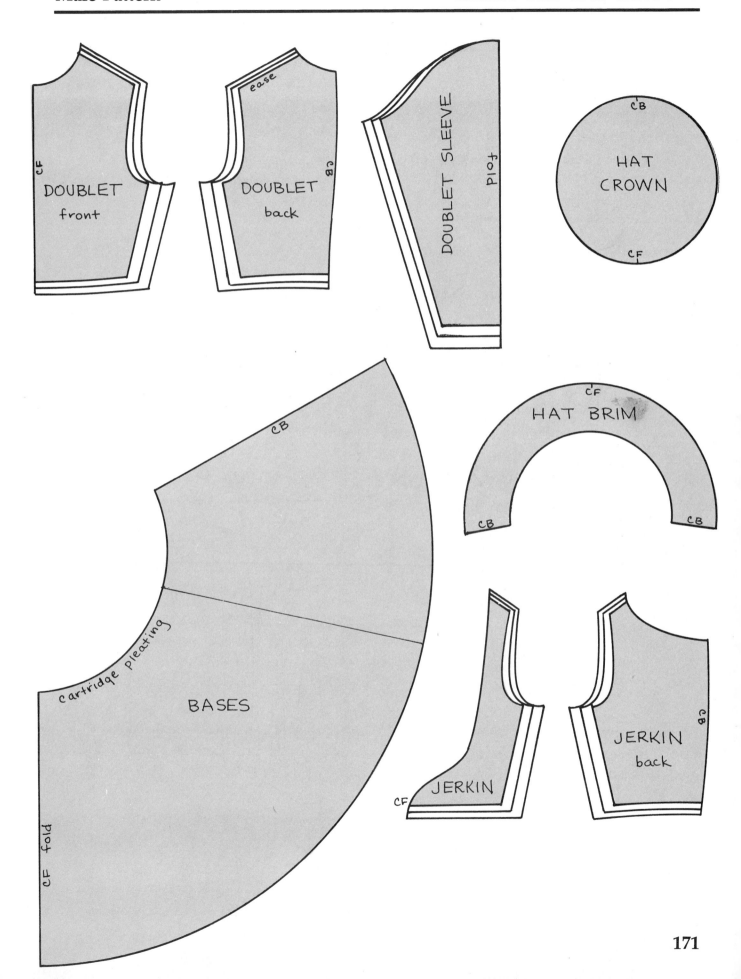

DOUBLET front

DOUBLET back

ease

CF

CB

DOUBLET SLEEVE

fold

HAT CROWN

CB

CF

CB

HAT BRIM

CF

CB

CB

BASES

CB

cartridge pleating

CF fold

JERKIN

CF

JERKIN back

CB

SURCOAT
circular overcoat with wide
revere usually lined in fur,
and short melon sleeves

CHAMARRE
square overcoat with
revere and added
rectangular collar

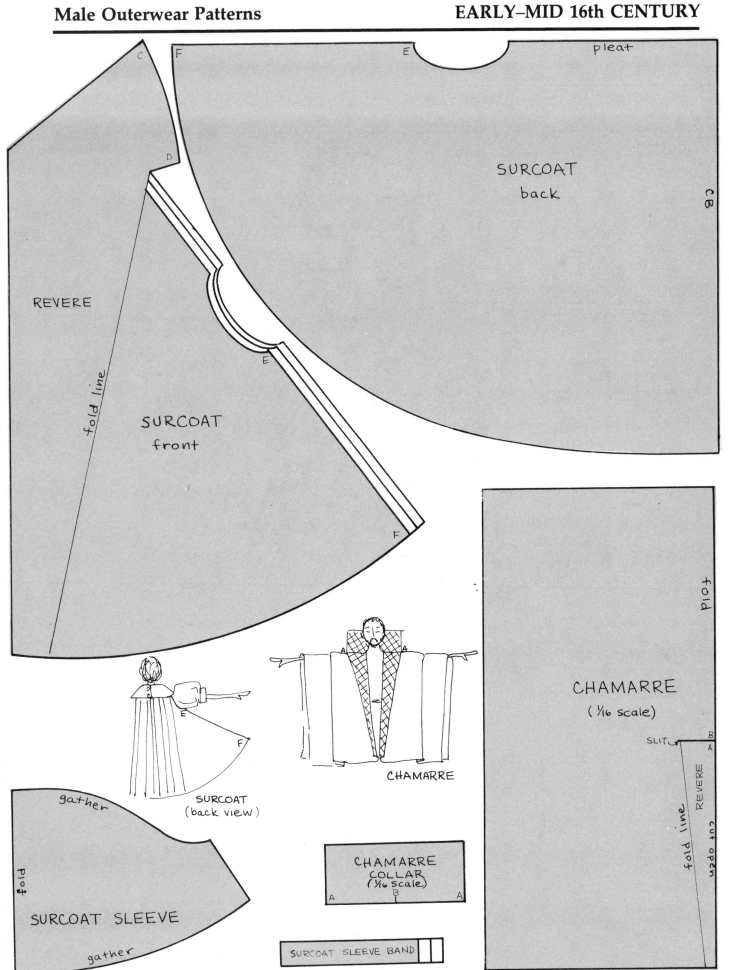

SURCOAT
back

pleat

C B

REVERE

fold line

SURCOAT
front

D

E

F

E

F

SURCOAT
(back view)

CHAMARRE

CHAMARRE
(¹⁄₁₆ scale)

fold

SLIT

B

A

REVERE

fold line

cut open

gather

fold

SURCOAT SLEEVE

gather

CHAMARRE
COLLAR
(¹⁄₁₆ scale)

A   B   A

SURCOAT SLEEVE BAND

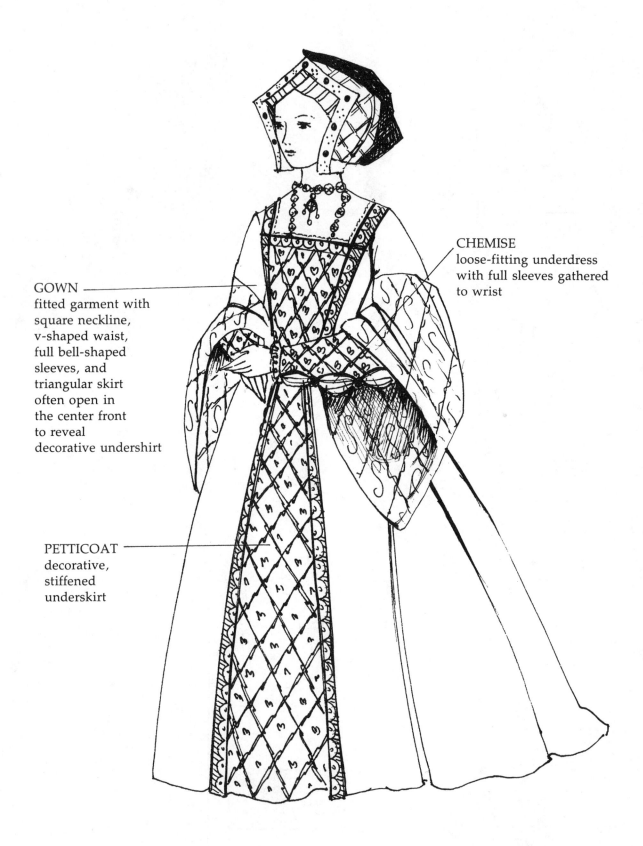

GOWN
fitted garment with
square neckline,
v-shaped waist,
full bell-shaped
sleeves, and
triangular skirt
often open in
the center front
to reveal
decorative undershirt

CHEMISE
loose-fitting underdress
with full sleeves gathered
to wrist

PETTICOAT
decorative,
stiffened
underskirt

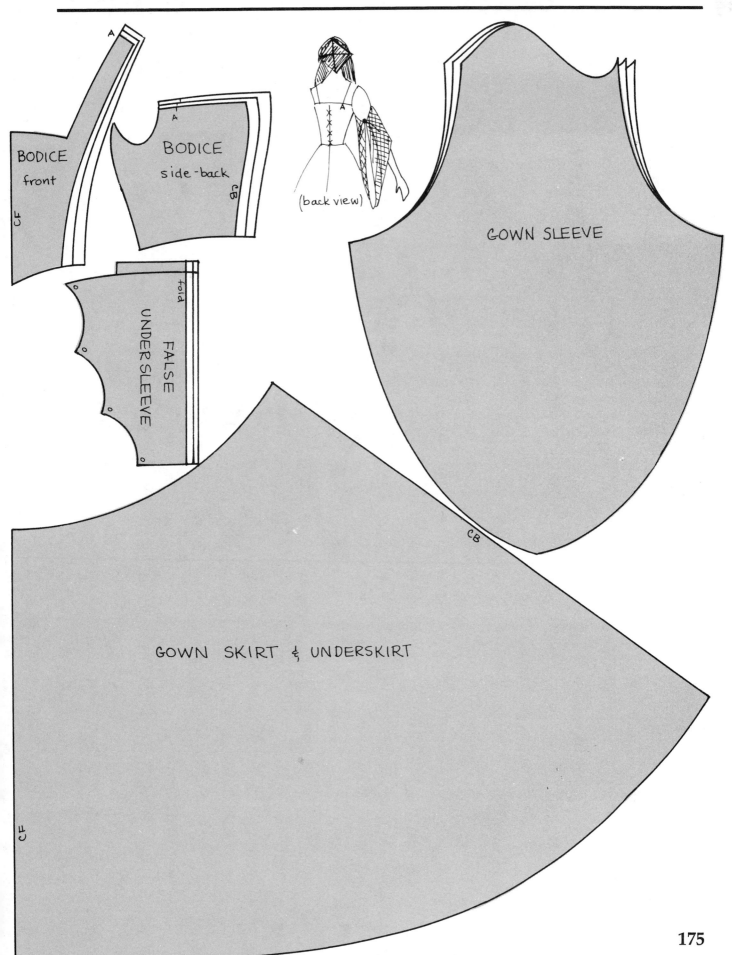

A

BODICE
front

CF

BODICE
side-back

A

CB

FALSE
UNDERSLEEVE

fold

(back view)
A

GOWN SLEEVE

CB

GOWN SKIRT & UNDERSKIRT

CF

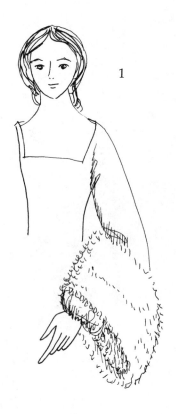

1

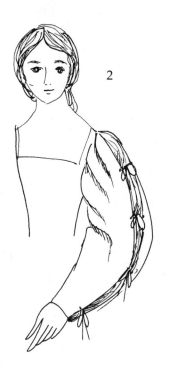

2

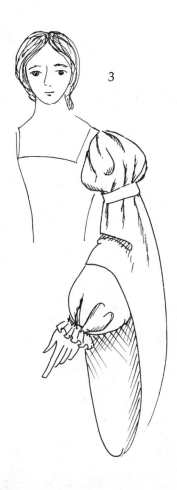

3

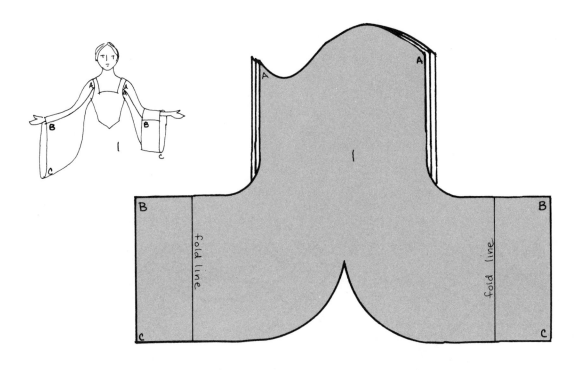

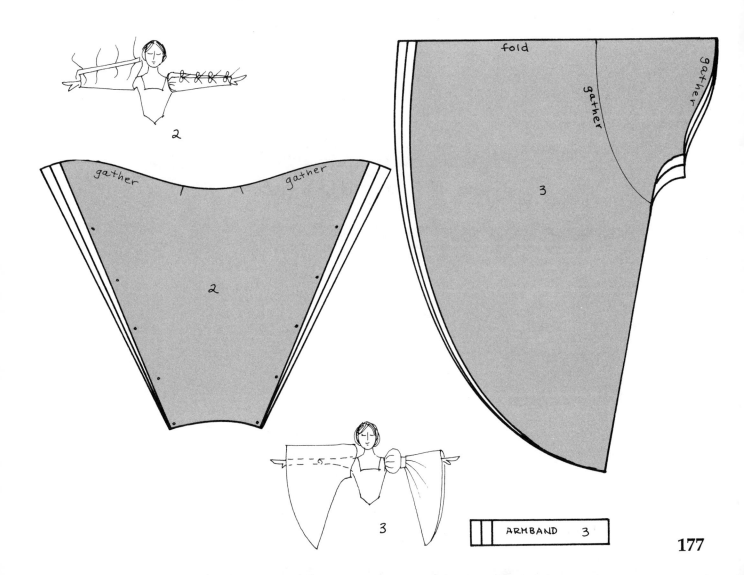

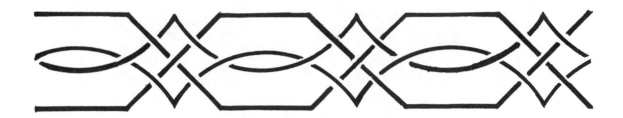

HAT
narrow brim; crown
stiffened to stand
up; decorated with
small plume

DOUBLET
with padded belly
(peascod belly)
and wings at
shoulder

VENETIANS
knee-length breeches
full at the waist,
narrowing to the knee

GARTERS

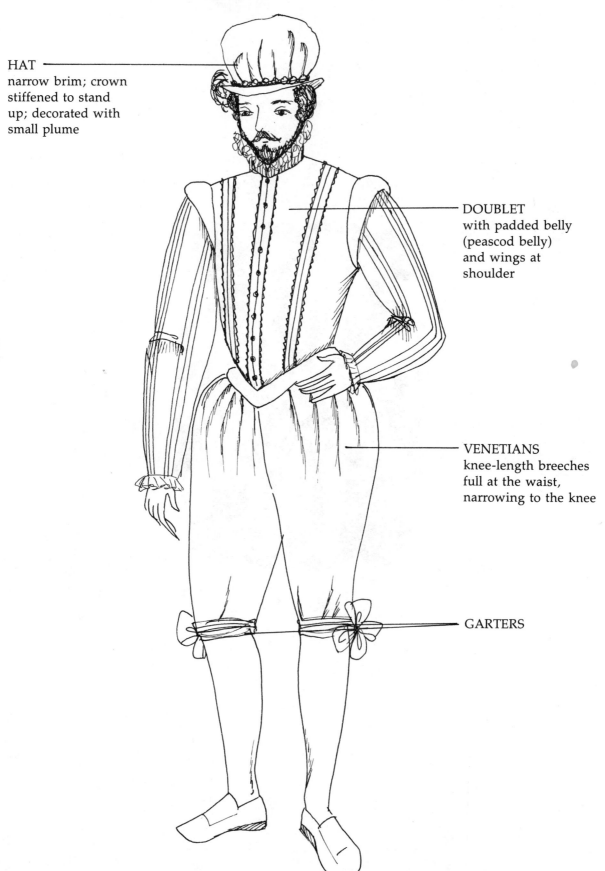

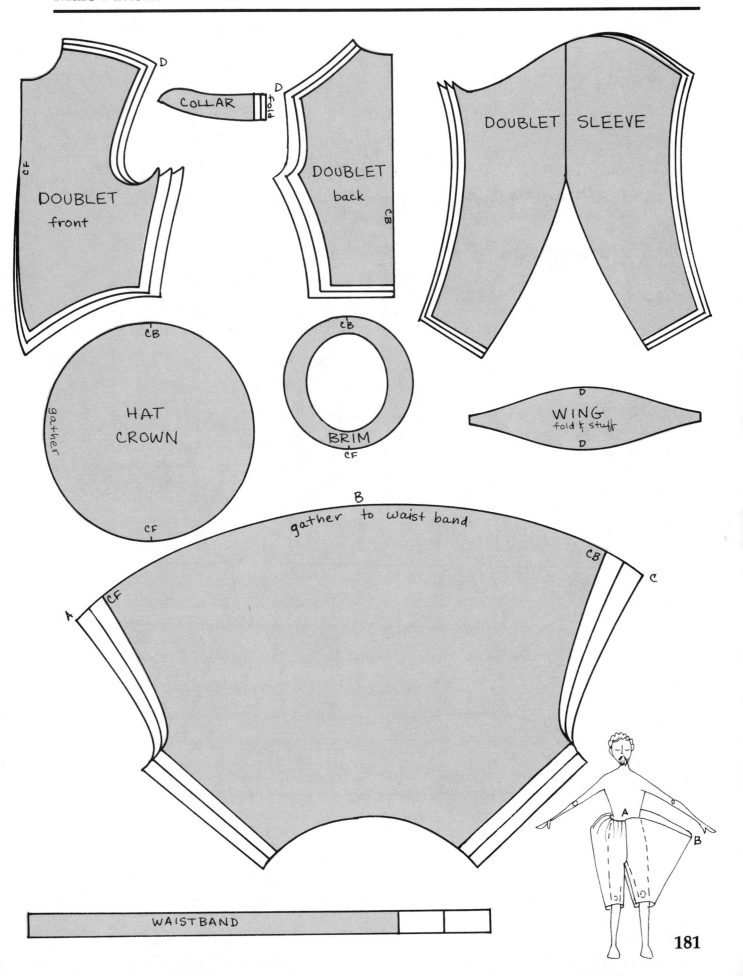

DOUBLET
front

CF

COLLAR

D

D
fold

DOUBLET
back

CB

DOUBLET　SLEEVE

HAT
CROWN

CB

gather

CF

BRIM

CB

CF

WING
fold & stuff

D

D

B

gather　to　waist　band

CF

CB

C

A

WAISTBAND

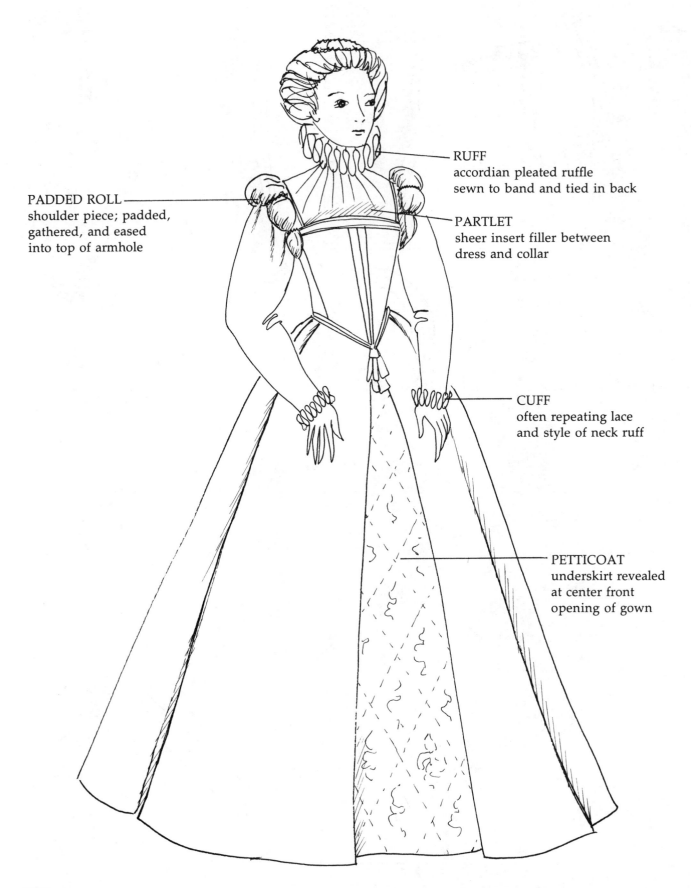

PADDED ROLL
shoulder piece; padded,
gathered, and eased
into top of armhole

RUFF
accordian pleated ruffle
sewn to band and tied in back

PARTLET
sheer insert filler between
dress and collar

CUFF
often repeating lace
and style of neck ruff

PETTICOAT
underskirt revealed
at center front
opening of gown

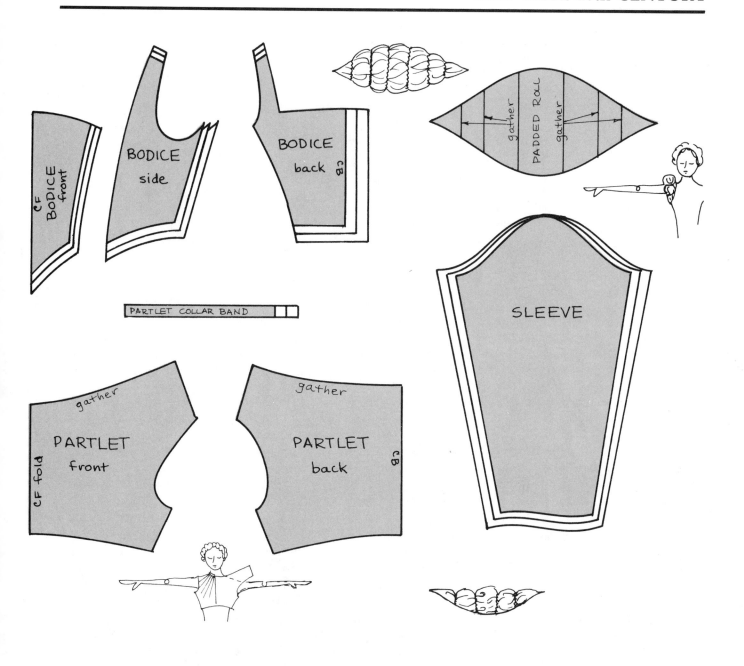

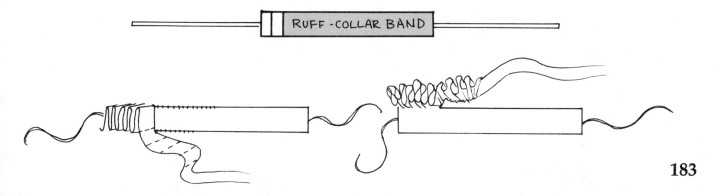

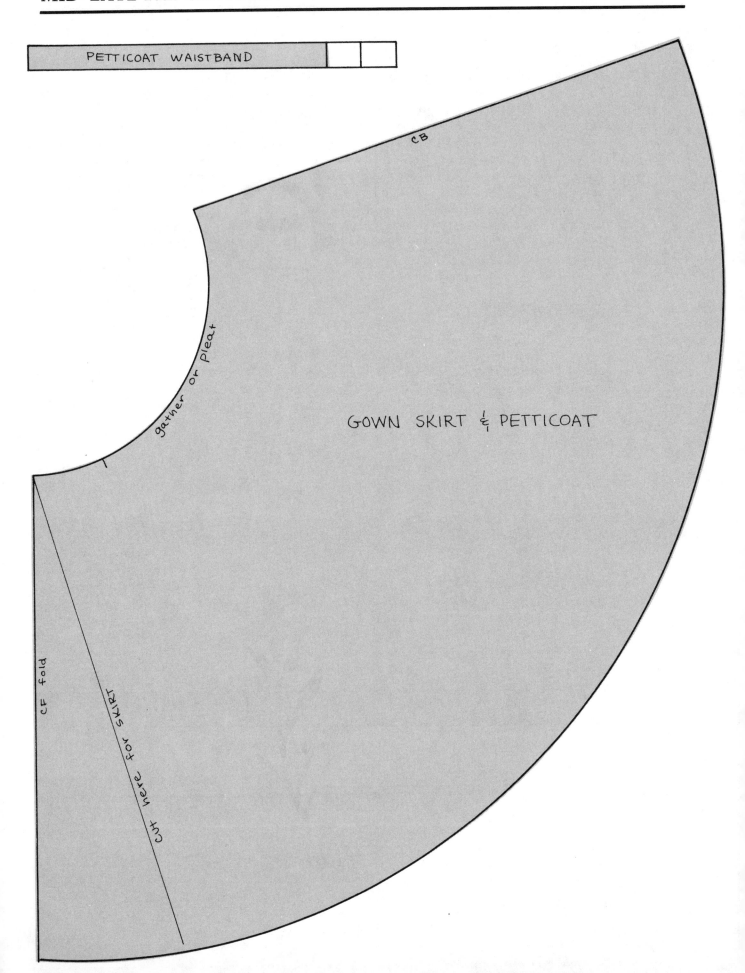

PETTICOAT WAISTBAND

CB

gather or pleat

GOWN SKIRT ¼ PETTICOAT

CF fold

Cut here for skirt

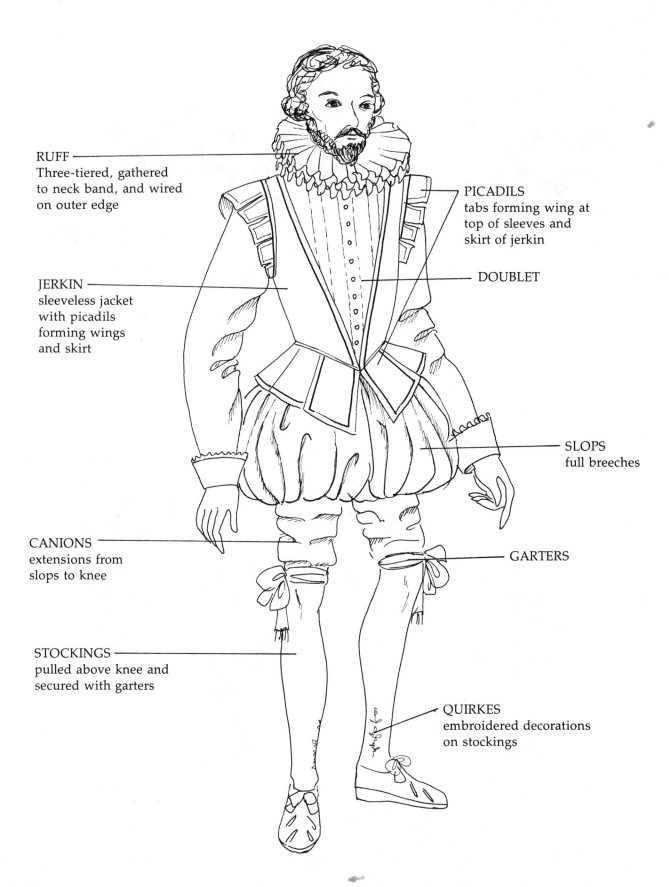

RUFF
Three-tiered, gathered
to neck band, and wired
on outer edge

PICADILS
tabs forming wing at
top of sleeves and
skirt of jerkin

DOUBLET

JERKIN
sleeveless jacket
with picadils
forming wings
and skirt

SLOPS
full breeches

CANIONS
extensions from
slops to knee

GARTERS

STOCKINGS
pulled above knee and
secured with garters

QUIRKES
embroidered decorations
on stockings

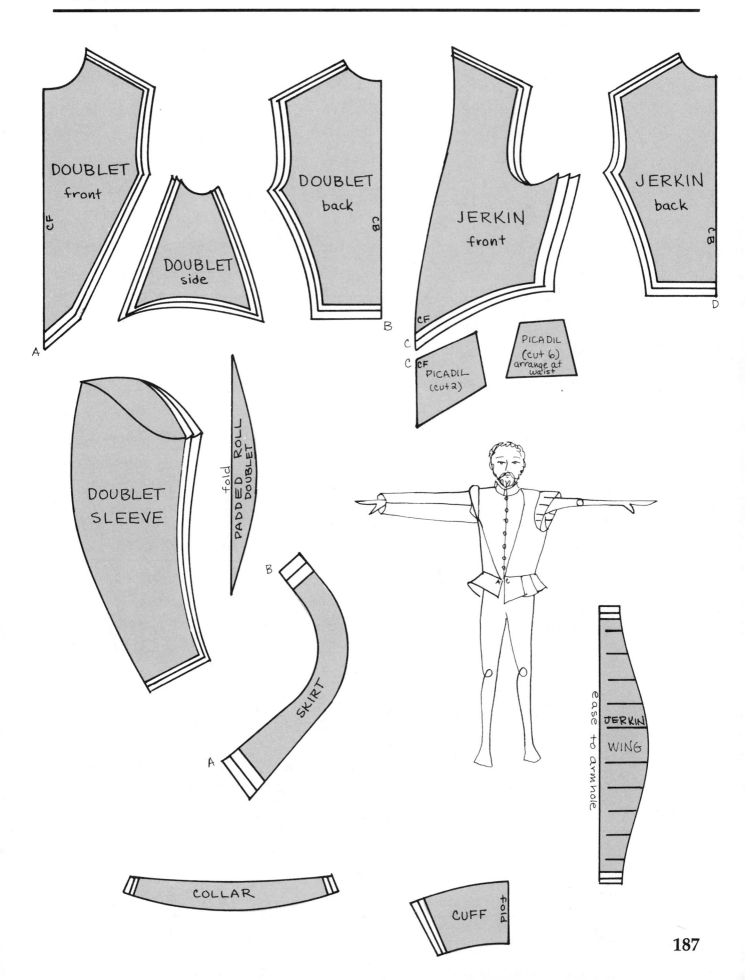

DOUBLET
front

CF

A

DOUBLET
side

DOUBLET
back

CB

B

JERKIN
front

CF

C

C

CF

PICADIL
(cut 2)

PICADIL
(cut 6)
arrange at
waist

JERKIN
back

CB

D

DOUBLET
SLEEVE

fold
PADDED ROLL
DOUBLET

B

SKIRT

A

COLLAR

CUFF   fold

ease to armhole

JERKIN
WING

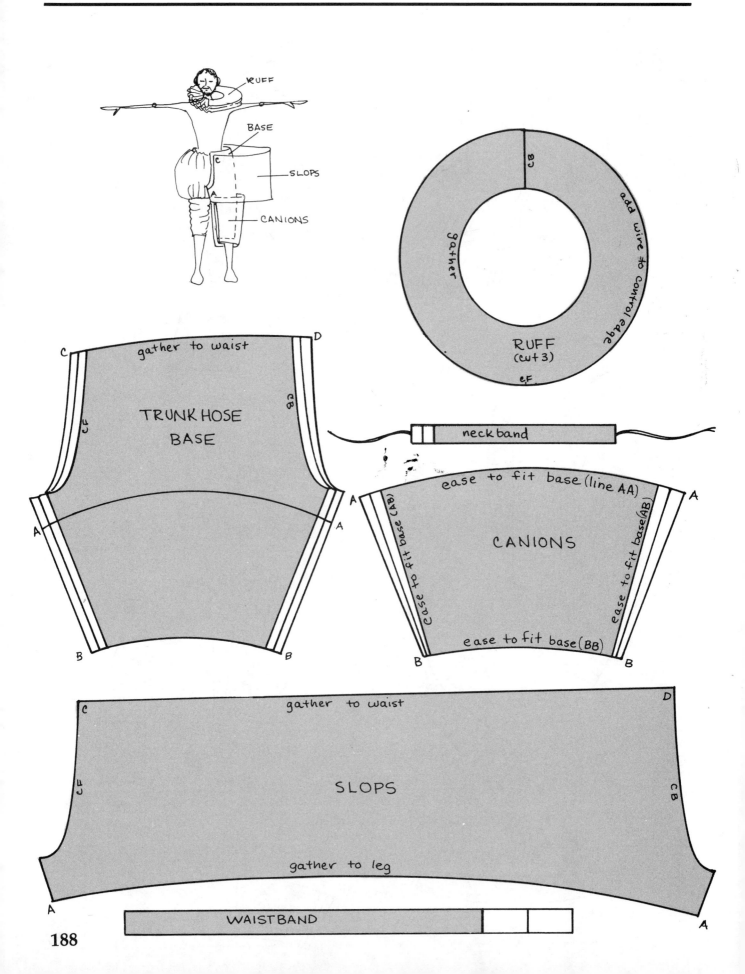

RUFF

BASE

SLOPS

CANIONS

CB

gather

add wire to controledge

RUFF
(cut 3)

CF

C — gather to waist — D

CF

TRUNK HOSE BASE

CB

A A A

B B

neckband

ease to fit base (line AA)

ease to fit base (AB)

ease to fit base (AB)

CANIONS

A A

ease to fit base (AB)

ease to fit base (AB)

ease to fit base (BB)

B B

C — gather to waist — D

CF

SLOPS

CB

gather to leg

A

A

WAISTBAND

1

CIRCULAR CAPE
worn with standing collar

2

SEMICIRCULAR CAPE
constructed with collar
and decorative
sleeves

3

HOODED CAPE
made of an elongated
semi-circle folded and fastened
in the back to form a hood

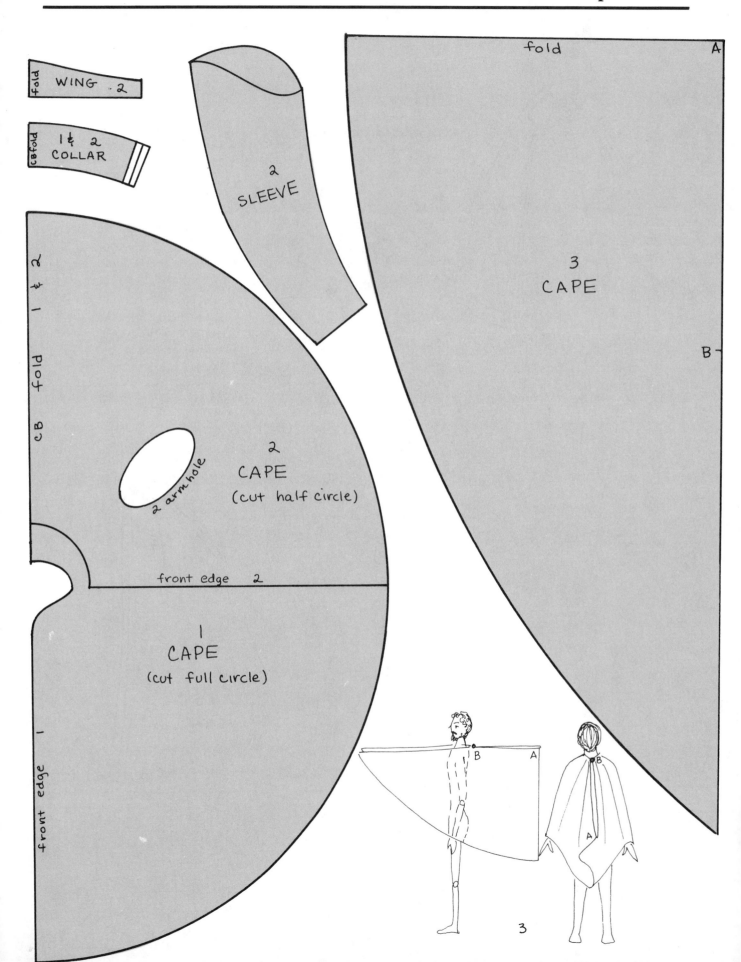

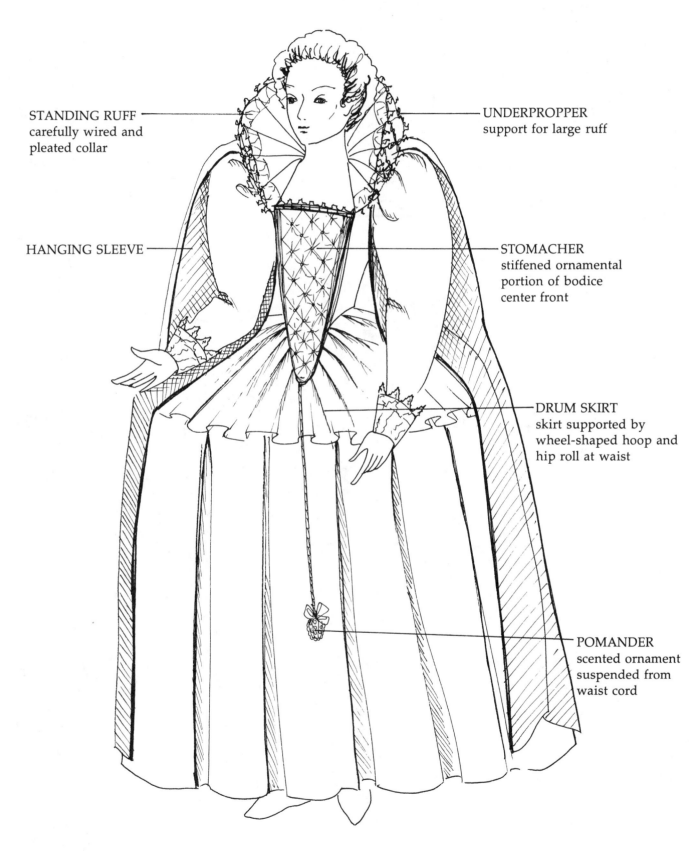

STANDING RUFF
carefully wired and
pleated collar

UNDERPROPPER
support for large ruff

HANGING SLEEVE

STOMACHER
stiffened ornamental
portion of bodice
center front

DRUM SKIRT
skirt supported by
wheel-shaped hoop and
hip roll at waist

POMANDER
scented ornament
suspended from
waist cord

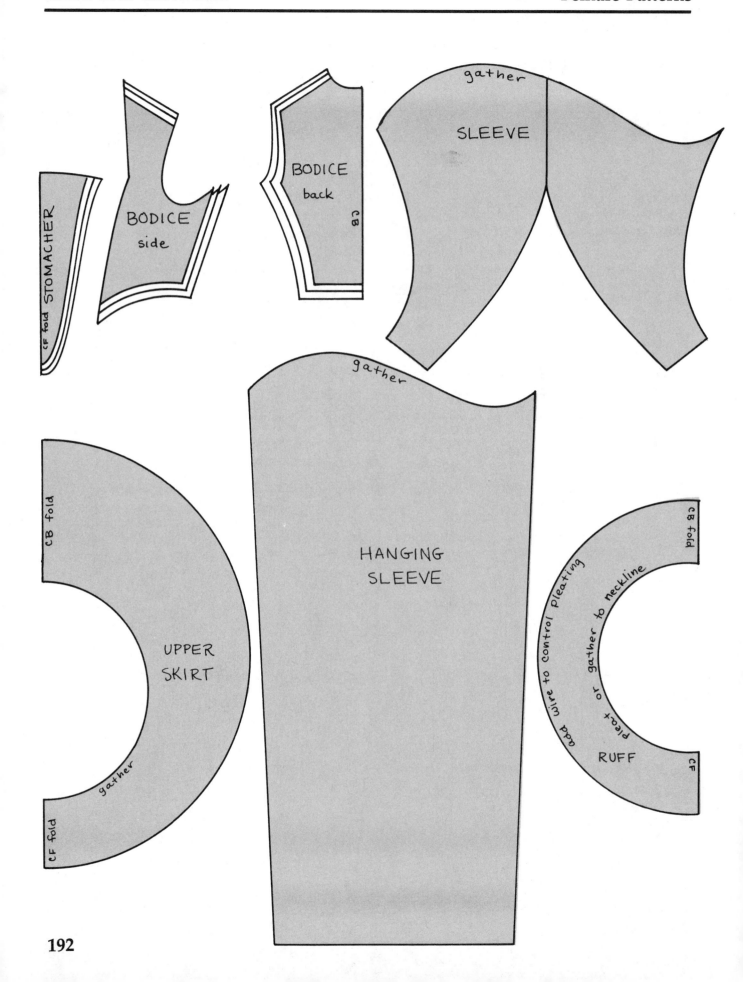

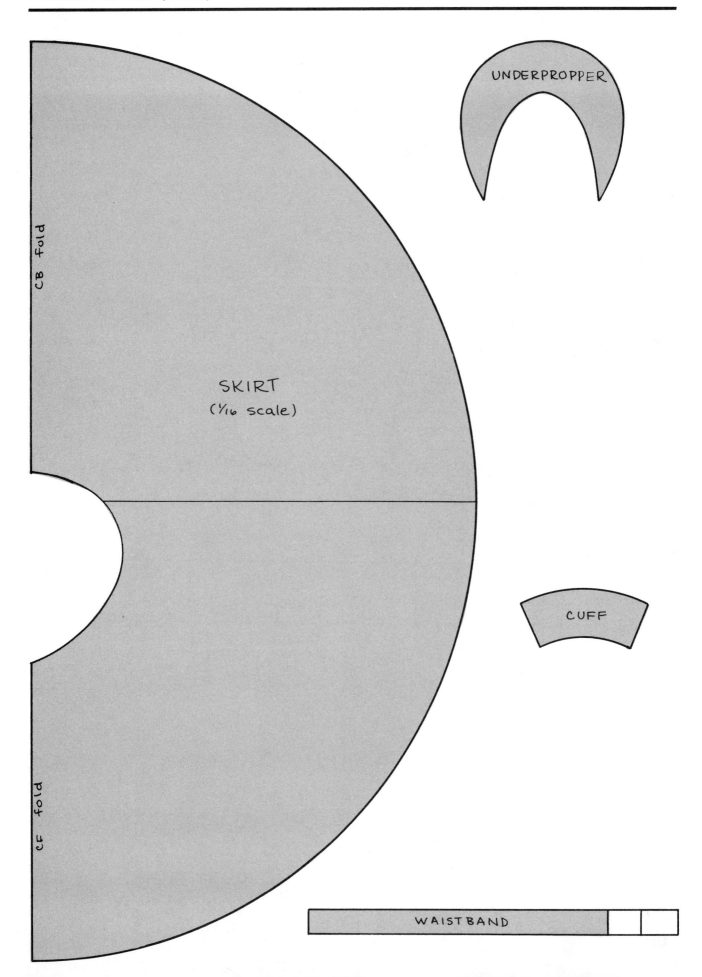

UNDERPROPPER

CB fold

SKIRT
(1/16 scale)

CF fold

CUFF

WAISTBAND

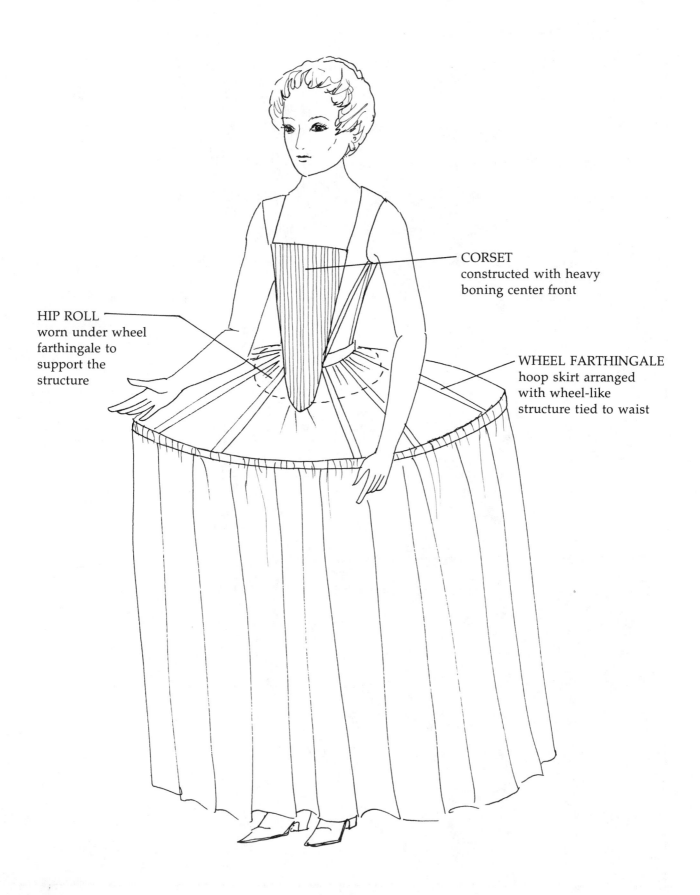

CORSET
constructed with heavy
boning center front

HIP ROLL
worn under wheel
farthingale to
support the
structure

WHEEL FARTHINGALE
hoop skirt arranged
with wheel-like
structure tied to waist

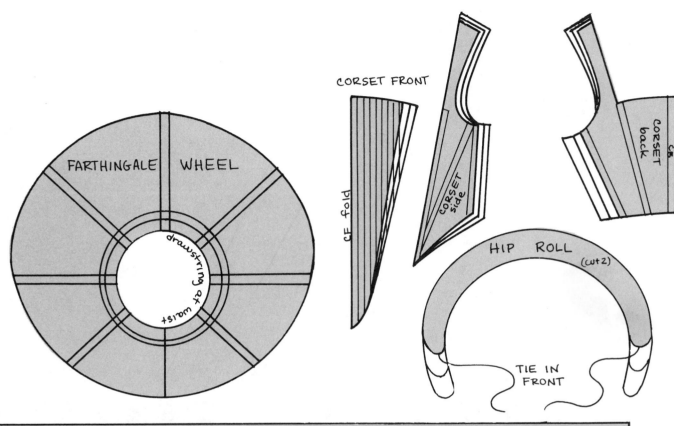

FARTHINGALE WHEEL

drawstring at waist

CORSET FRONT

CF fold

CORSET side

CORSET back

C.B.

HIP ROLL (cut 2)

TIE IN FRONT

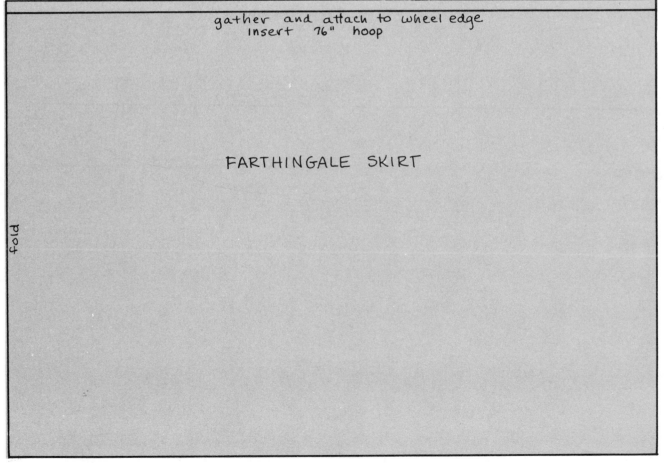

gather and attach to wheel edge
insert 76" hoop

FARTHINGALE SKIRT

fold

1

SLEEVELESS SURCOAT

2

SURCOAT WITH HANGING SLEEVES

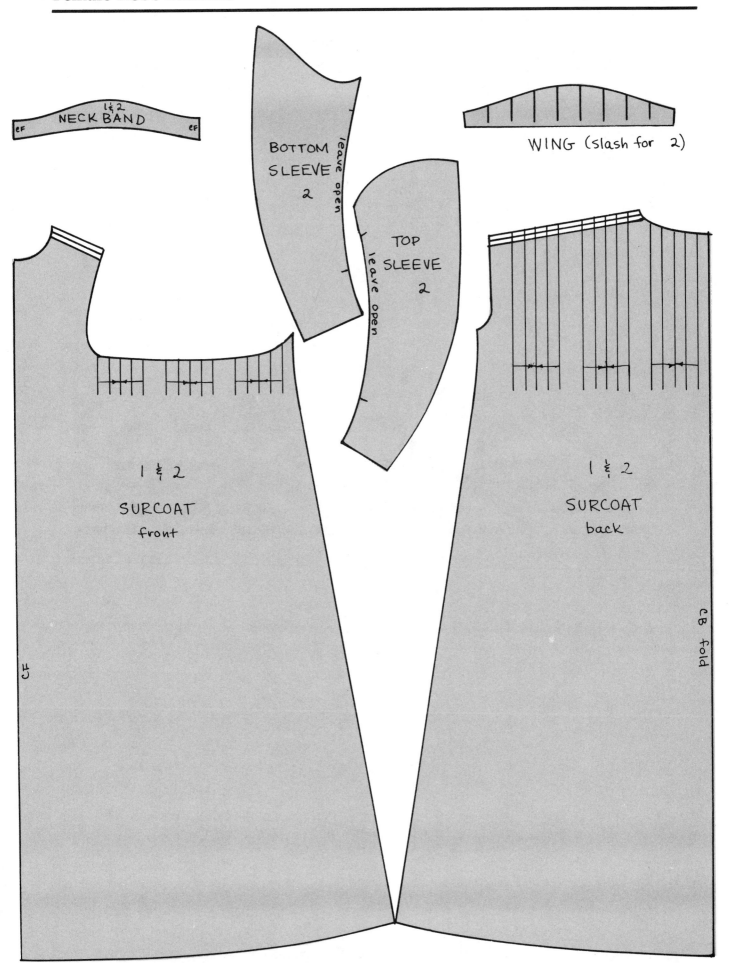

NECK BAND 1 & 2 CF CF

BOTTOM SLEEVE 2 leave open

WING (slash for 2)

TOP SLEEVE 2 leave open

1 & 2 SURCOAT front CF

1 & 2 SURCOAT back CB fold

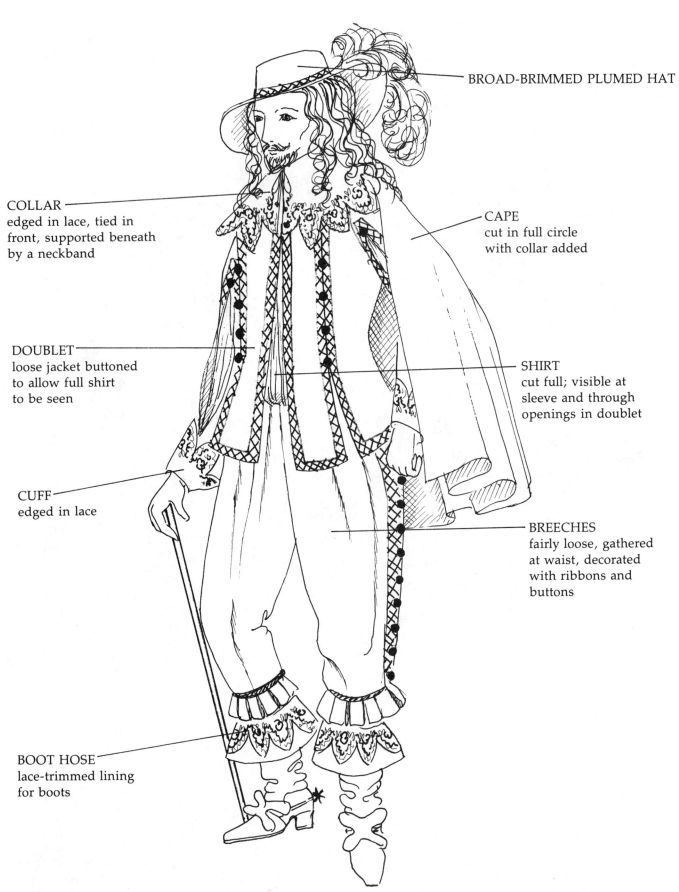

COLLAR
edged in lace, tied in
front, supported beneath
by a neckband

CAPE
cut in full circle
with collar added

DOUBLET
loose jacket buttoned
to allow full shirt
to be seen

SHIRT
cut full; visible at
sleeve and through
openings in doublet

CUFF
edged in lace

BROAD-BRIMMED PLUMED HAT

BREECHES
fairly loose, gathered
at waist, decorated
with ribbons and
buttons

BOOT HOSE
lace-trimmed lining
for boots

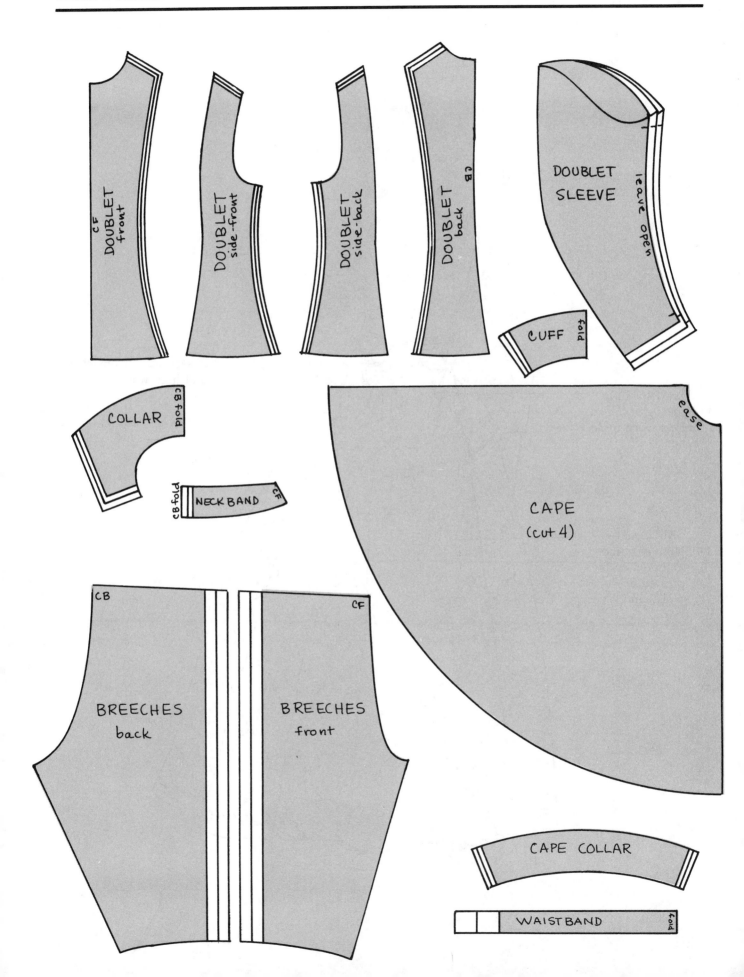

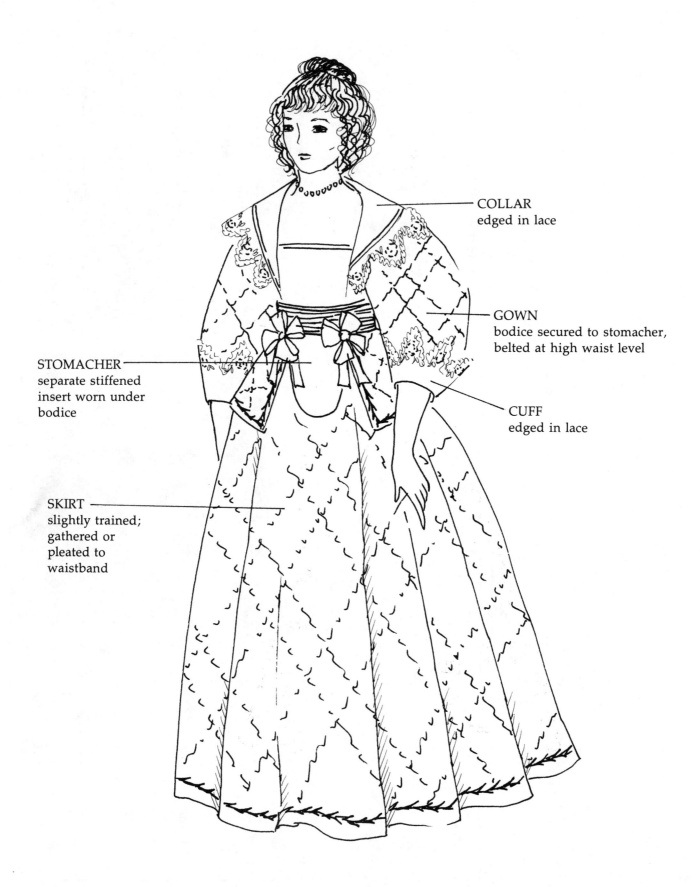

COLLAR
edged in lace

GOWN
bodice secured to stomacher,
belted at high waist level

CUFF
edged in lace

STOMACHER
separate stiffened
insert worn under
bodice

SKIRT
slightly trained;
gathered or
pleated to
waistband

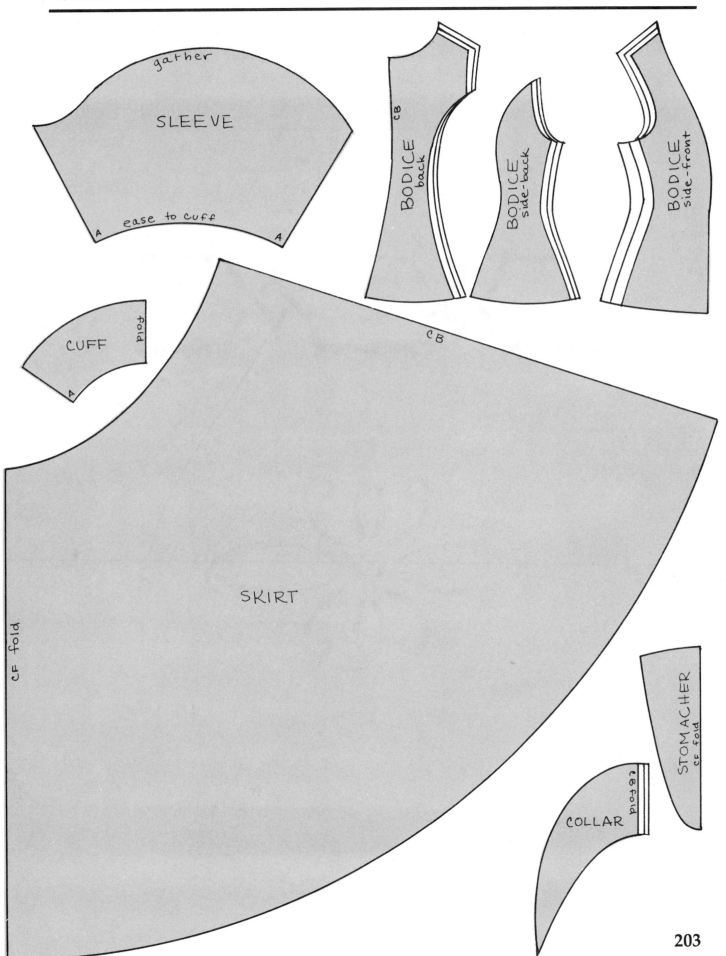

gather

SLEEVE

ease to cuff

A　　　　A

CUFF

fold

A

BODICE
back

CB

BODICE
side-back

BODICE
side-front

SKIRT

CB

CF fold

STOMACHER
cf fold

COLLAR

cB fold

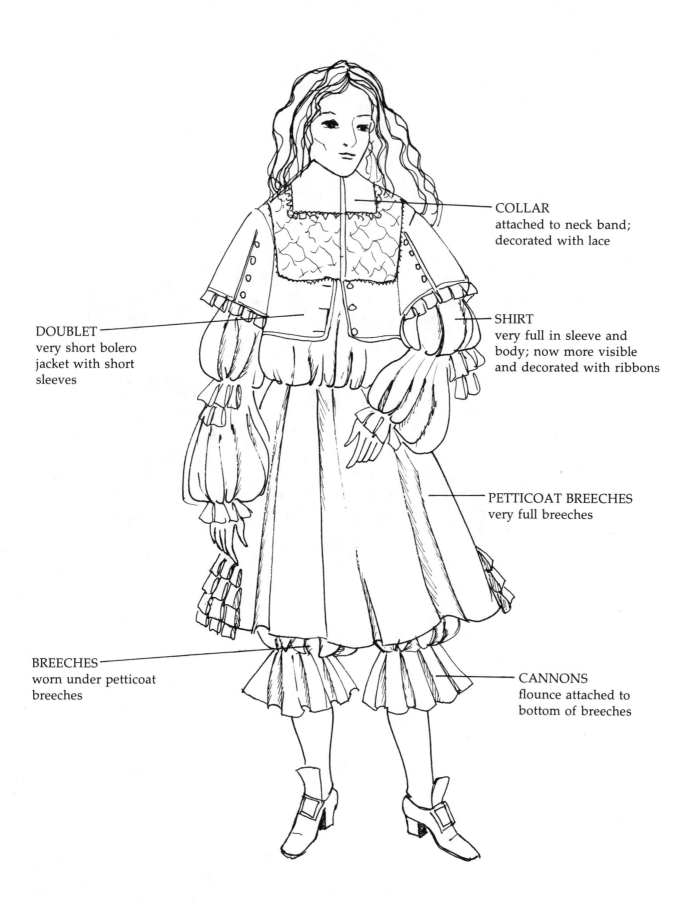

COLLAR
attached to neck band;
decorated with lace

SHIRT
very full in sleeve and
body; now more visible
and decorated with ribbons

DOUBLET
very short bolero
jacket with short
sleeves

PETTICOAT BREECHES
very full breeches

BREECHES
worn under petticoat
breeches

CANNONS
flounce attached to
bottom of breeches

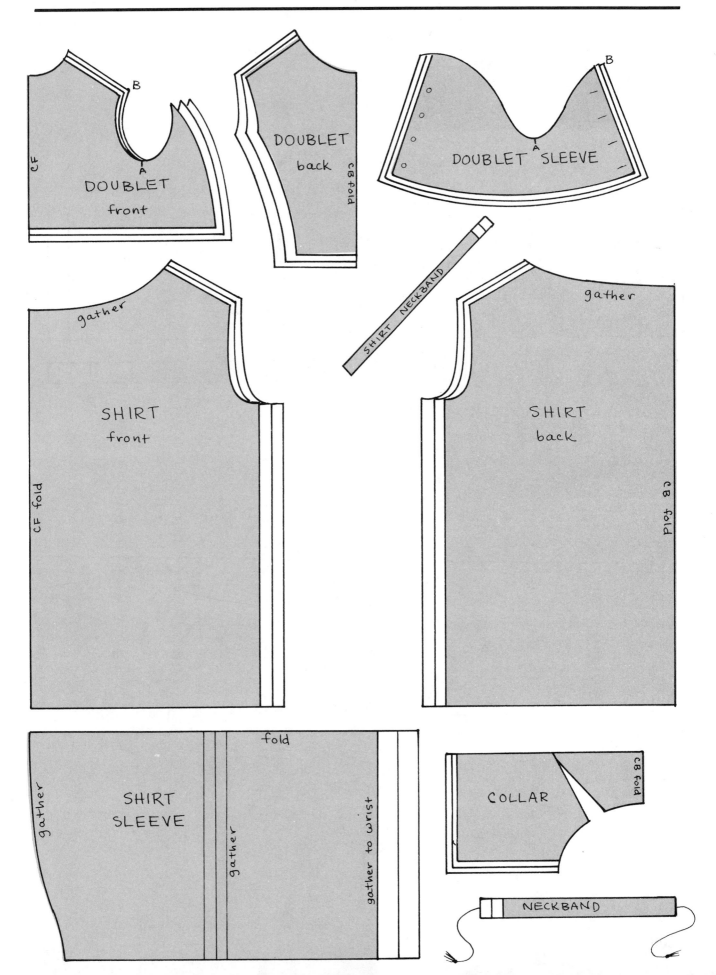

DOUBLET front

B

CF

A

DOUBLET back

CB fold

DOUBLET SLEEVE

B

A

SHIRT NECKBAND

gather

SHIRT front

CF fold

gather

SHIRT back

CB fold

SHIRT SLEEVE

gather

fold

gather

gather to wrist

COLLAR

CB fold

NECKBAND

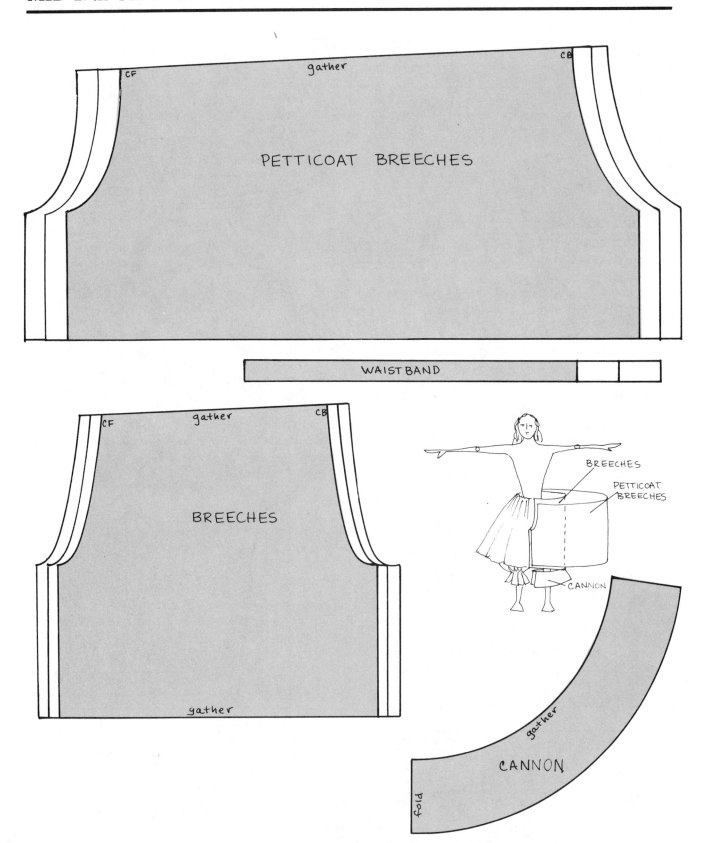

PETTICOAT BREECHES

WAISTBAND

BREECHES

BREECHES
PETTICOAT BREECHES

CANNON

CANNON

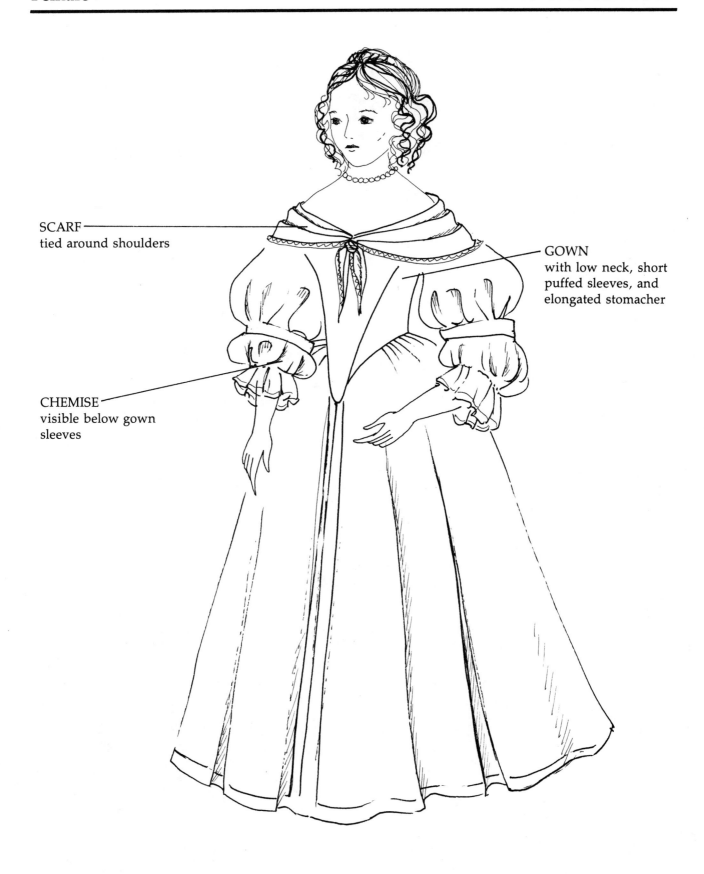

SCARF
tied around shoulders

GOWN
with low neck, short
puffed sleeves, and
elongated stomacher

CHEMISE
visible below gown
sleeves

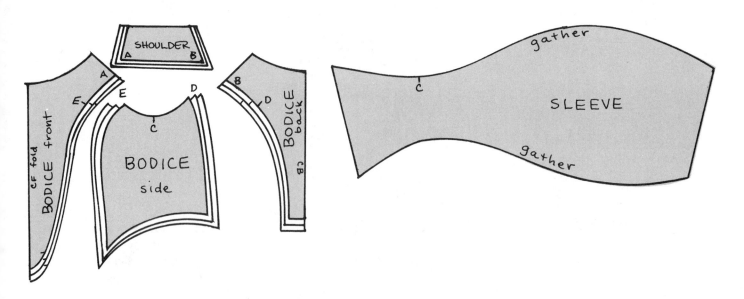

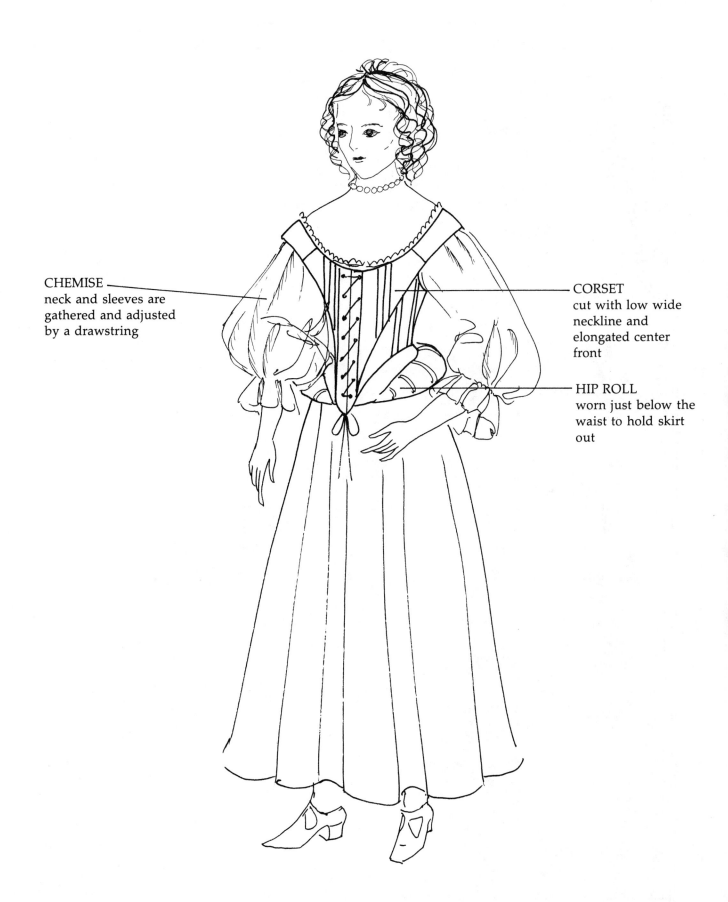

CHEMISE
neck and sleeves are
gathered and adjusted
by a drawstring

CORSET
cut with low wide
neckline and
elongated center
front

HIP ROLL
worn just below the
waist to hold skirt
out

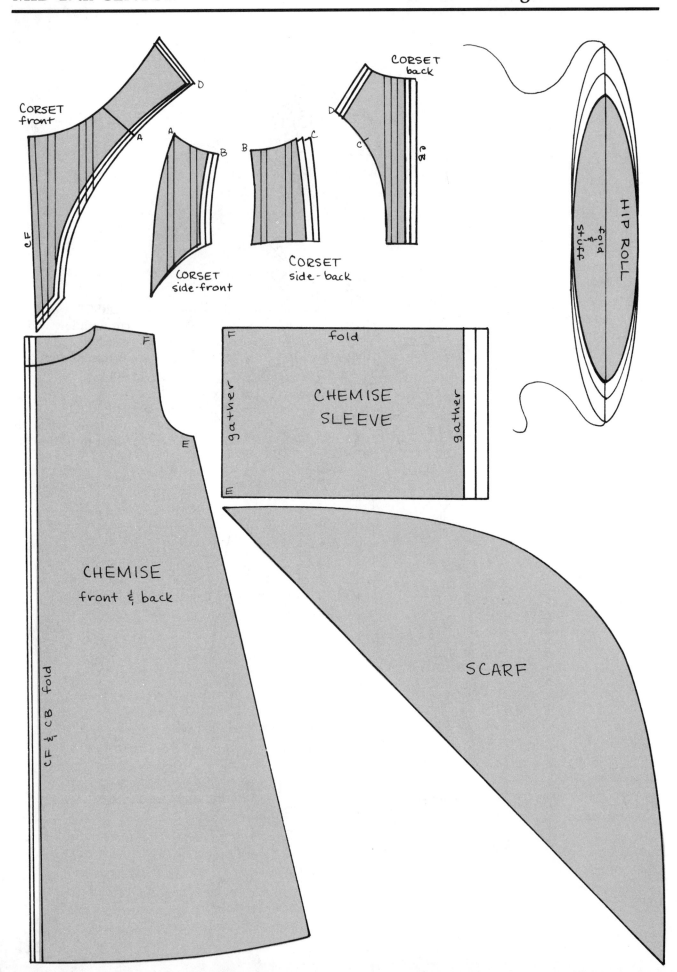

CORSET
front

CORSET
side-front

CORSET
side-back

CORSET
back

HIP ROLL

fold & stuff

CHEMISE
SLEEVE

fold

gather

gather

CHEMISE
front & back

C F & C B fold

SCARF

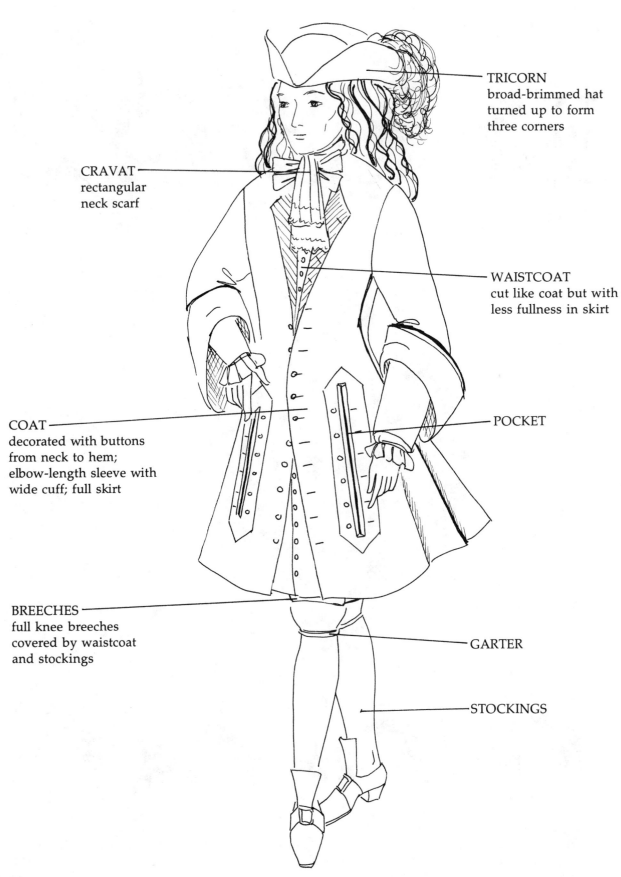

TRICORN
broad-brimmed hat
turned up to form
three corners

CRAVAT
rectangular
neck scarf

WAISTCOAT
cut like coat but with
less fullness in skirt

COAT
decorated with buttons
from neck to hem;
elbow-length sleeve with
wide cuff; full skirt

POCKET

BREECHES
full knee breeches
covered by waistcoat
and stockings

GARTER

STOCKINGS

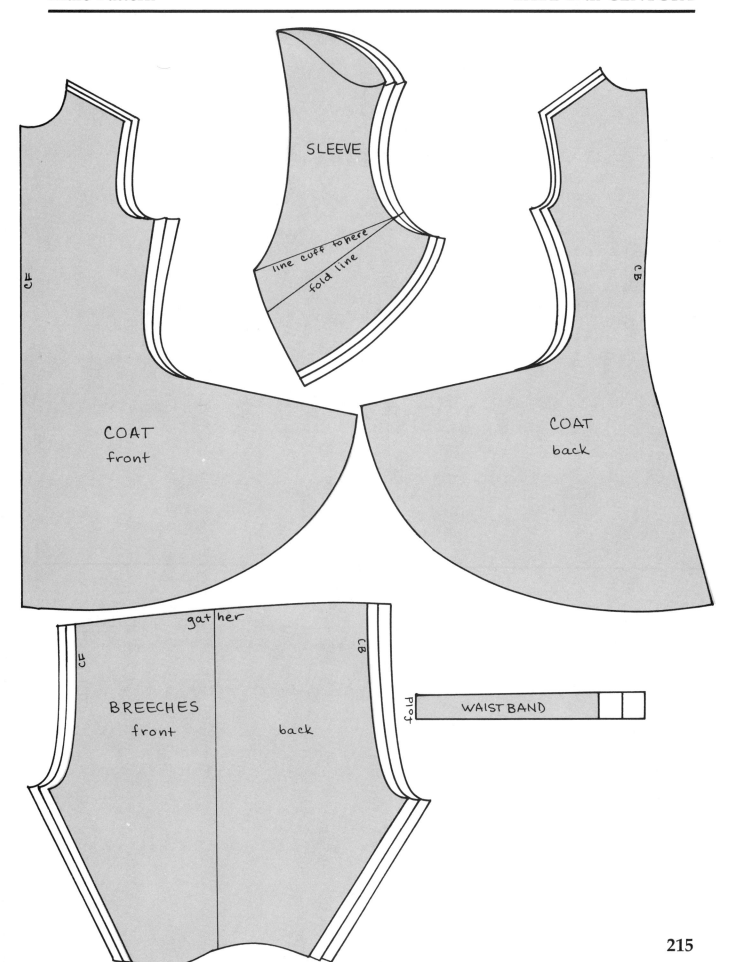

SLEEVE

line cuff to here

fold line

CF

COAT
front

CB

COAT
back

gather

CF

CB

BREECHES
front

back

fold

WAIST BAND

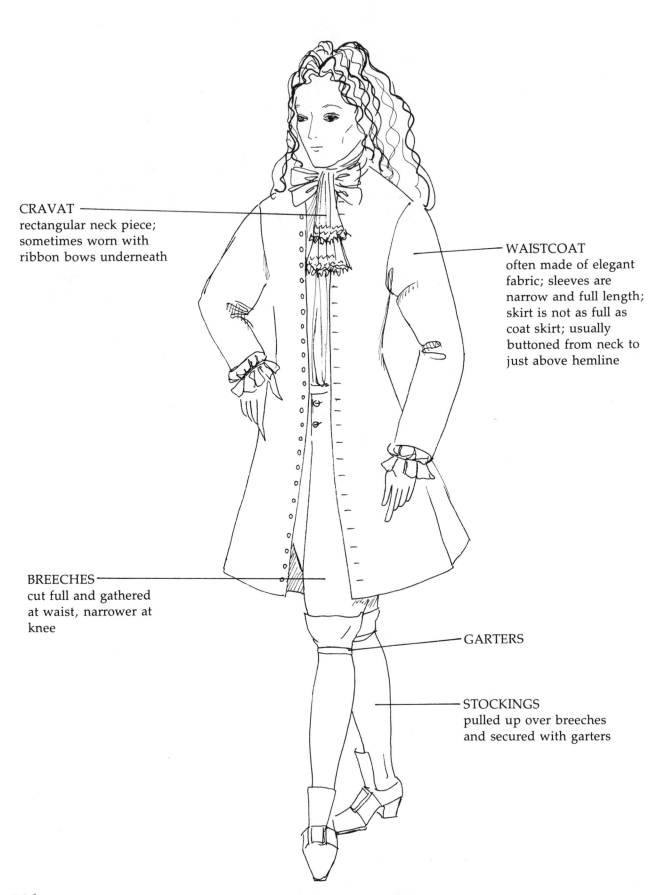

CRAVAT
rectangular neck piece;
sometimes worn with
ribbon bows underneath

WAISTCOAT
often made of elegant
fabric; sleeves are
narrow and full length;
skirt is not as full as
coat skirt; usually
buttoned from neck to
just above hemline

BREECHES
cut full and gathered
at waist, narrower at
knee

GARTERS

STOCKINGS
pulled up over breeches
and secured with garters

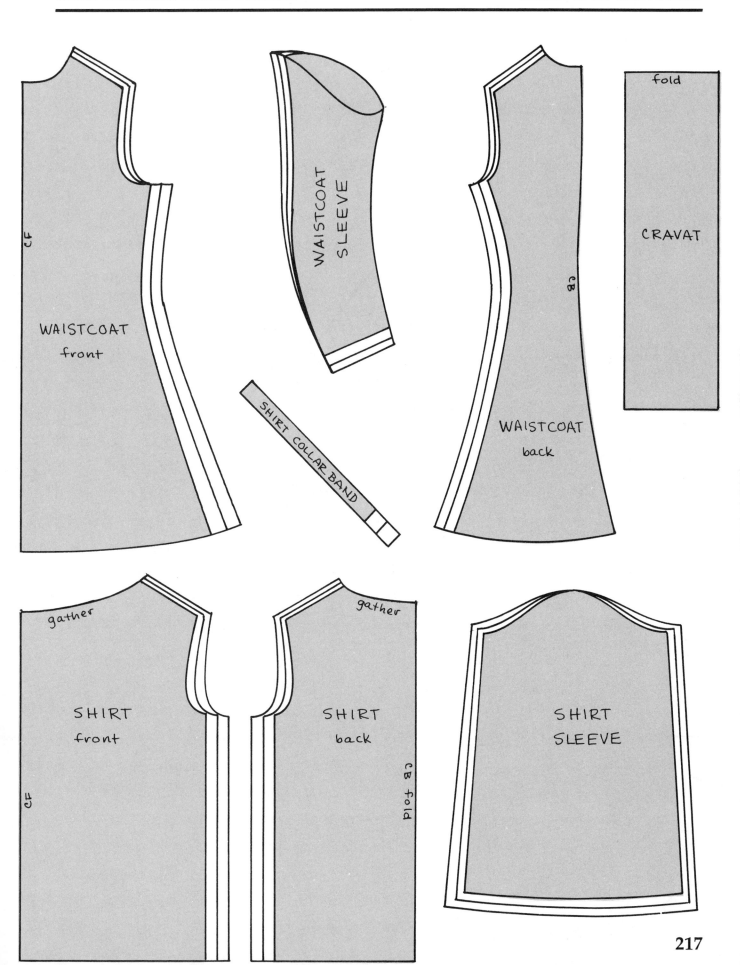

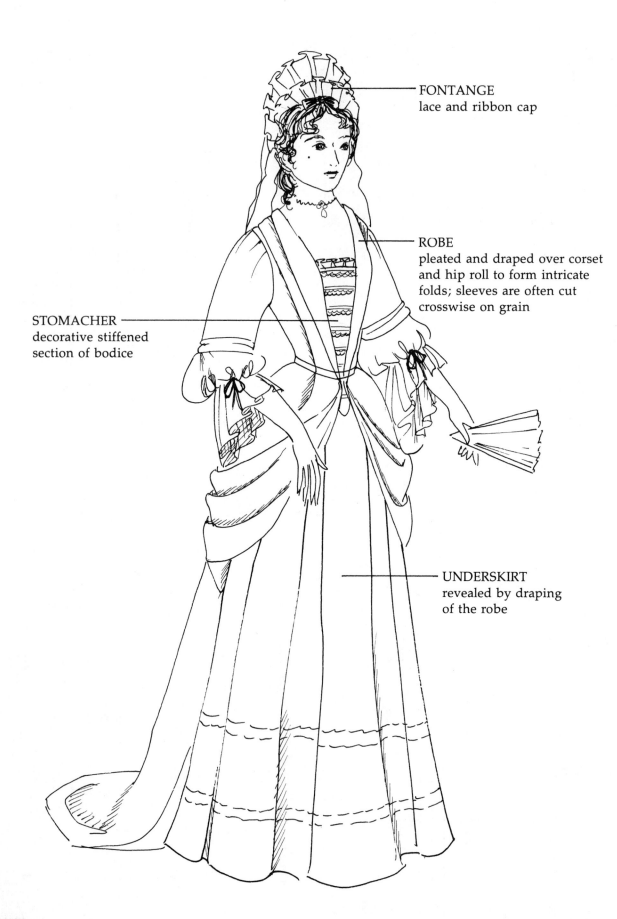

FONTANGE
lace and ribbon cap

ROBE
pleated and draped over corset
and hip roll to form intricate
folds; sleeves are often cut
crosswise on grain

STOMACHER
decorative stiffened
section of bodice

UNDERSKIRT
revealed by draping
of the robe

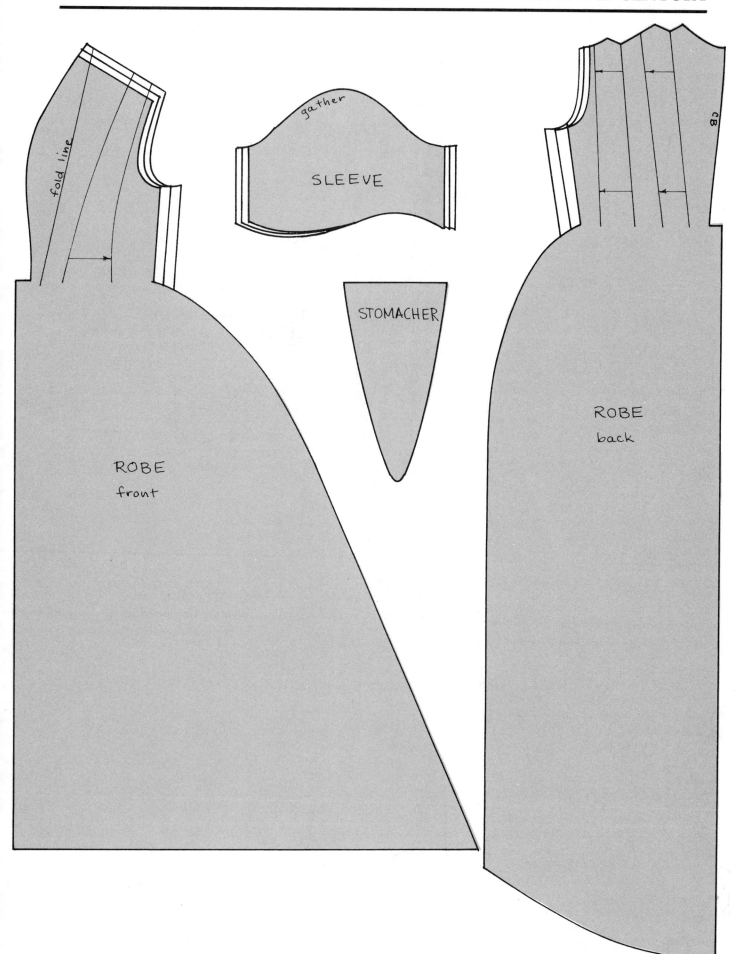

fold line

gather

SLEEVE

cB

STOMACHER

ROBE
front

ROBE
back

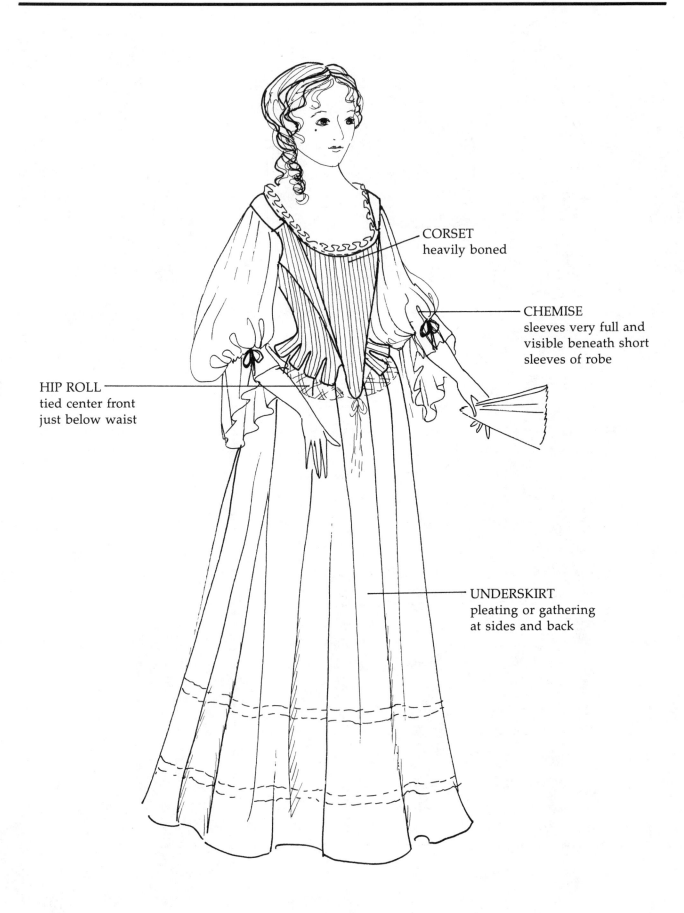

CORSET
heavily boned

CHEMISE
sleeves very full and
visible beneath short
sleeves of robe

HIP ROLL
tied center front
just below waist

UNDERSKIRT
pleating or gathering
at sides and back

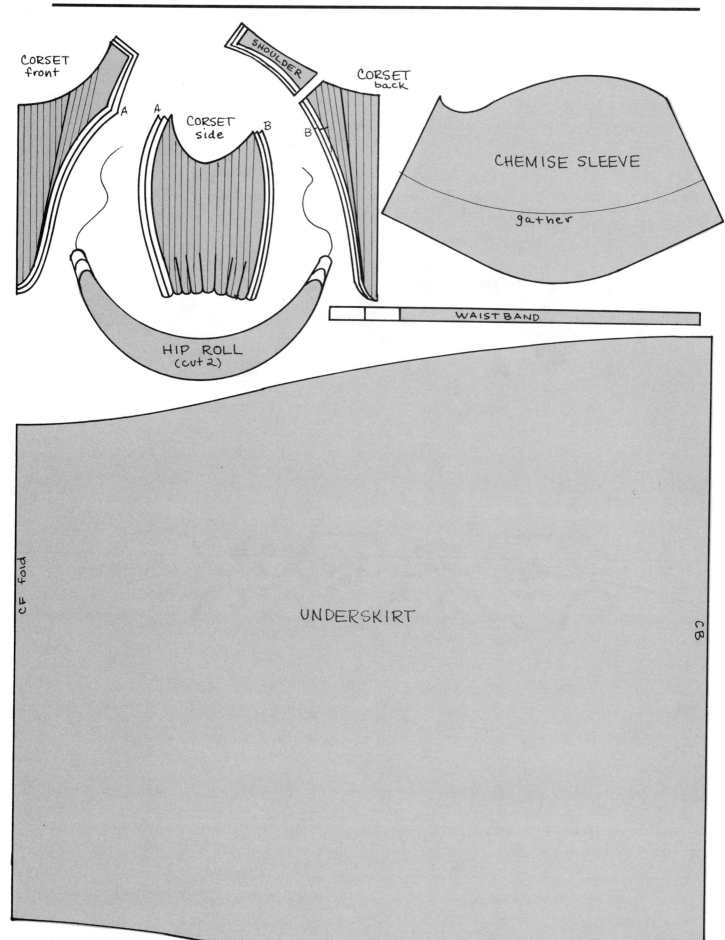

CORSET front

SHOULDER

CORSET back

CORSET side

A   A   B   B

CHEMISE SLEEVE

gather

HIP ROLL
(cut 2)

WAISTBAND

CF fold

UNDERSKIRT

CB

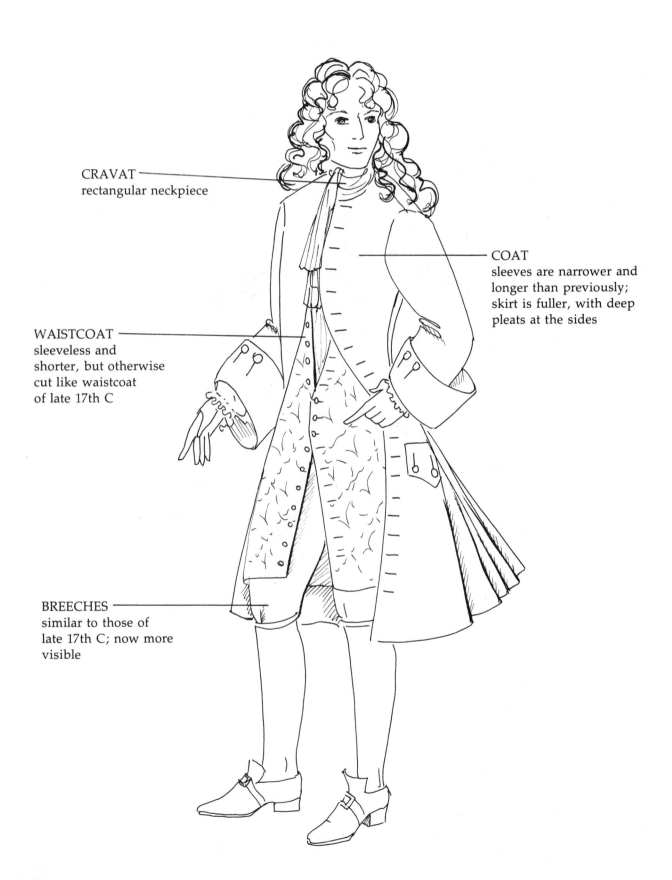

CRAVAT
rectangular neckpiece

COAT
sleeves are narrower and
longer than previously;
skirt is fuller, with deep
pleats at the sides

WAISTCOAT
sleeveless and
shorter, but otherwise
cut like waistcoat
of late 17th C

BREECHES
similar to those of
late 17th C; now more
visible

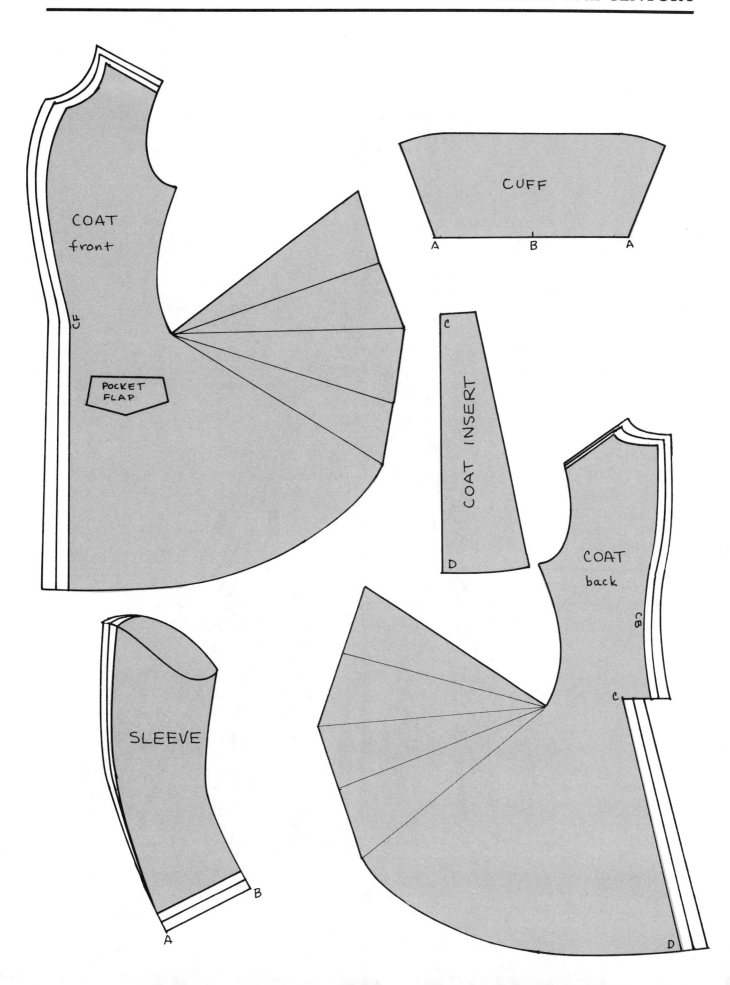

COAT
front

CF

POCKET
FLAP

CUFF

A　　　　　　B　　　　　　A

C

COAT INSERT

D

COAT
back

CB

C

SLEEVE

A

B

D

STOMACHER

CHEMISE
sleeveless visible
beneath gown sleeves

GOWN
bodice fitted to stomacher
in the front, falling into
full box pleats from
shoulder to hem in the
back; worn over hoop
petticoat

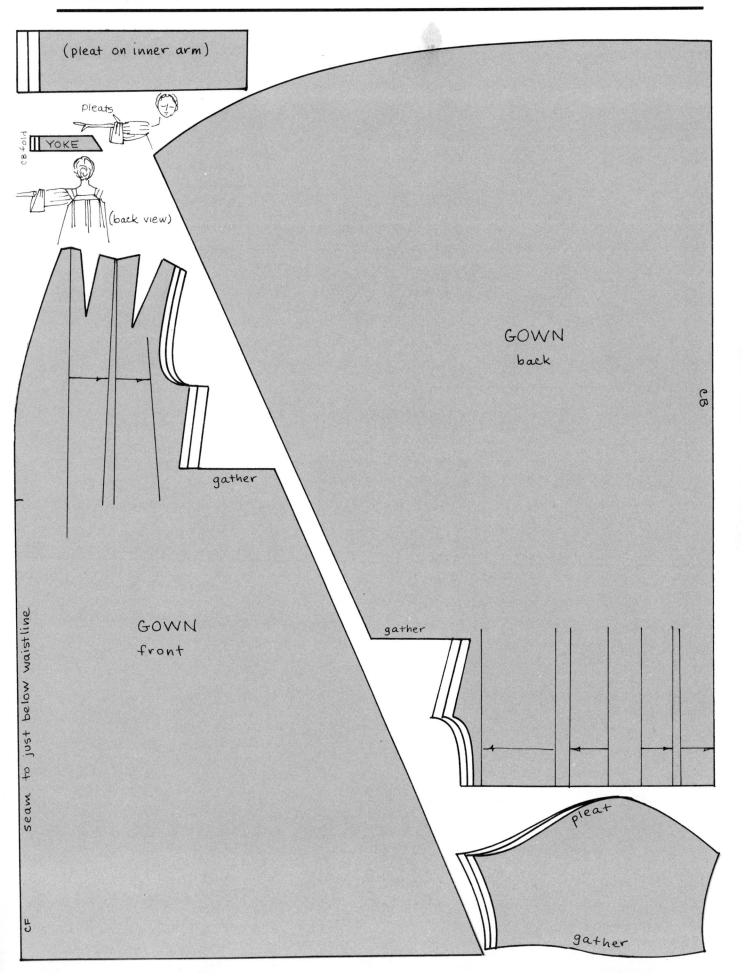

(pleat on inner arm)

pleats

CB fold

YOKE

(back view)

GOWN
back

CB

gather

gather

GOWN
front

seam to just below waistline

CF

gather

pleat

gather

CAP
small gathered cap
decorated with lace

NECK RUFFLE
small gathered ruffle
tied in the back

CHEMISE

STOMACHER

GOWN LINING
fitted under-bodice to
which gown pleats are
secured

HOOP PETTICOAT
petticoat silhouette
varied by strings
tied on inside to
flatten or widen oval
shape

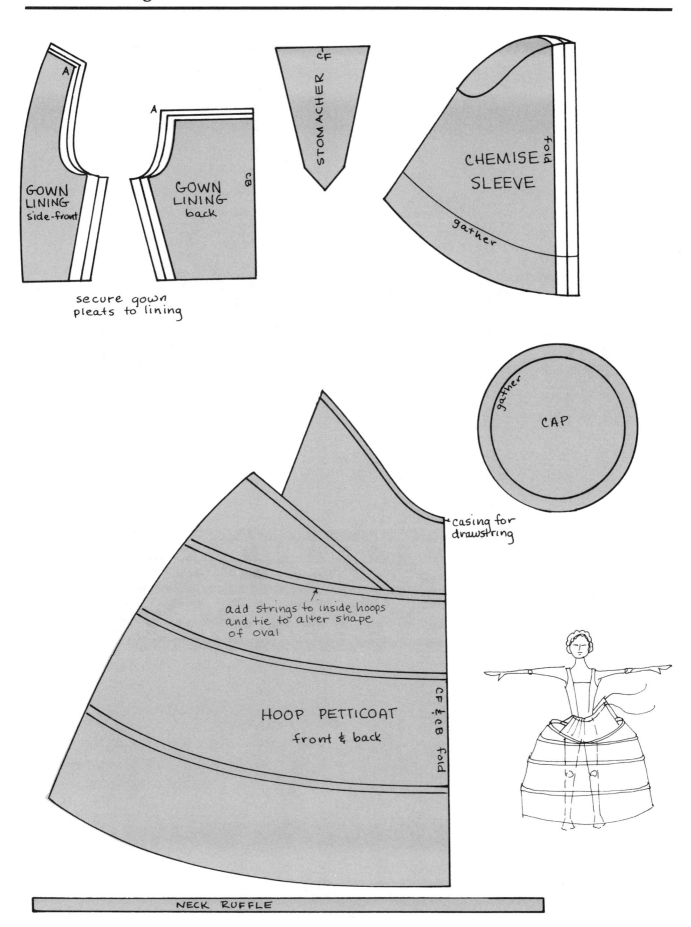

A

GOWN
LINING
side-front

A

CB

GOWN
LINING
back

secure gown
pleats to lining

CF

STOMACHER

CHEMISE
SLEEVE

fold

gather

CAP

gather

casing for
drawstring

add strings to inside hoops
and tie to alter shape
of oval

CF & CB fold

HOOP PETTICOAT

front & back

NECK RUFFLE

gather and sew to ribbon

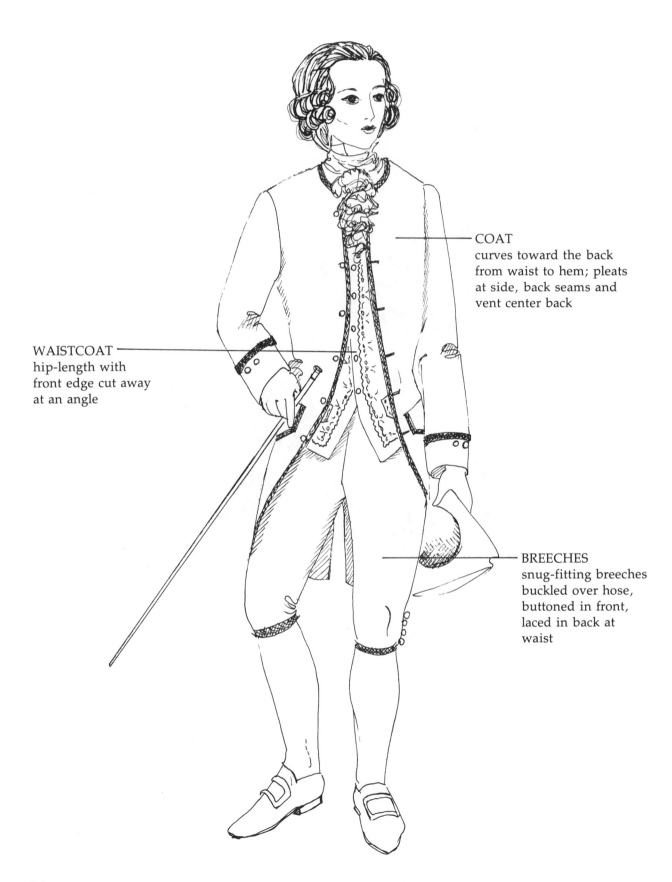

COAT
curves toward the back
from waist to hem; pleats
at side, back seams and
vent center back

WAISTCOAT
hip-length with
front edge cut away
at an angle

BREECHES
snug-fitting breeches
buckled over hose,
buttoned in front,
laced in back at
waist

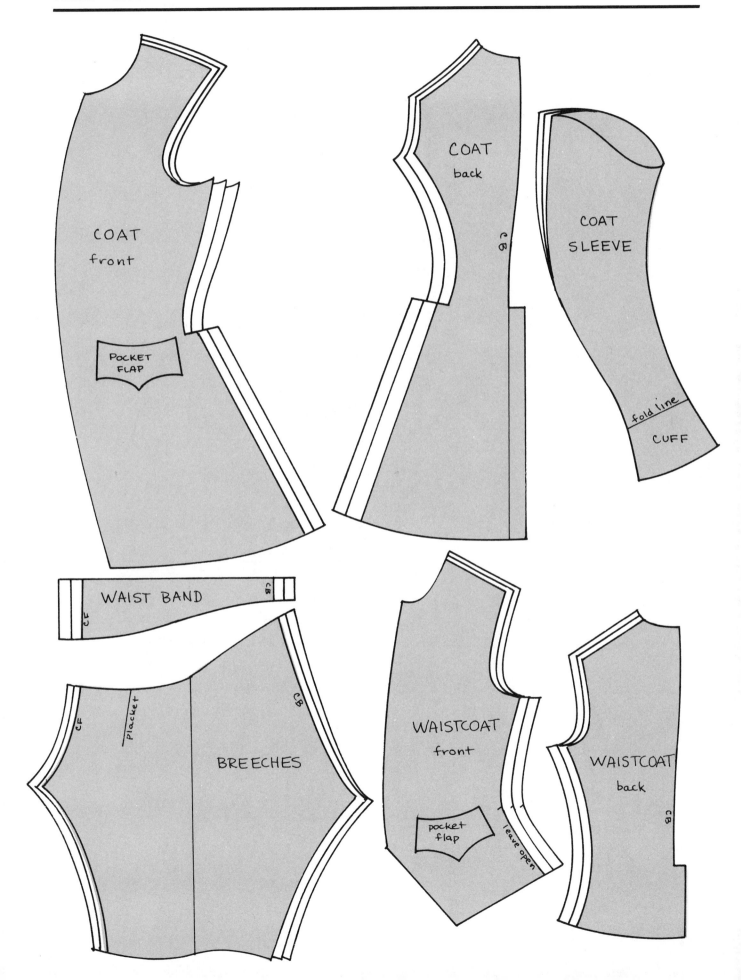

MOB CAP
large gathered cap set
on full dressed hairstyle

ROBE
bodice pleated and fitted
across back and fastened
to stomacker in front

CHEMISE RUFFLE

UNDERSKIRT
very elaborately
decorated; gathered
or pleated to
waistband

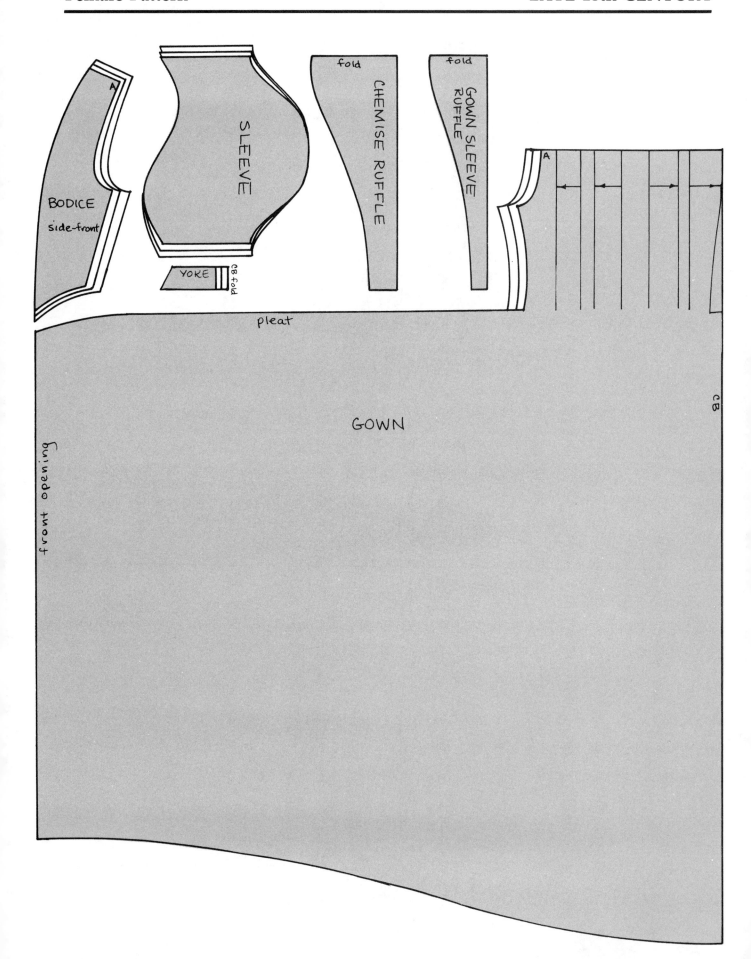

BODICE
side-front

A

SLEEVE

YOKE

CB fold

fold

CHEMISE RUFFLE

fold

GOWN SLEEVE RUFFLE

A

CB

pleat

front opening

GOWN

MOB CAP

CHEMISE

CORSET

POCKET HOOP
worn at each hip; tied
at waist and hip; used
to increase width only
at sides of skirt

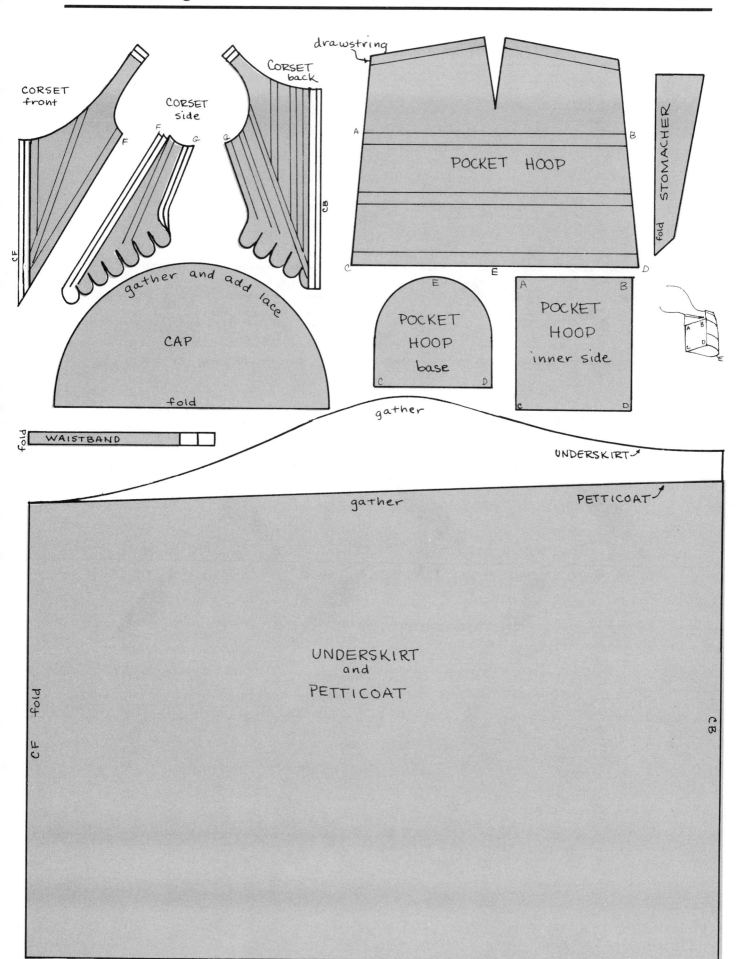

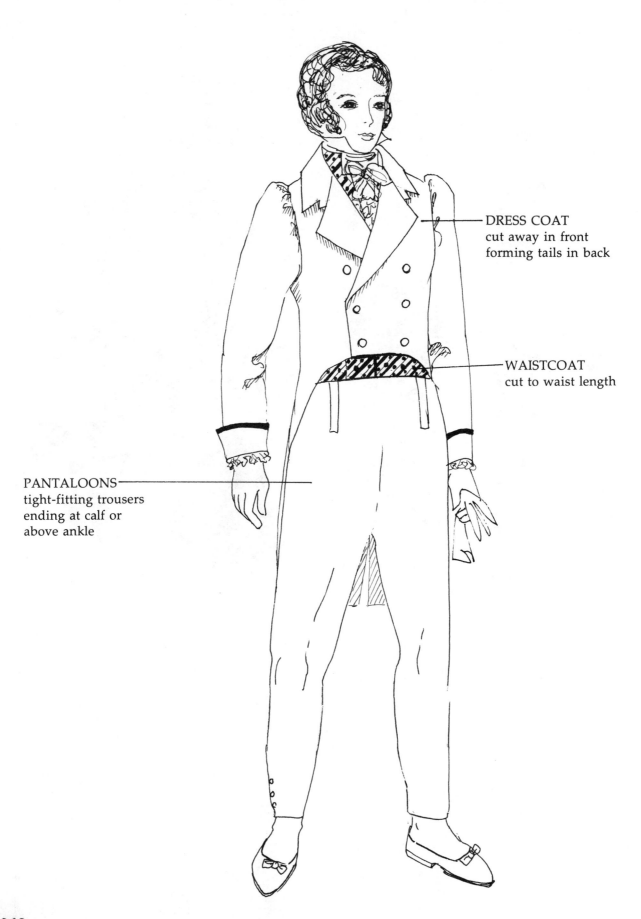

DRESS COAT
cut away in front
forming tails in back

WAISTCOAT
cut to waist length

PANTALOONS
tight-fitting trousers
ending at calf or
above ankle

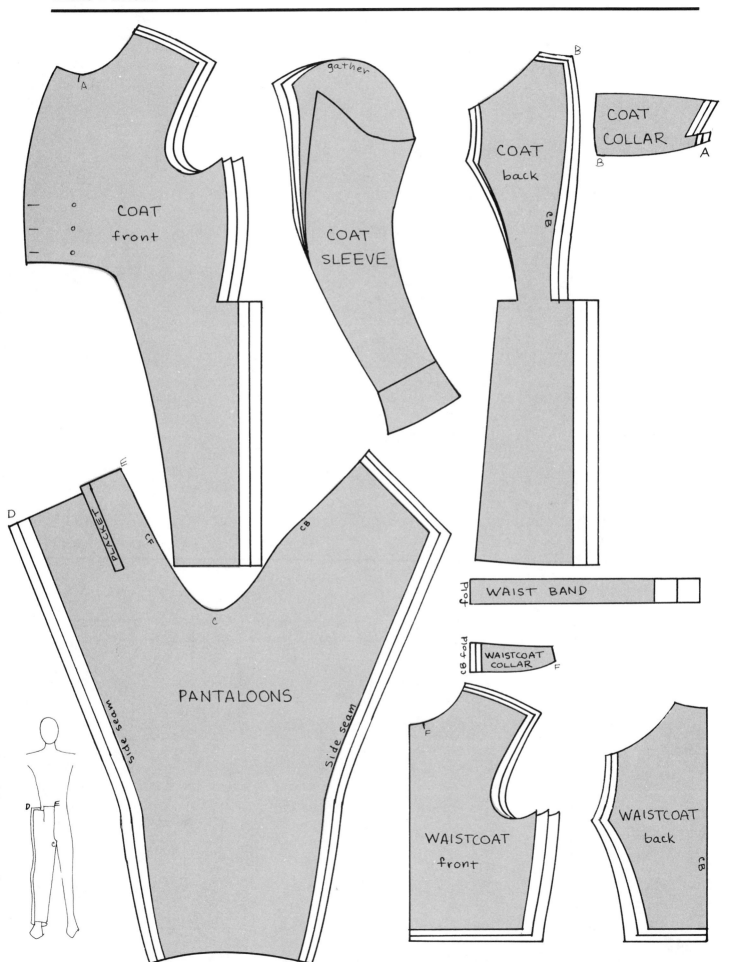

COAT front

A

COAT SLEEVE

gather

COAT back

CB

B

COAT COLLAR

B

B

A

PLACKET

E

D

CF

CB

C

side seam

Side seam

PANTALOONS

D E

C

WAIST BAND

fold

CB fold

WAISTCOAT COLLAR

F

F

WAISTCOAT front

WAISTCOAT back

CB

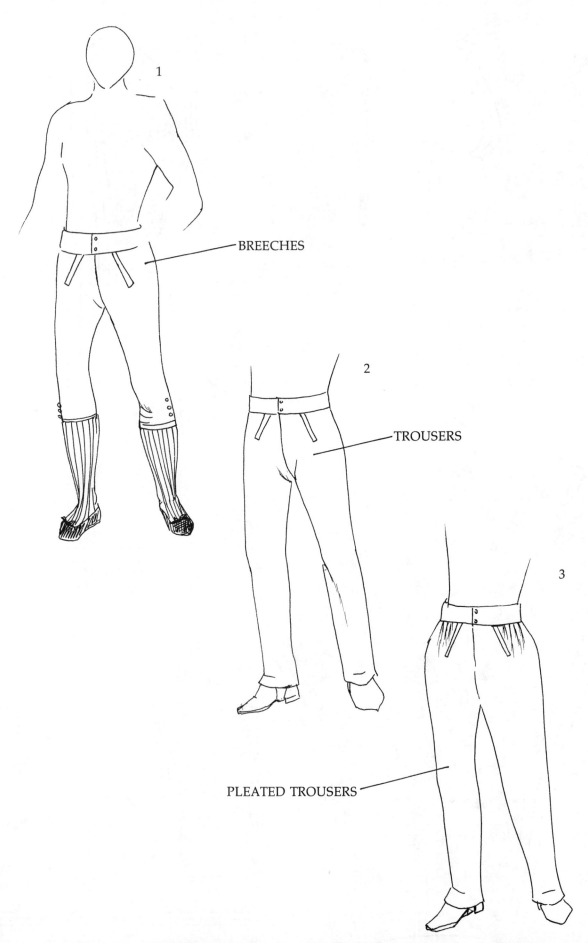

BREECHES

TROUSERS

PLEATED TROUSERS

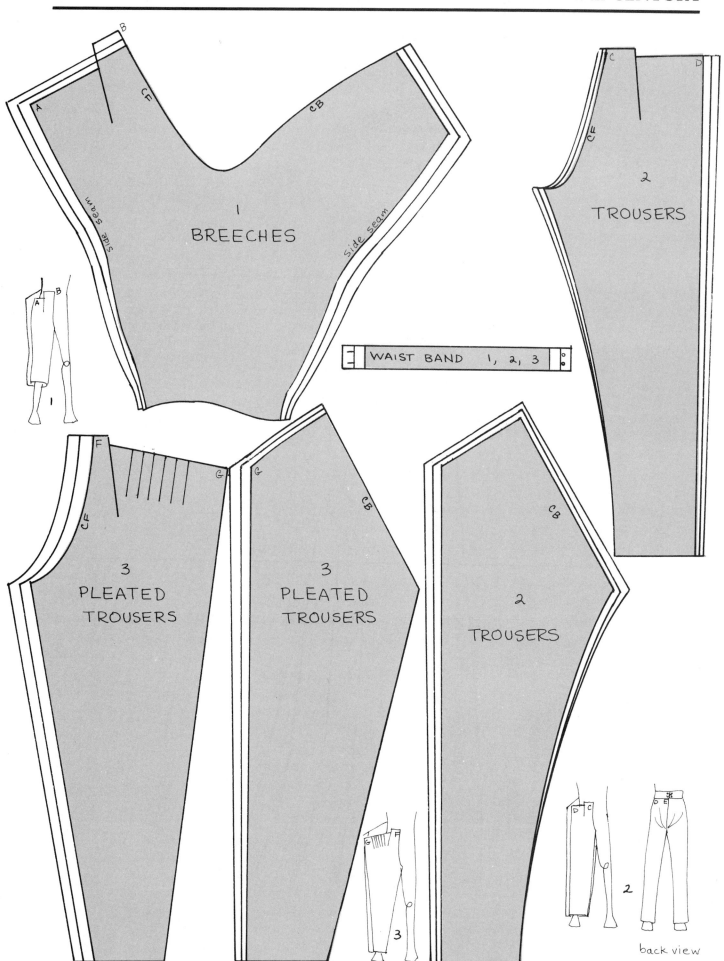

B

A

CF

CB

side seam

Side seam

1

BREECHES

C

D

CF

2

TROUSERS

A B

1

WAIST BAND   1, 2, 3

F

G G

CF

3
**PLEATED
TROUSERS**

3
**PLEATED
TROUSERS**

CB

CB

2

TROUSERS

G

3

D C

D E

2

back view

NECK RUFFLE

GOWN
with trained skirt and
gathered bodice; belted
under bustline

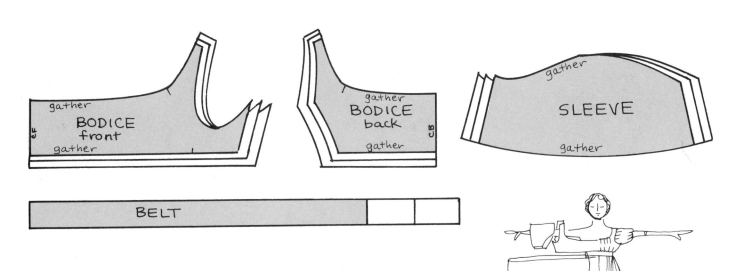

gather
BODICE
front
gather

gather
BODICE
back
gather

gather
SLEEVE
gather

BELT

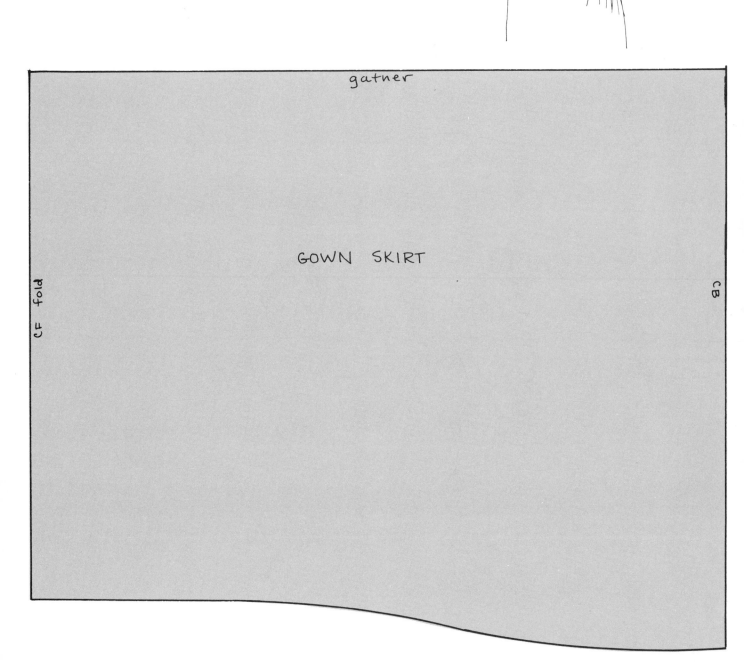

gather

GOWN SKIRT

CF fold

CB

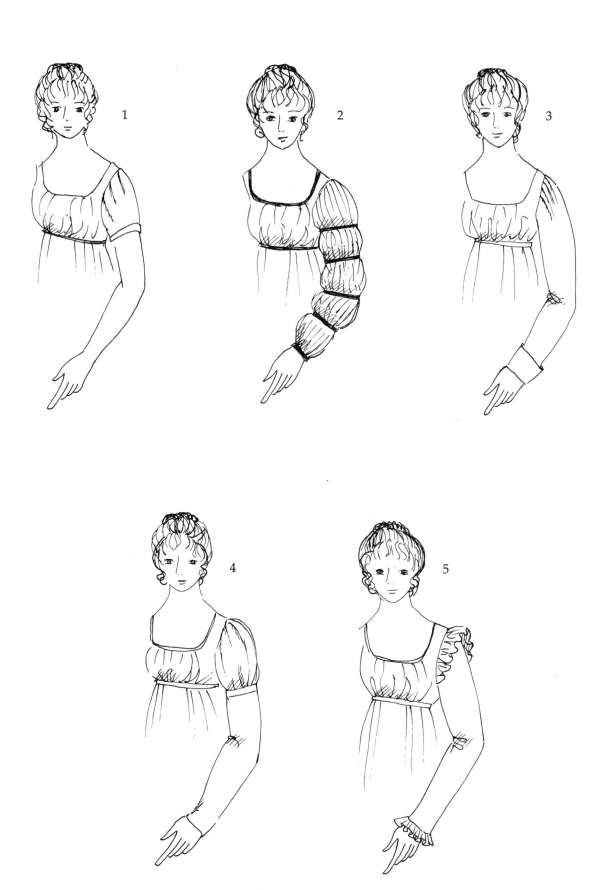

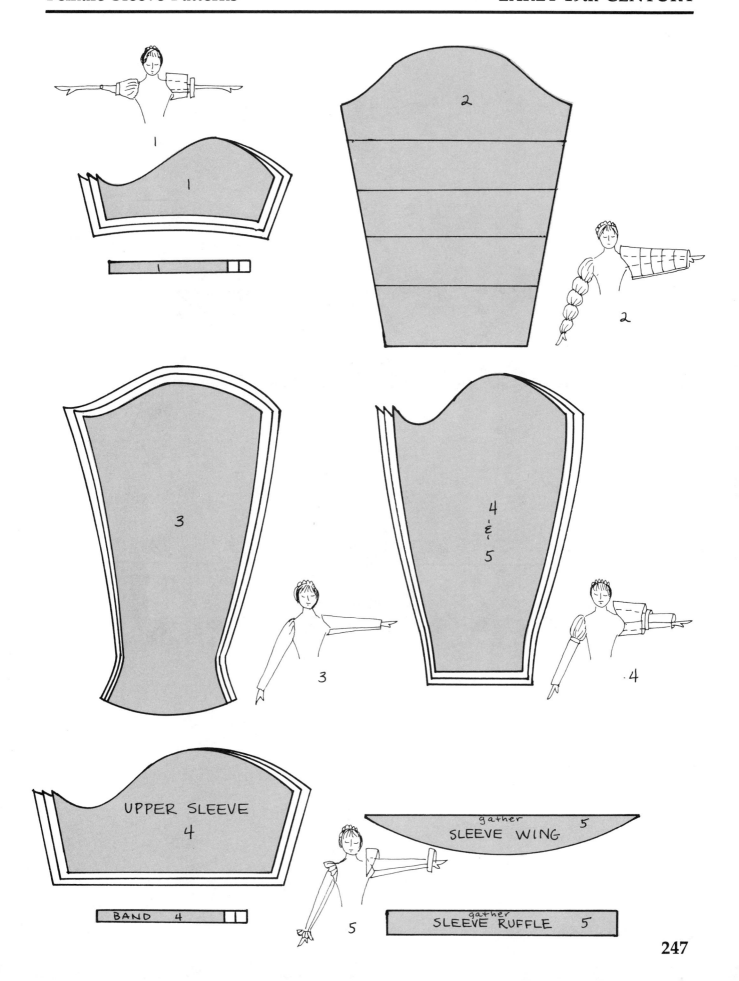

UPPER SLEEVE
4

BAND   4

gather
SLEEVE WING   5

gather
SLEEVE RUFFLE   5

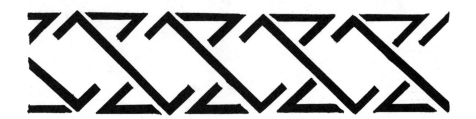

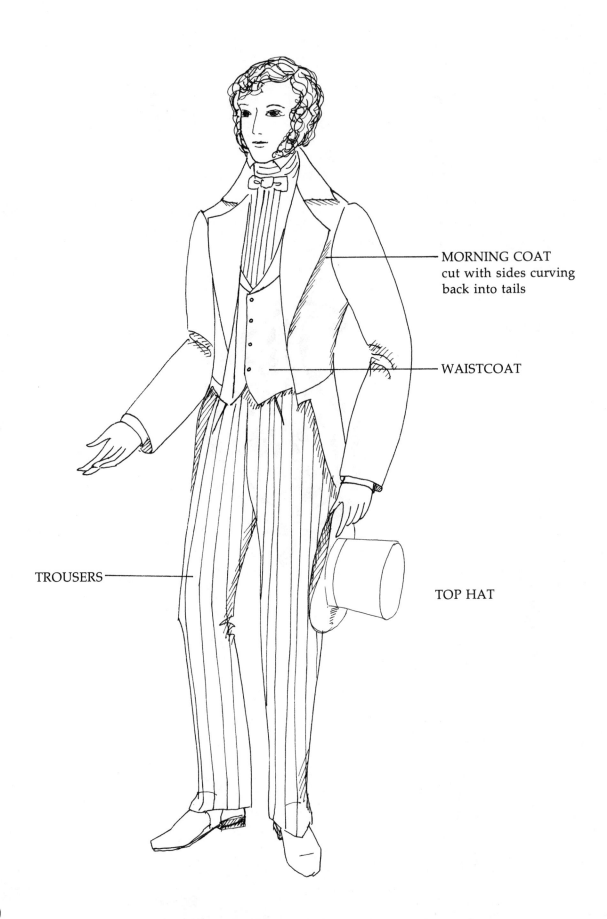

MORNING COAT
cut with sides curving
back into tails

WAISTCOAT

TROUSERS

TOP HAT

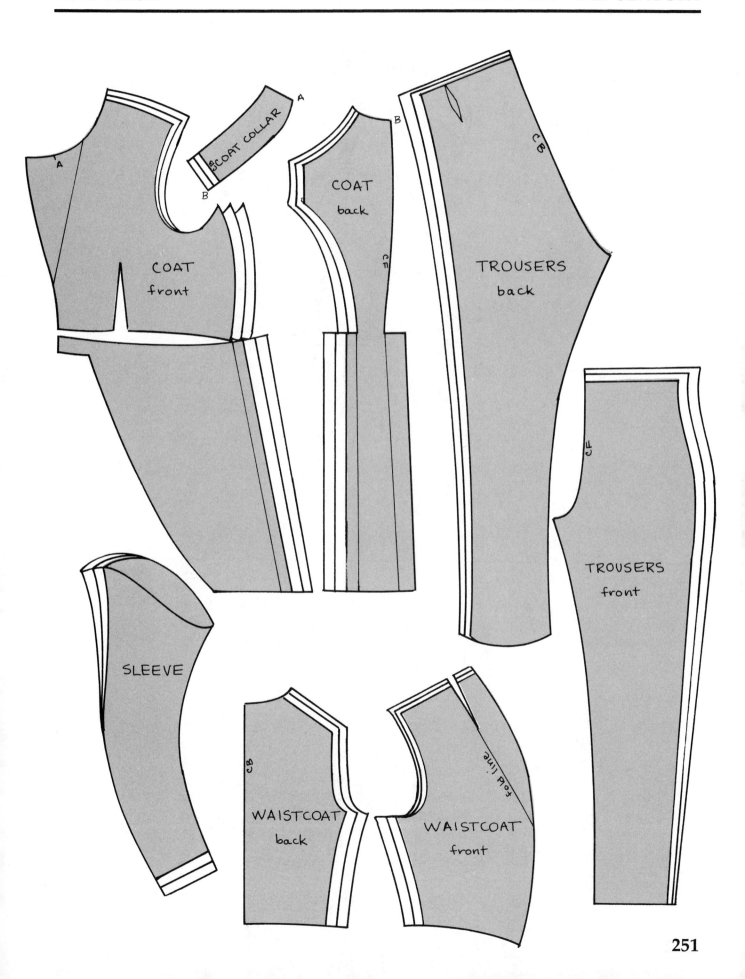

BONNET

DRESS
ankle length; belted a
bit above the waist
with leg-o-mutton
sleeves

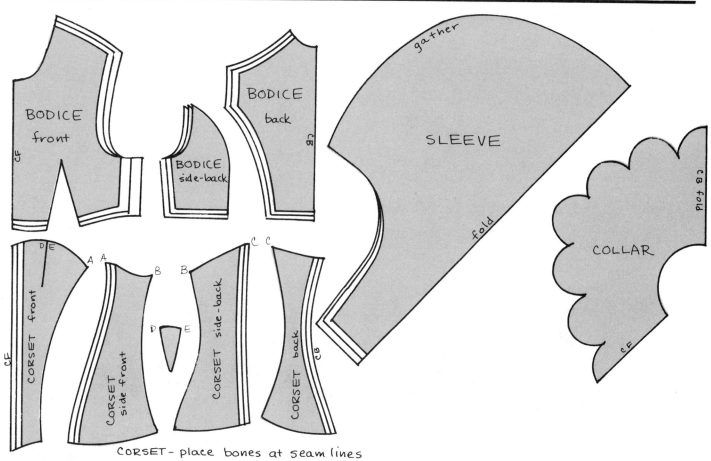

BODICE front

CF

BODICE side-back

BODICE back

CB

SLEEVE

gather

fold

COLLAR

CB fold

CF

CORSET front

CF

D E

A A

B B

D E

CORSET side front

C C

CORSET side-back

CORSET back

CB

CORSET – place bones at seam lines

gather

SKIRT

CF fold

CB

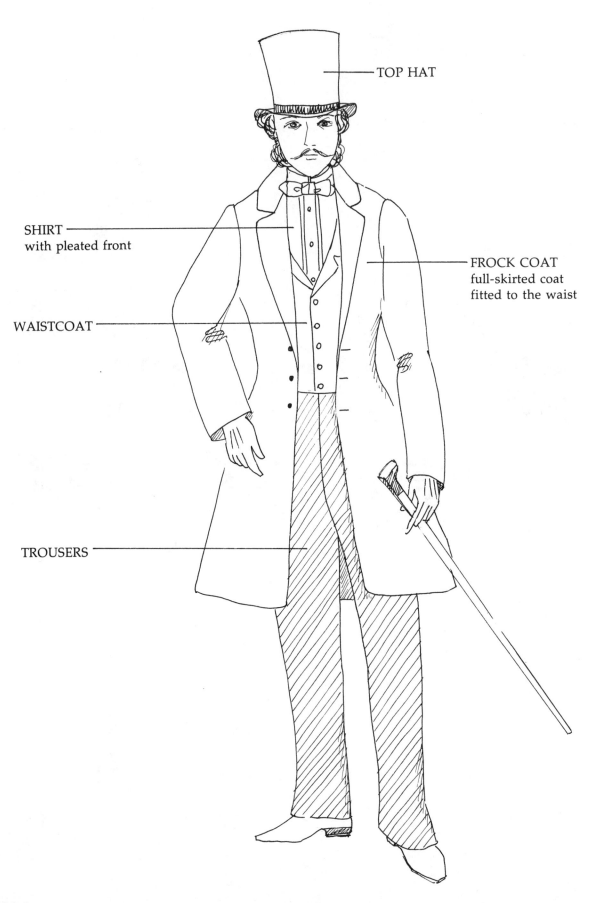

TOP HAT

SHIRT
with pleated front

WAISTCOAT

TROUSERS

FROCK COAT
full-skirted coat
fitted to the waist

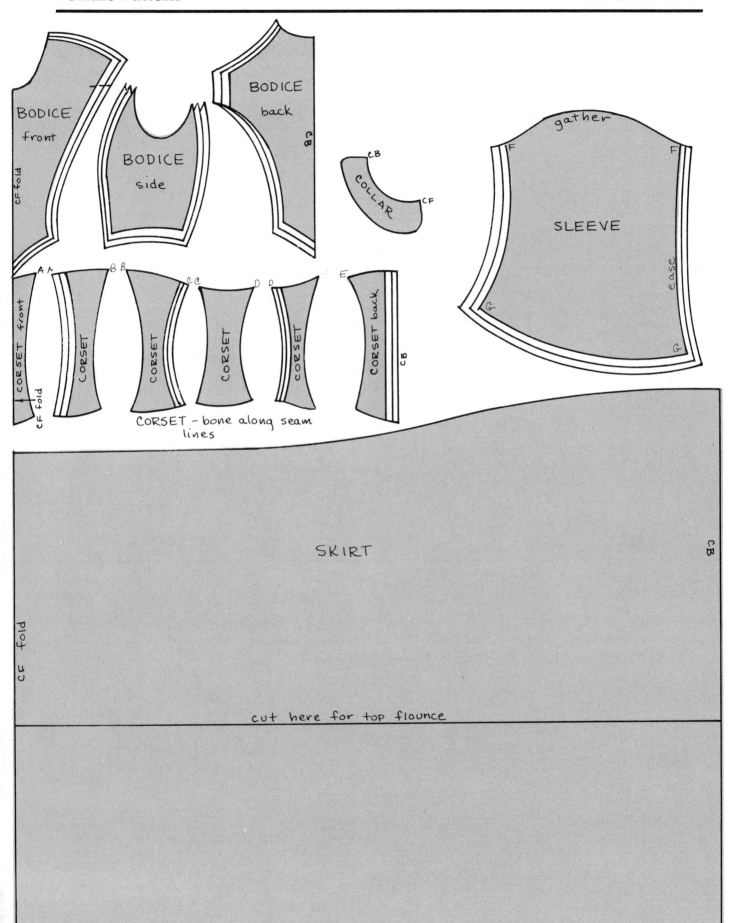

BODICE front

BODICE side

BODICE back

CF fold

CB

COLLAR

CB

CF

SLEEVE

gather

F

F

ease

G

G

A A

B B

C C

D D

E

CORSET front

CORSET

CORSET

CORSET

CORSET

CORSET back

CF fold

CB

CORSET – bone along seam lines

SKIRT

CF fold

CB

cut here for top flounce

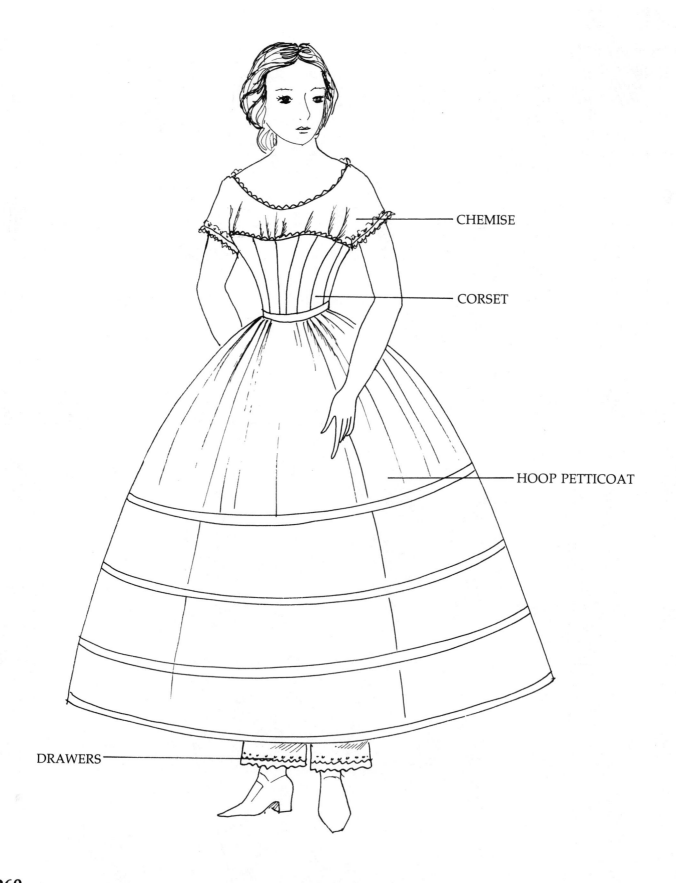

CHEMISE

CORSET

HOOP PETTICOAT

DRAWERS

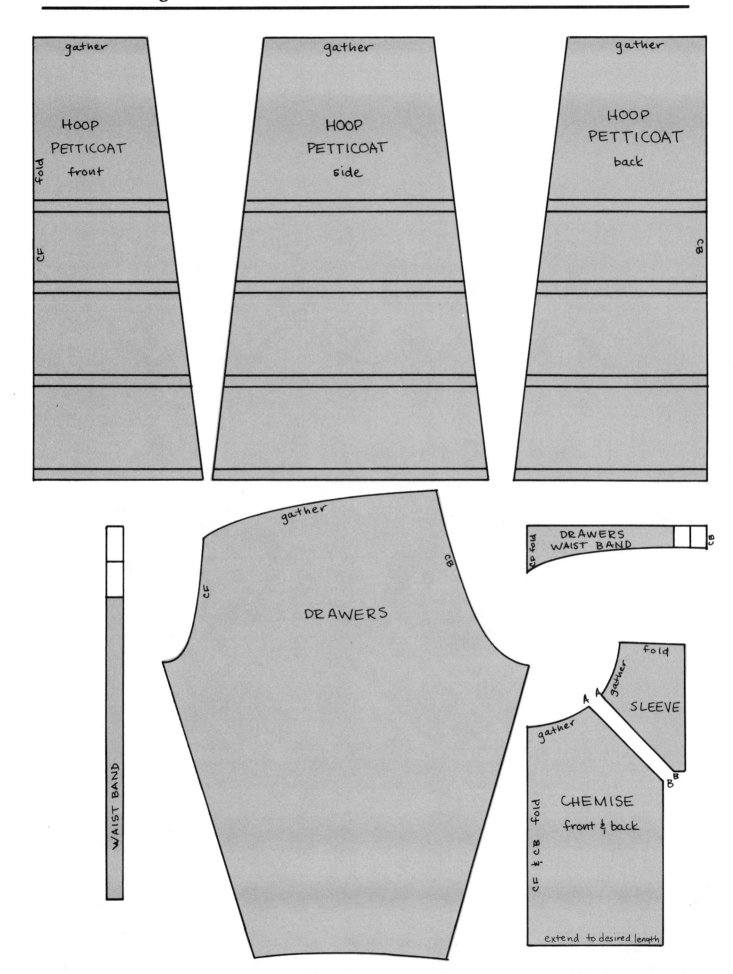

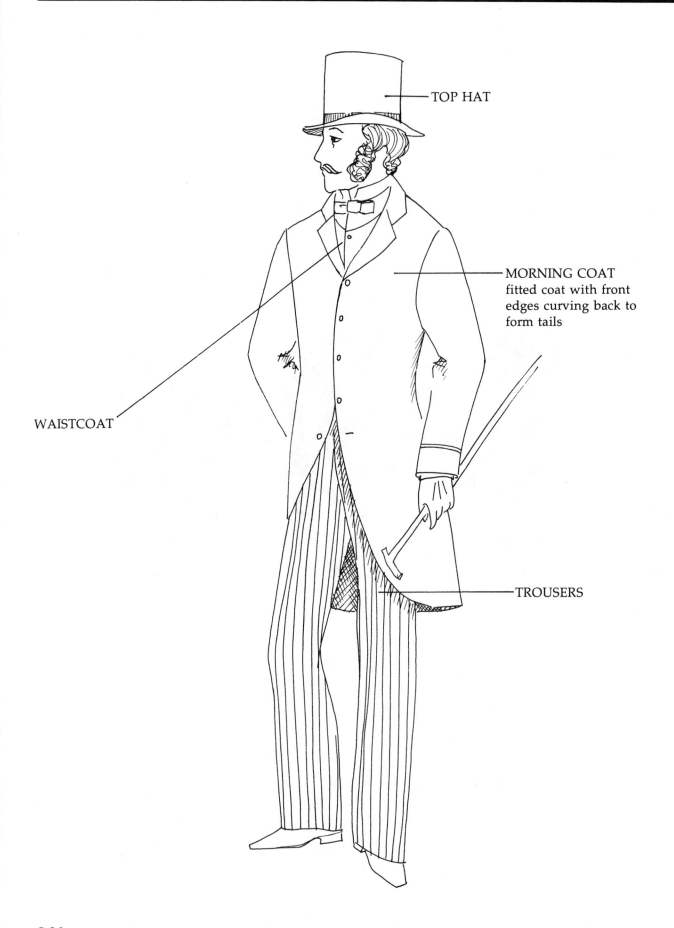

TOP HAT

MORNING COAT
fitted coat with front
edges curving back to
form tails

WAISTCOAT

TROUSERS

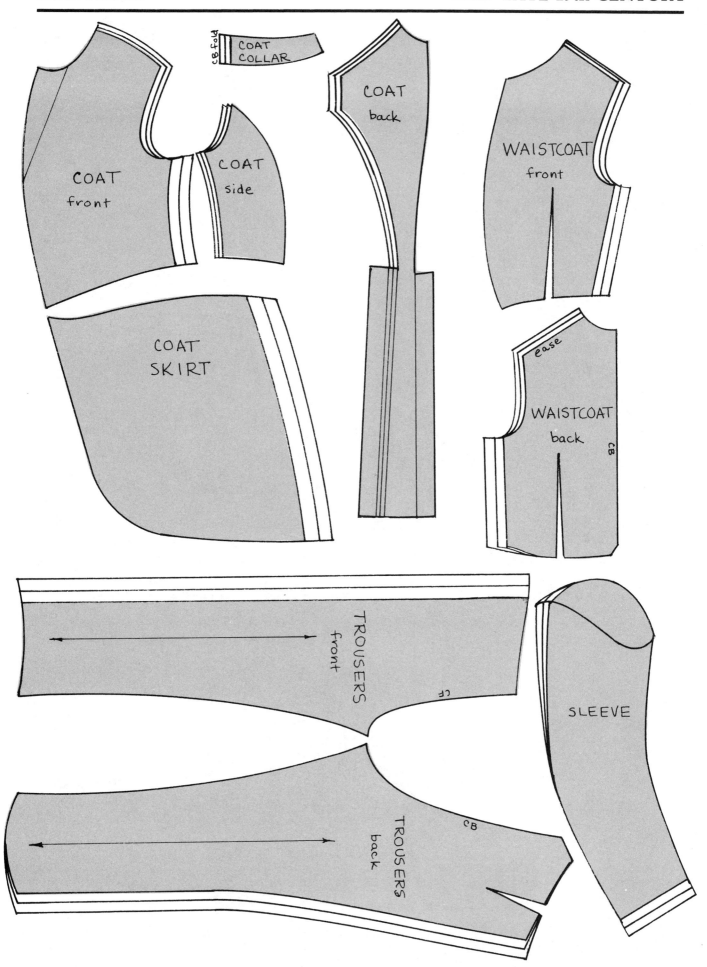

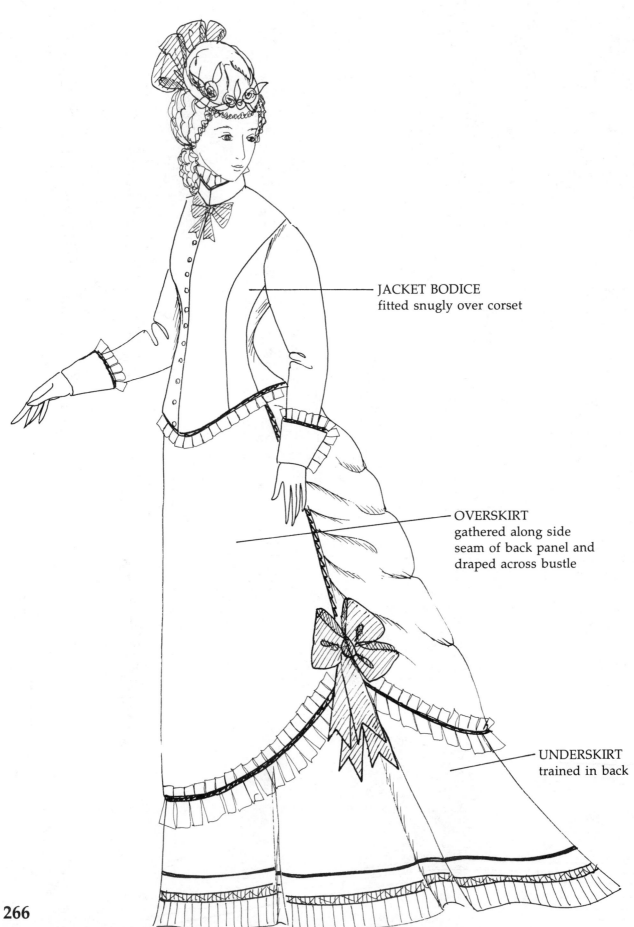

JACKET BODICE
fitted snugly over corset

OVERSKIRT
gathered along side
seam of back panel and
draped across bustle

UNDERSKIRT
trained in back

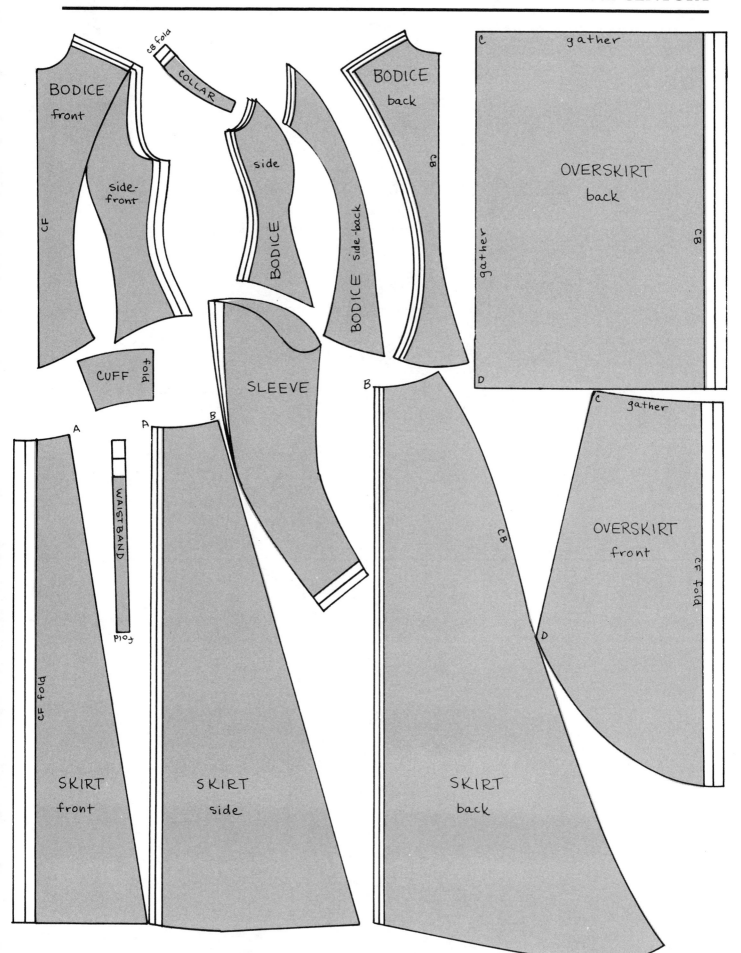

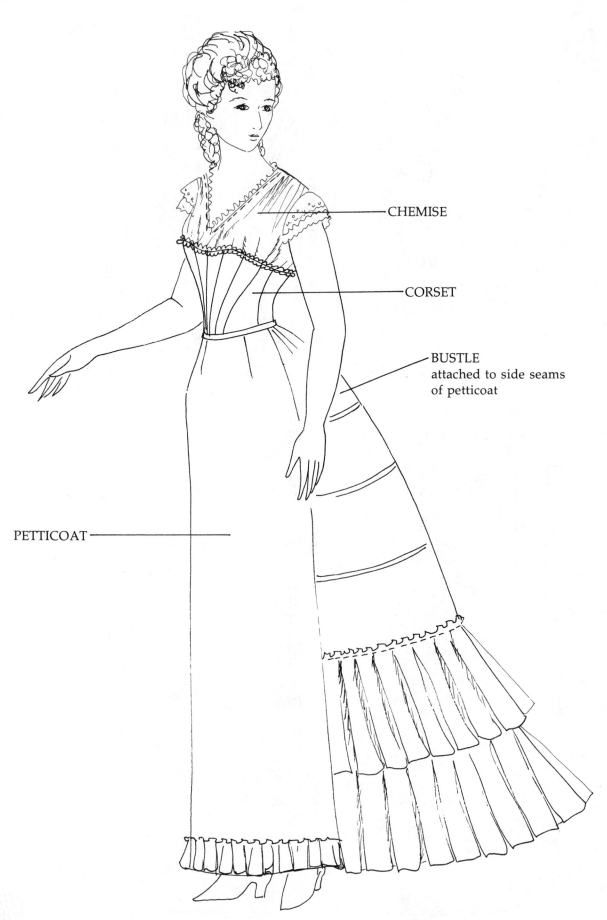

CHEMISE

CORSET

BUSTLE
attached to side seams
of petticoat

PETTICOAT

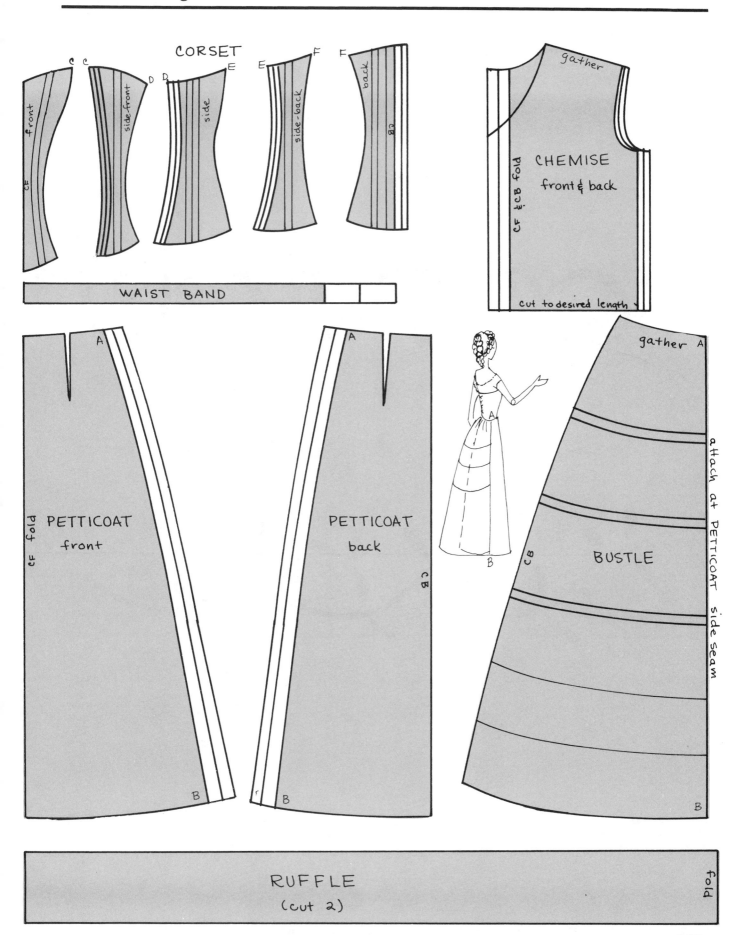

CORSET

front

C C

side-front

D D

E E

side

F F

E E

side-back

back

WAIST BAND

CHEMISE

front & back

CF & CB fold

gather

cut to desired length

PETTICOAT

front

CF fold

A

B

PETTICOAT

back

A

CB

B

A

B

BUSTLE

gather A

CB

attach at PETTICOAT side seam

B

RUFFLE

(cut 2)

fold

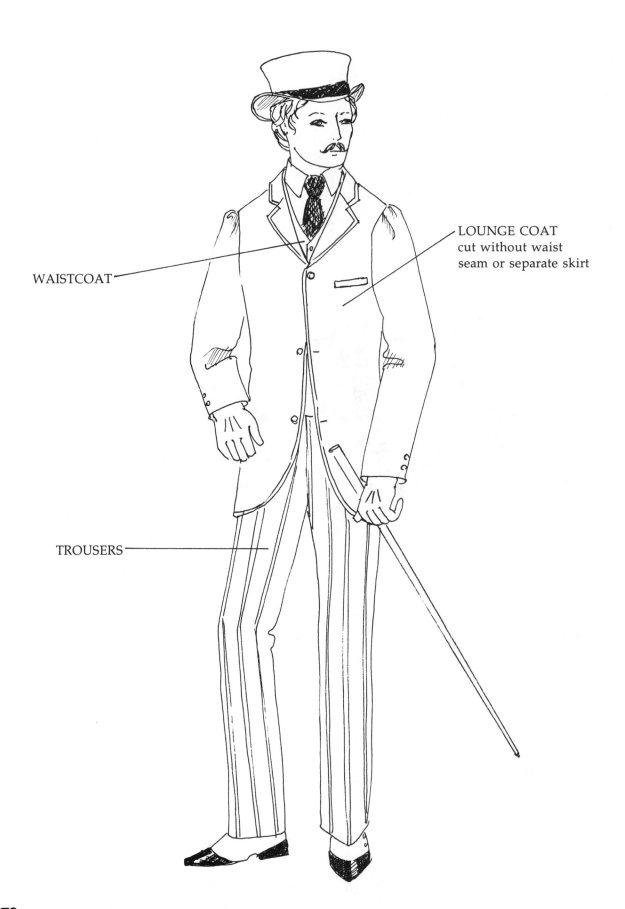

WAISTCOAT

LOUNGE COAT
cut without waist
seam or separate skirt

TROUSERS

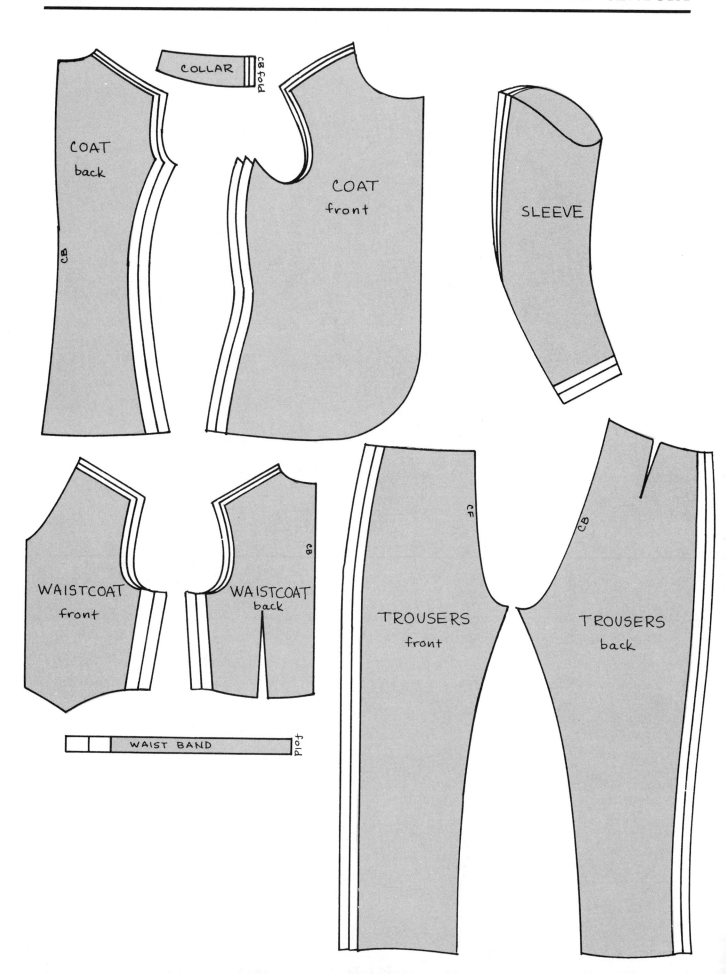

COLLAR

CB fold

COAT
back

CB

COAT
front

SLEEVE

WAISTCOAT
front

WAISTCOAT
back

CB

TROUSERS
front

CF

TROUSERS
back

CB

WAIST BAND

fold

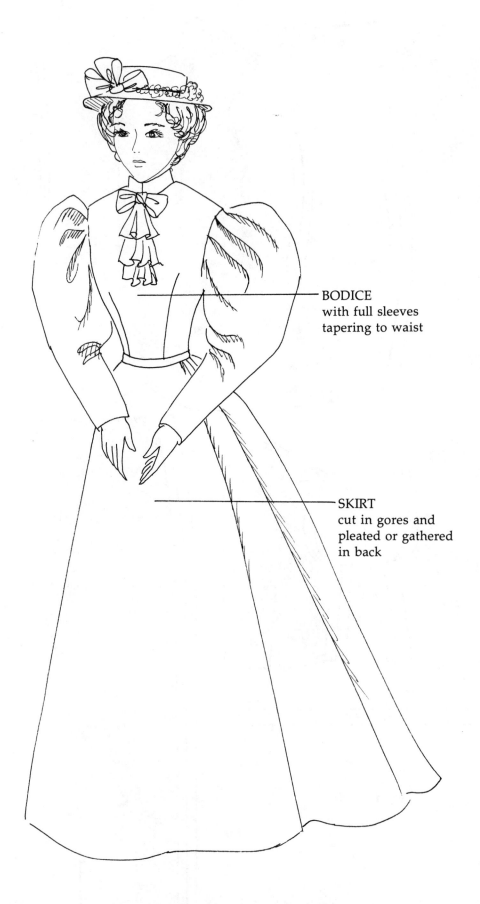

BODICE
with full sleeves
tapering to waist

SKIRT
cut in gores and
pleated or gathered
in back

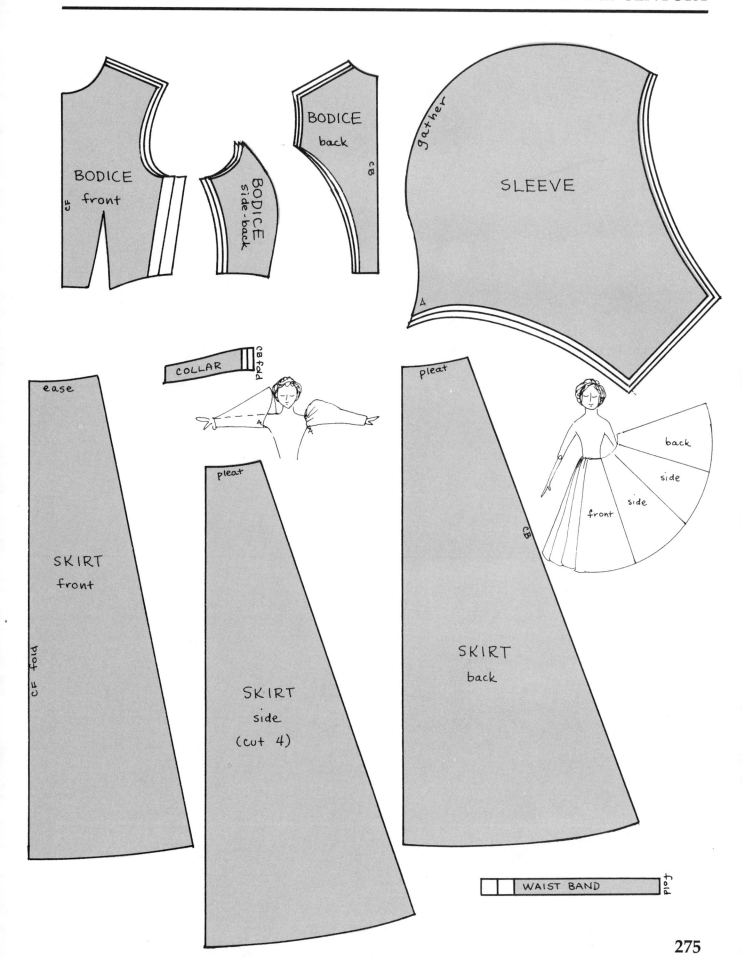

BODICE front

BODICE side-back

BODICE back

SLEEVE

gather

COLLAR

ease

SKIRT front

SKIRT side (cut 4)

pleat

pleat

SKIRT back

back

side

side

front

WAIST BAND

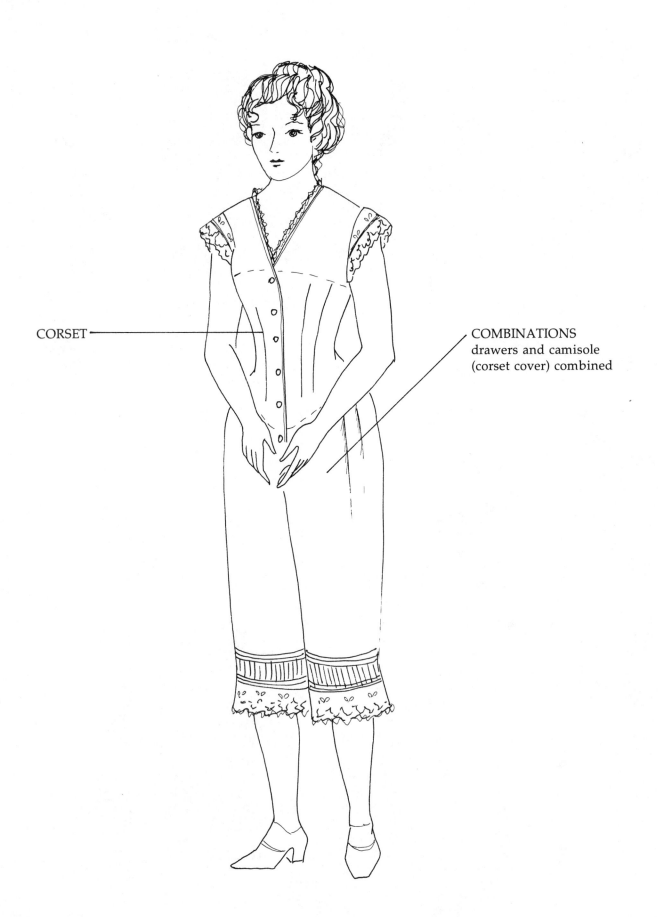

CORSET

COMBINATIONS
drawers and camisole
(corset cover) combined

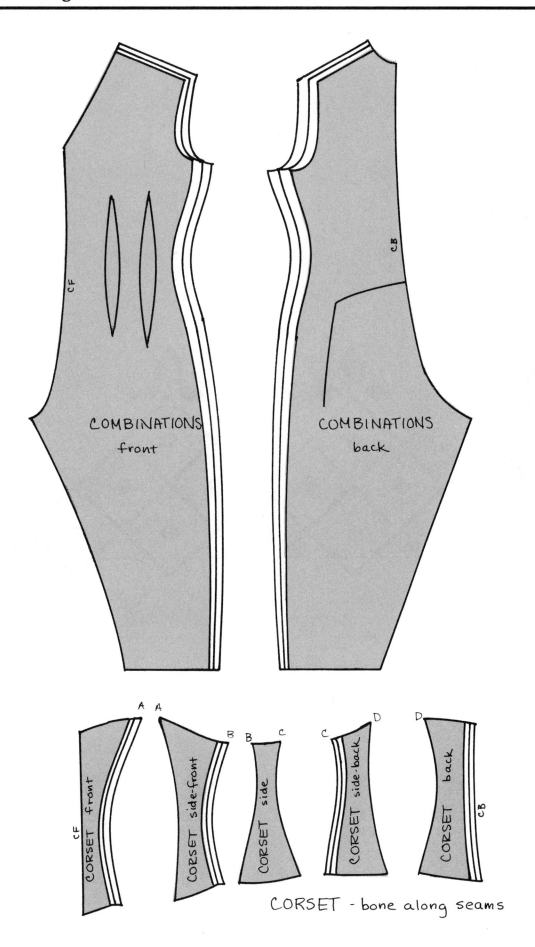

COMBINATIONS
front

CF

COMBINATIONS
back

CB

A A

B   B   C

C   D   D

CORSET front

CF

CORSET side-front

CORSET side

CORSET side-back

CORSET back

CB

CORSET - bone along seams

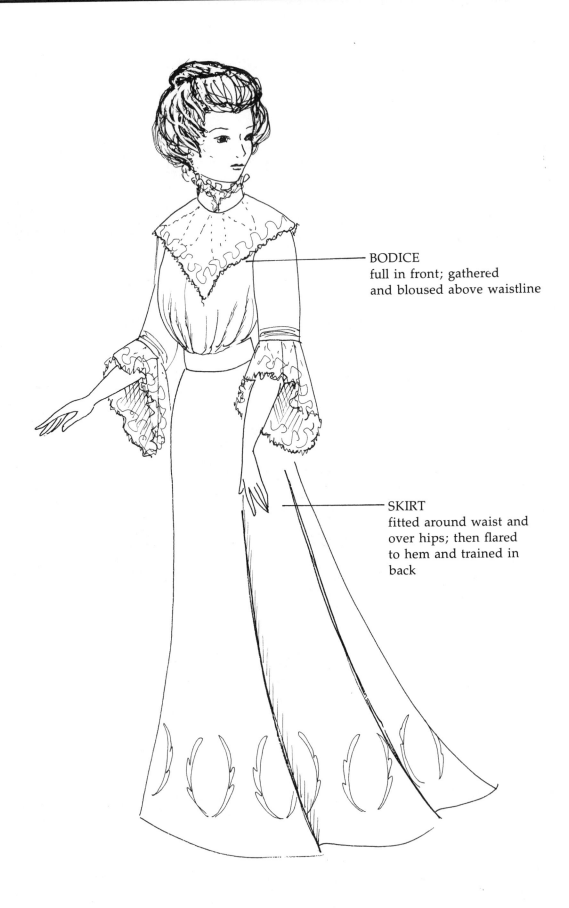

BODICE
full in front; gathered
and bloused above waistline

SKIRT
fitted around waist and
over hips; then flared
to hem and trained in
back

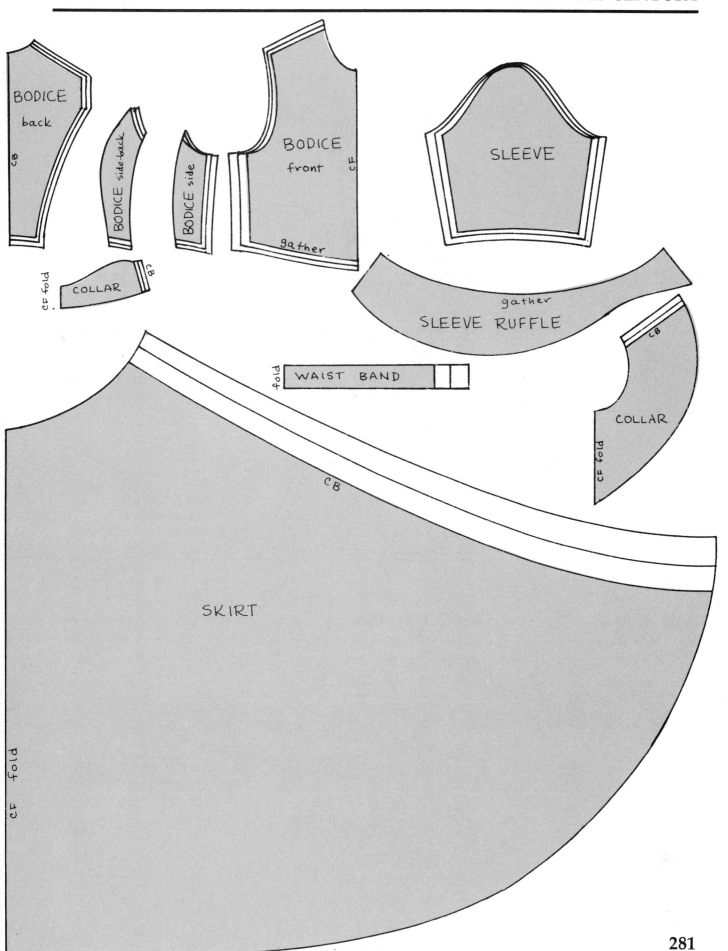

BODICE back

CB fold

BODICE side-back

BODICE side

BODICE front

CF

gather

SLEEVE

cf fold

COLLAR

CB

SLEEVE RUFFLE

gather

fold

WAIST BAND

CB

COLLAR

CF fold

CB

CB fold

SKIRT

CF fold

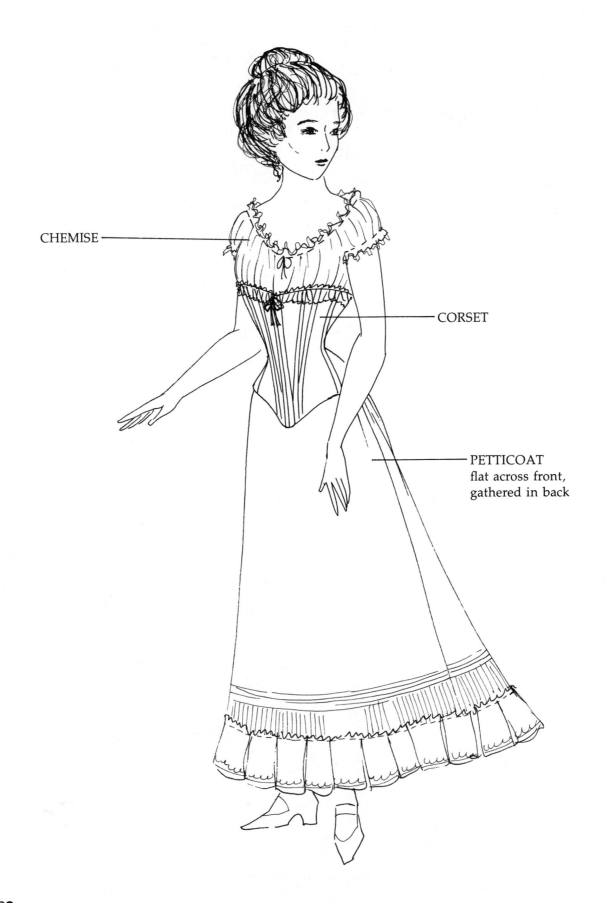

CHEMISE

CORSET

PETTICOAT
flat across front,
gathered in back

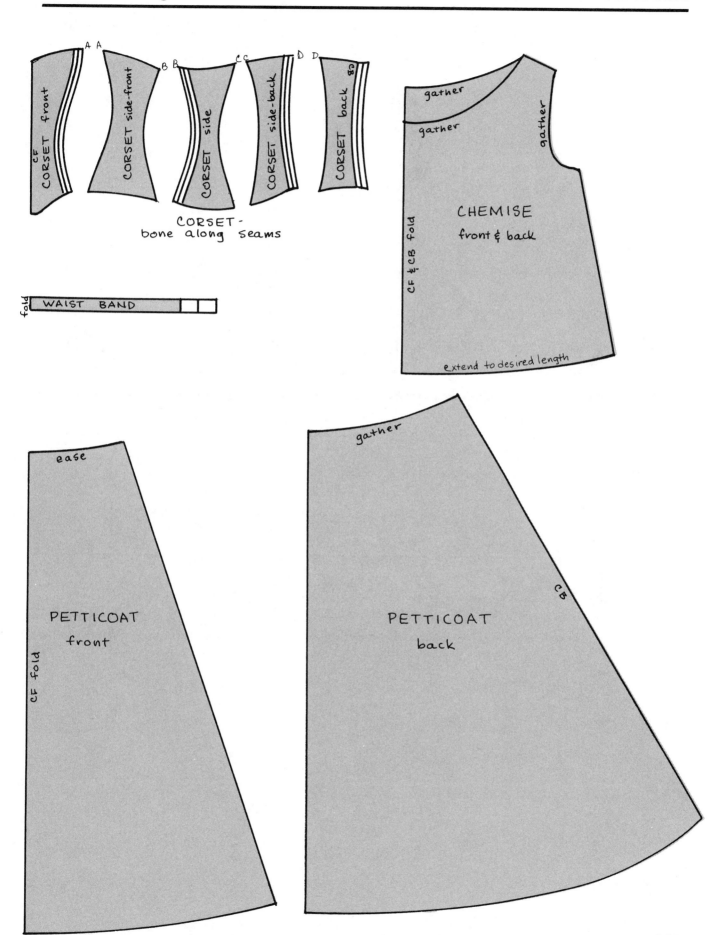

CORSET front

CORSET side-front

CORSET side

CORSET side-back

CORSET back

CORSET -
bone along seams

WAIST BAND

CHEMISE
front & back

extend to desired length

PETTICOAT
front

ease

PETTICOAT
back

gather

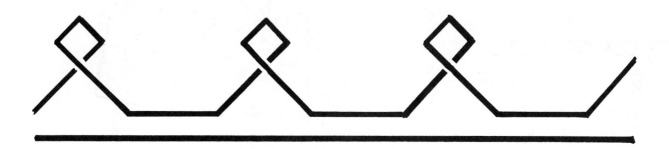

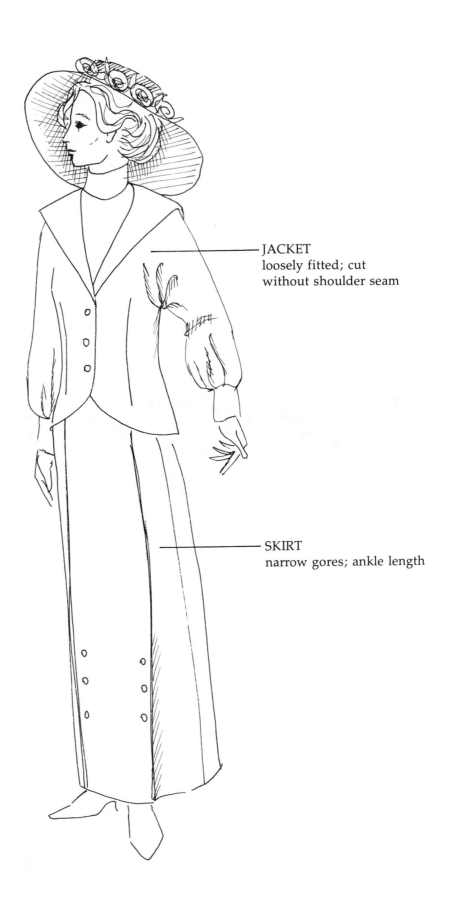

JACKET
loosely fitted; cut
without shoulder seam

SKIRT
narrow gores; ankle length

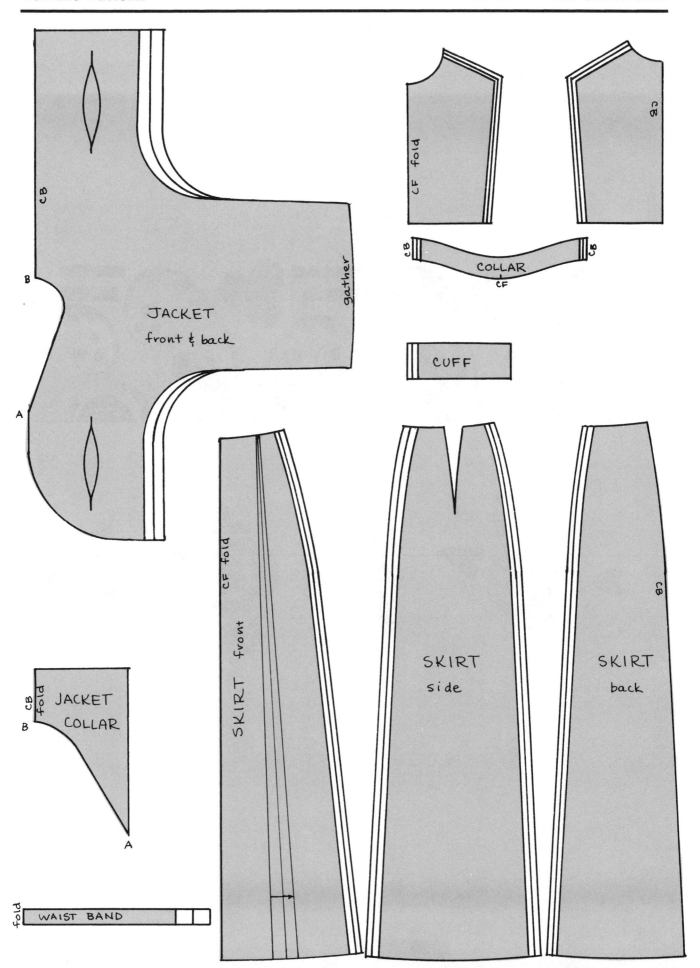

JACKET
front & back

gather

COLLAR

CUFF

JACKET
COLLAR

SKIRT front
CF fold

SKIRT
side

SKIRT
back

WAIST BAND

Specialty Costume Patterns

VEIL

WIMPLE

COLLAR

TUNIC

HOOD

SCAPULAR

ROBE

MITRE

LAPPET

CHASUBLE

DALMATIC

ALB

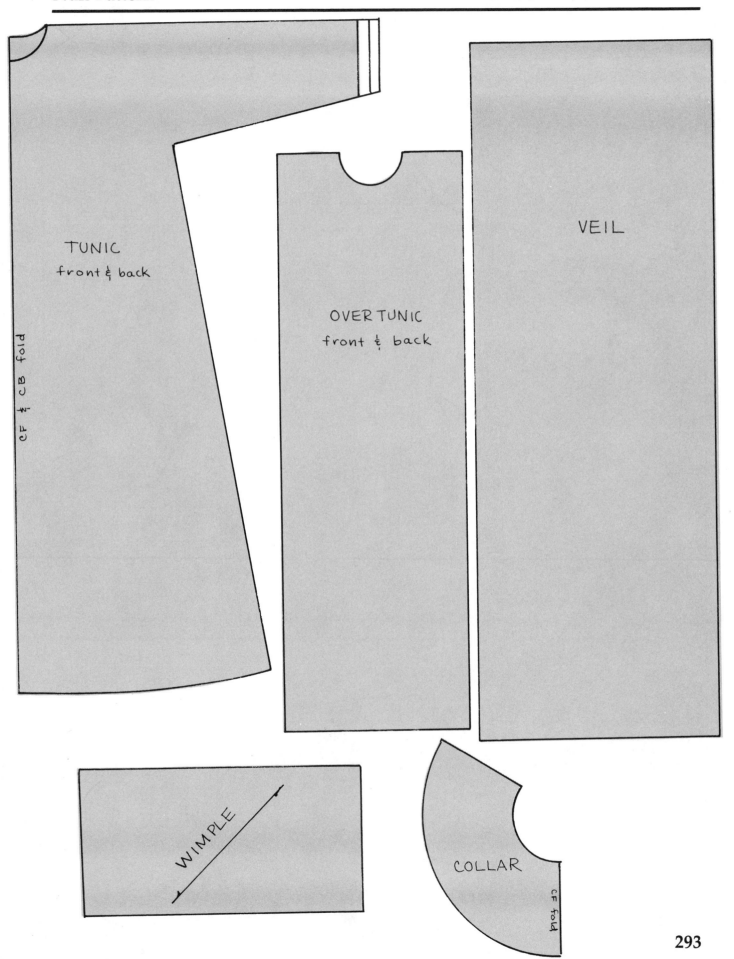

TUNIC
front & back

CF & CB fold

OVER TUNIC
front & back

VEIL

WIMPLE

COLLAR

CF fold

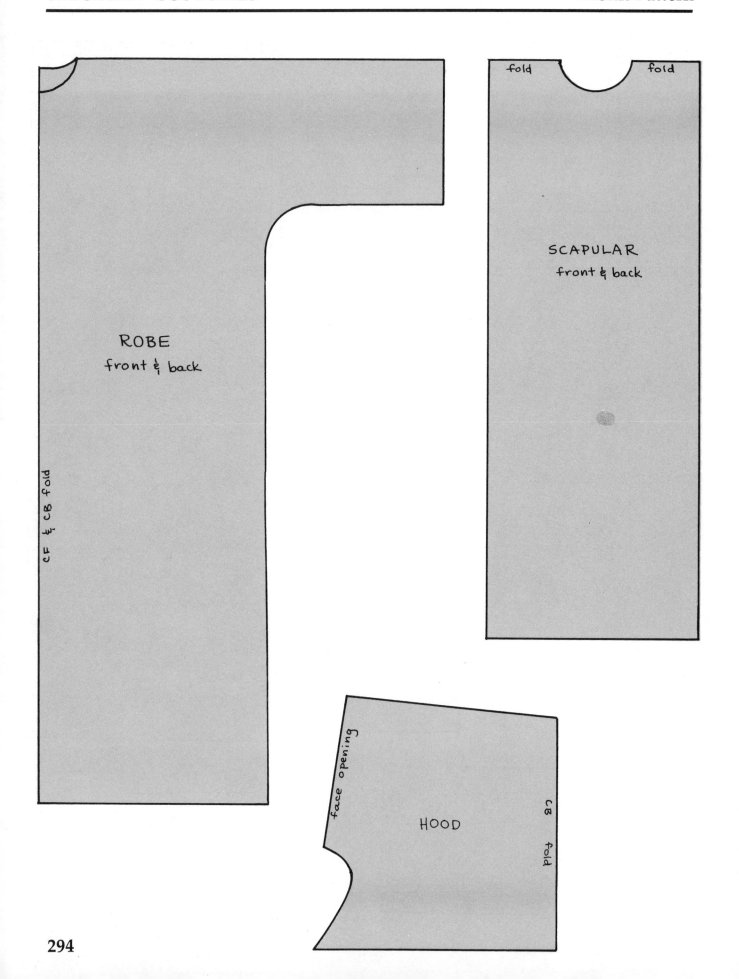

ROBE
front & back

CF & CB fold

SCAPULAR
front & back

fold

fold

fold

fold

face opening

HOOD

CB fold

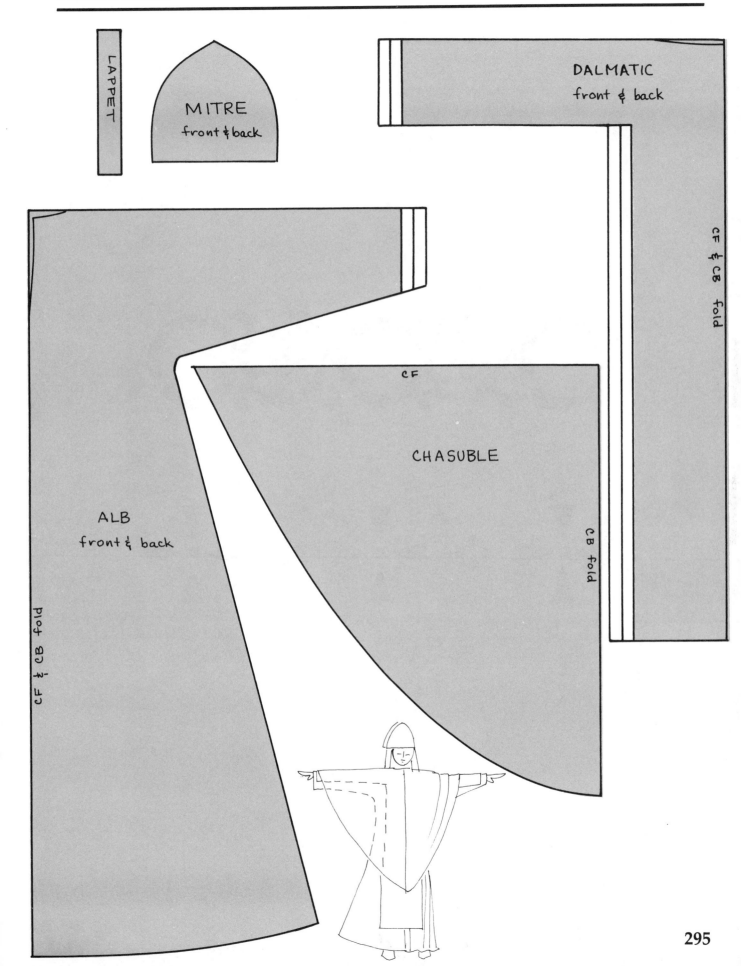

LAPPET

MITRE
front & back

DALMATIC
front & back

CF & CB fold

CF

CHASUBLE

CB fold

ALB
front & back

CF & CB fold

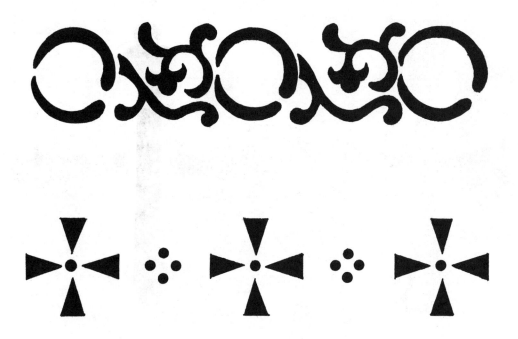

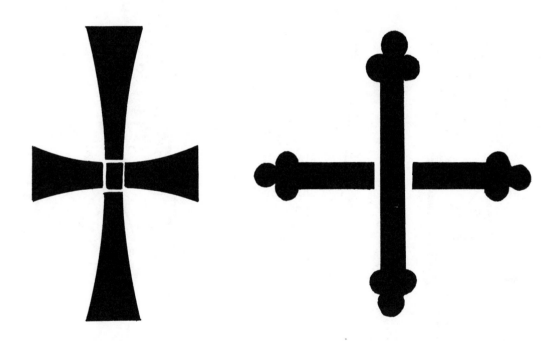

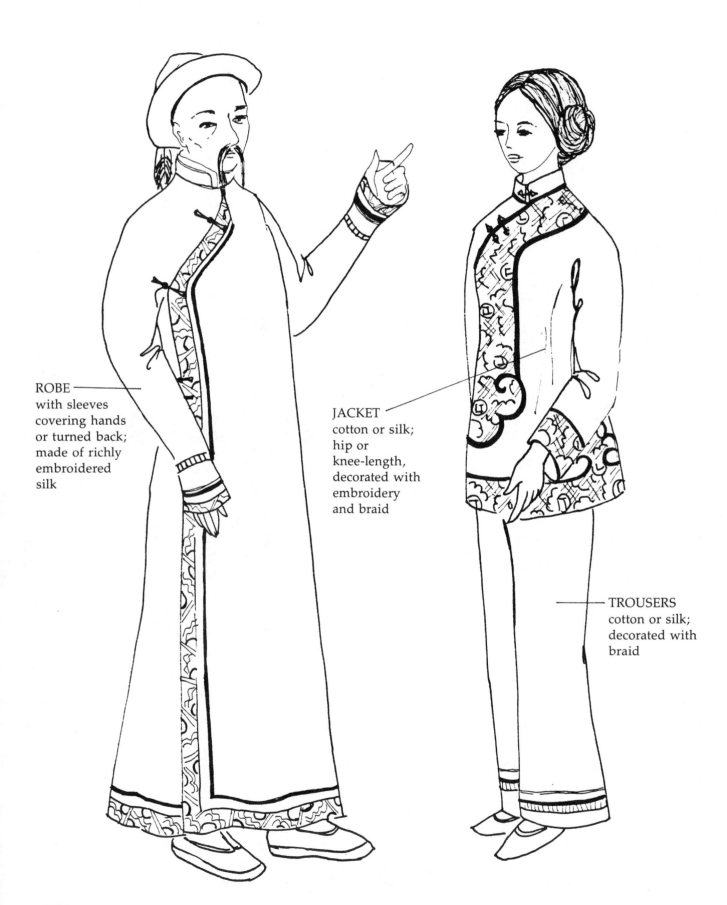

ROBE
with sleeves
covering hands
or turned back;
made of richly
embroidered
silk

JACKET
cotton or silk;
hip or
knee-length,
decorated with
embroidery
and braid

TROUSERS
cotton or silk;
decorated with
braid

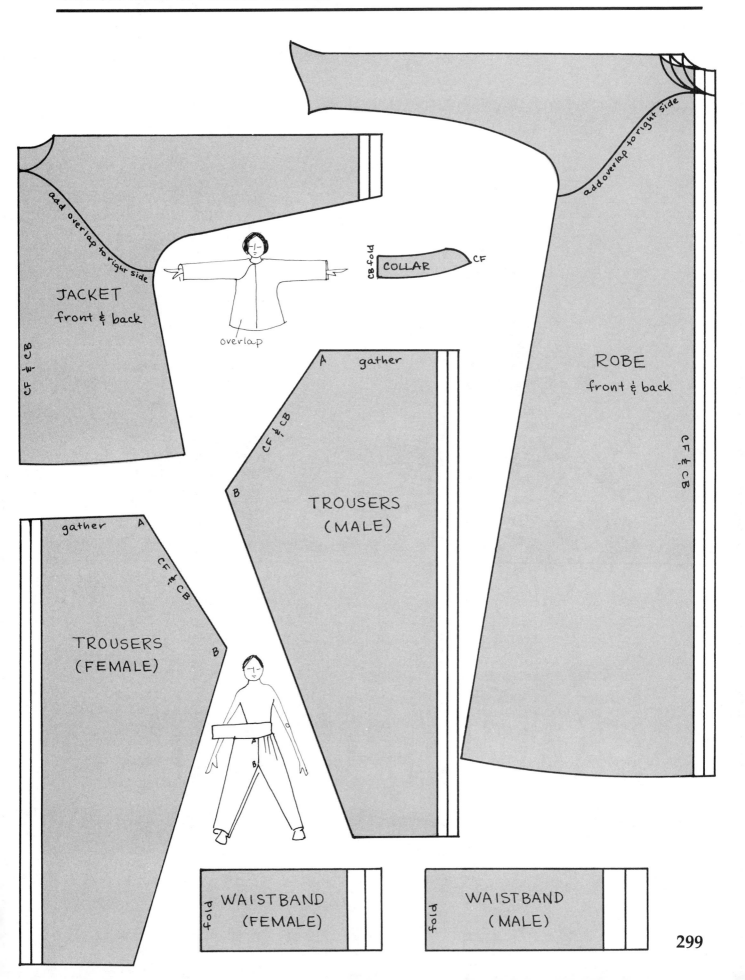

JACKET
front & back

add overlap to right side

CF & CB

COLLAR

CB-fold

CF

overlap

ROBE
front & back

add overlap to right side

CF & CB

A gather

CF & CB

B

TROUSERS
(MALE)

gather A

CF & CB

B

TROUSERS
(FEMALE)

WAISTBAND
(FEMALE)

fold

WAISTBAND
(MALE)

fold

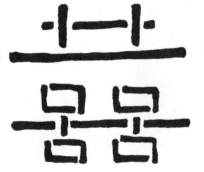

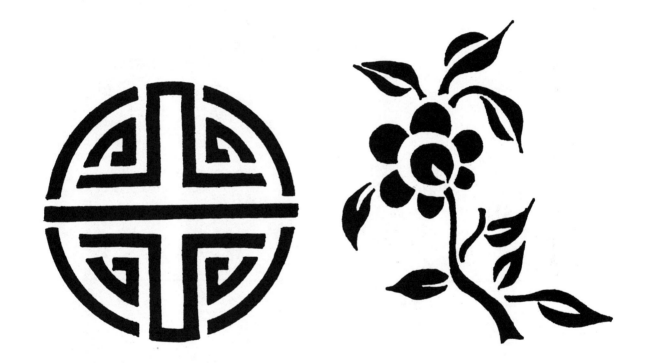

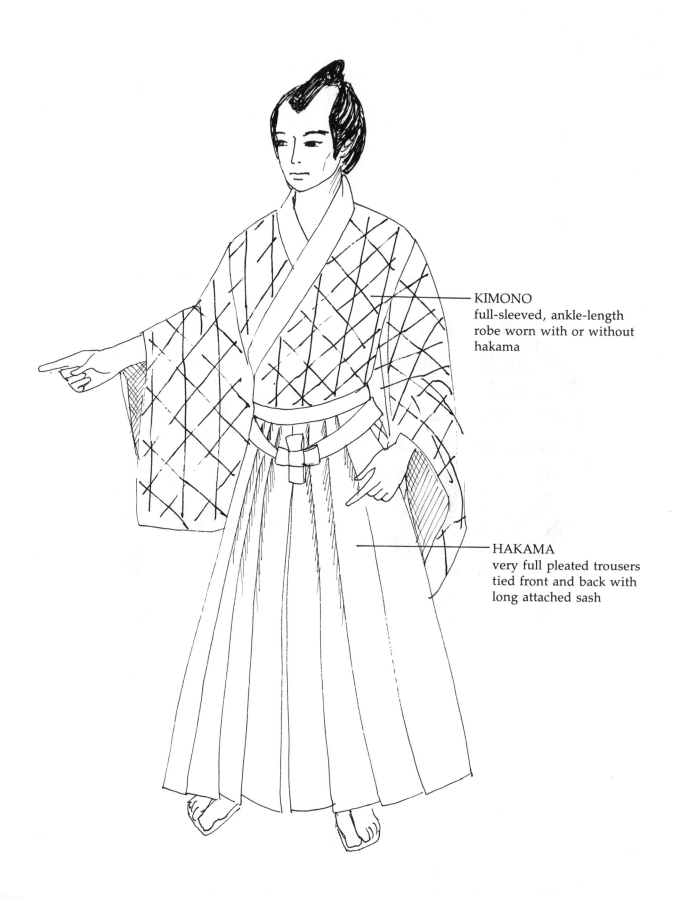

KIMONO
full-sleeved, ankle-length
robe worn with or without
hakama

HAKAMA
very full pleated trousers
tied front and back with
long attached sash

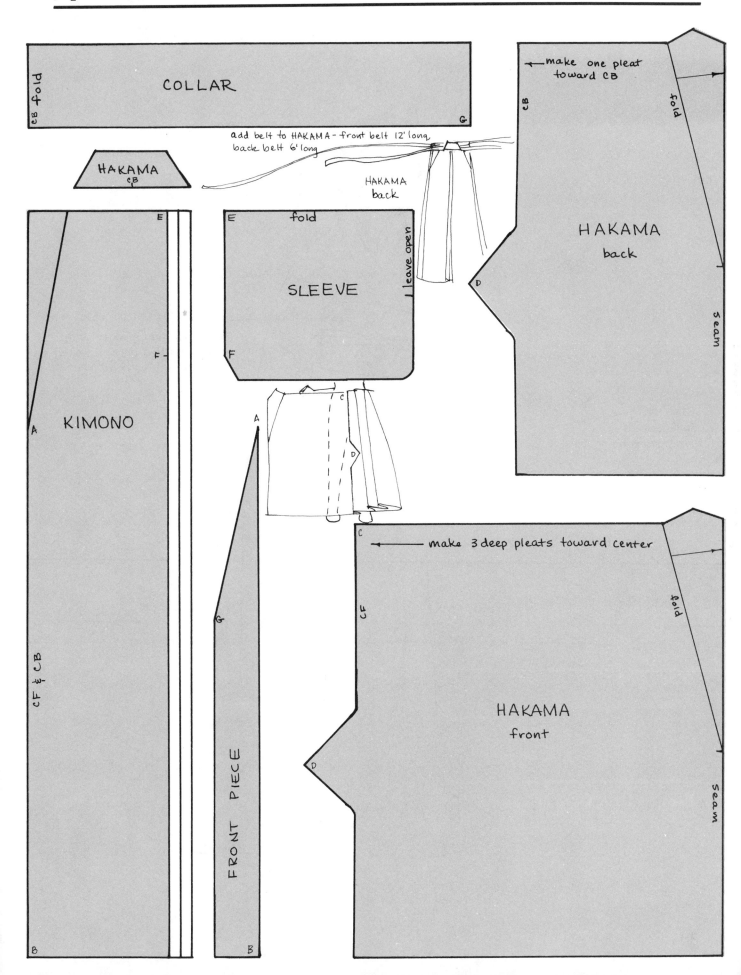

COLLAR

CB fold

HAKAMA
CB

add belt to HAKAMA – front belt 12' long
back belt 6' long

HAKAMA
back

make one pleat
toward CB

CB

fold

HAKAMA
back

seam

KIMONO

E

F

A

CF & CB

B

SLEEVE

fold

E

F

leave open

C

D

FRONT PIECE

A

G

B

make 3 deep pleats toward center

C

CF

D

HAKAMA
front

fold

seam

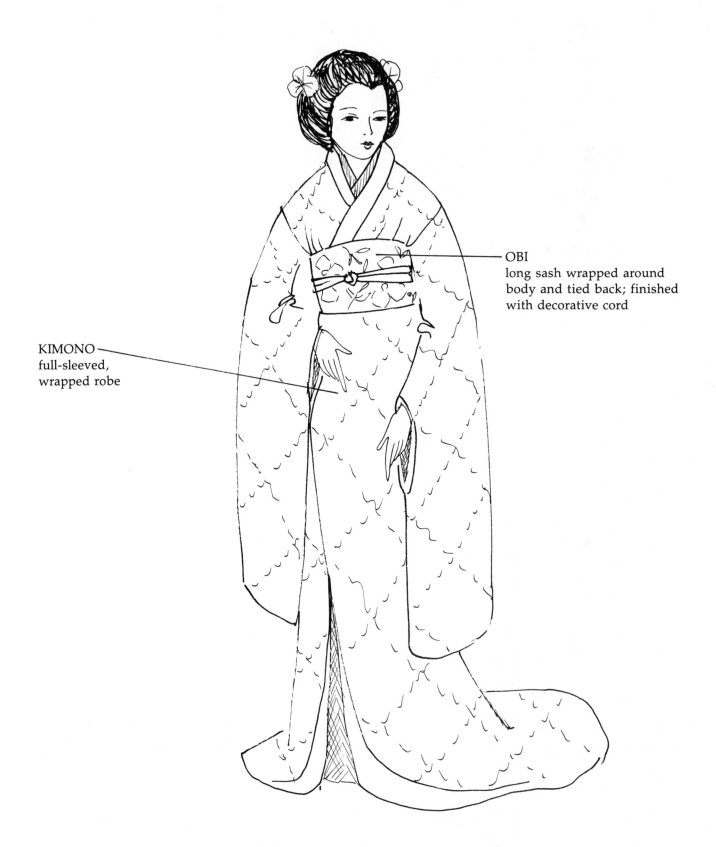

OBI
long sash wrapped around
body and tied back; finished
with decorative cord

KIMONO
full-sleeved,
wrapped robe

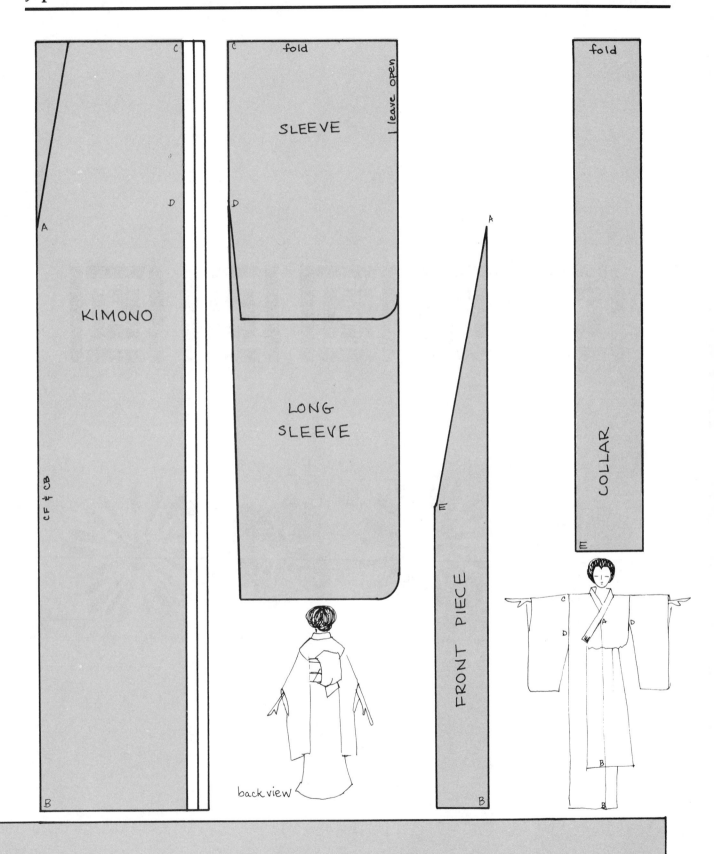

KIMONO

CF & CB

SLEEVE

leave open

LONG SLEEVE

back view

FRONT PIECE

fold

COLLAR

fold

OBI

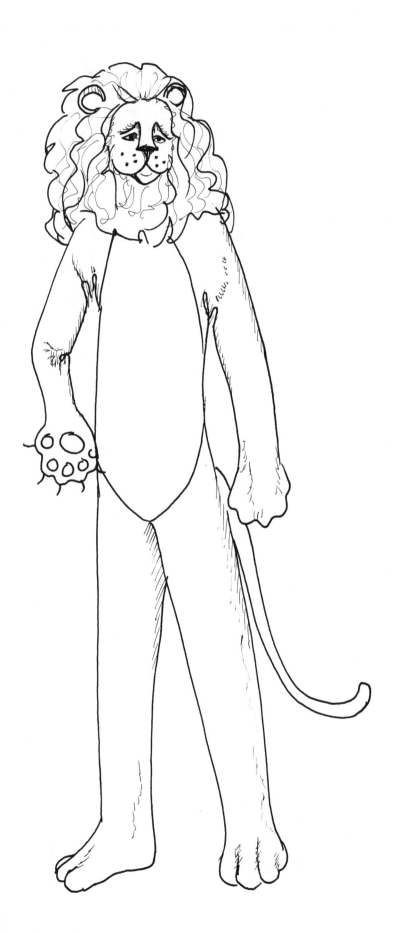

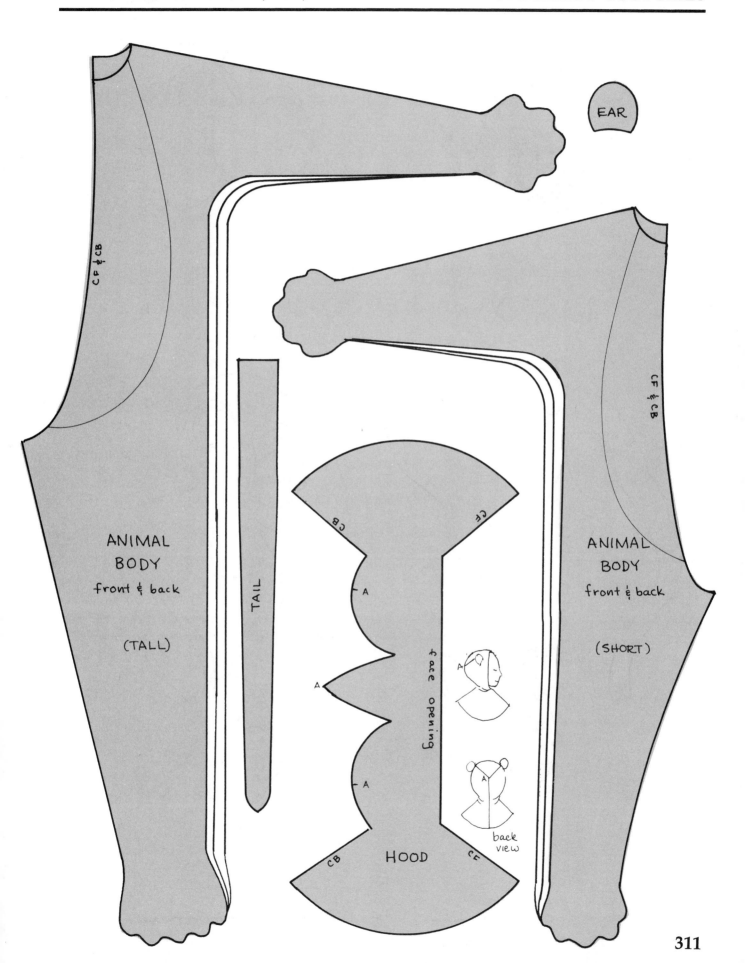

EAR

CF & CB

ANIMAL
BODY
front & back

(TALL)

TAIL

CB

A

A

A

CB

face opening

CF

A

A

CF

HOOD

back
view

ANIMAL
BODY
front & back

(SHORT)

CF & CB

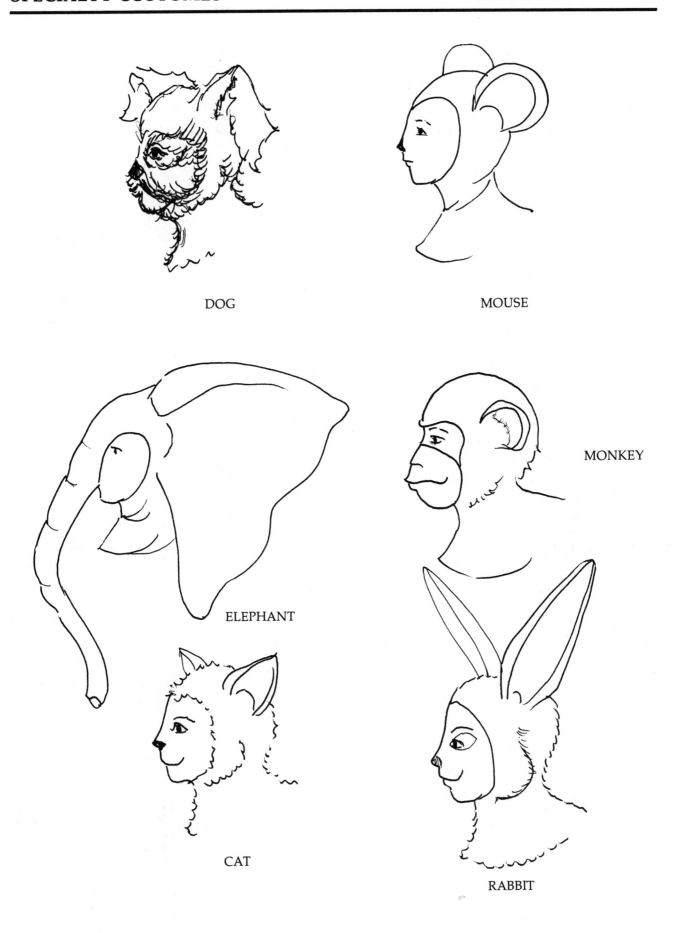

DOG

MOUSE

MONKEY

ELEPHANT

CAT

RABBIT

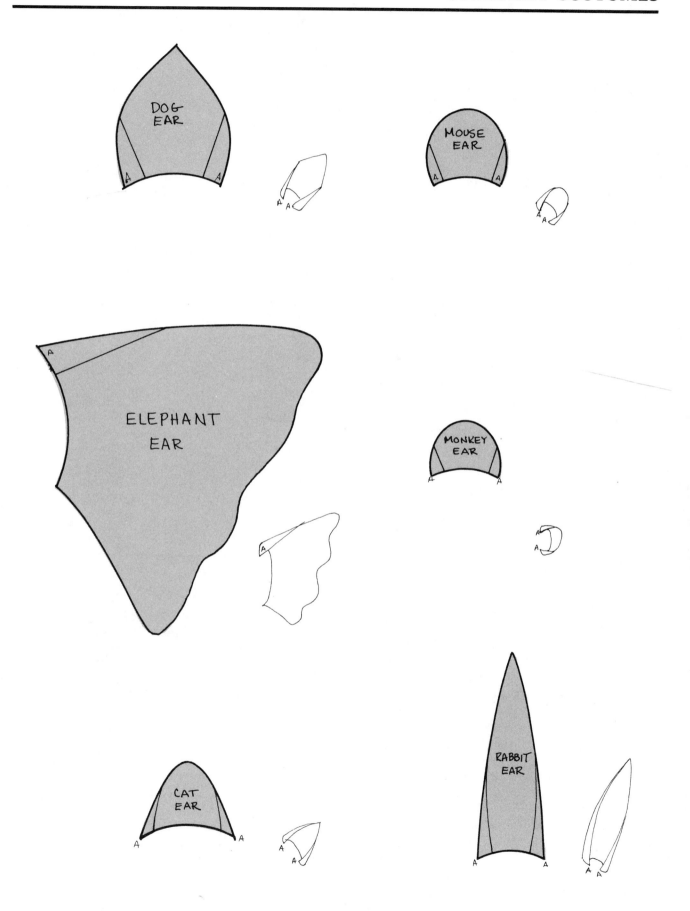

Construction of Special Costume Pieces

CORSETS

Corsets are intended not only to slim a figure, but to mold it into the proper silhouette and to effect the appropriate posture and movement for a specific period. Corsets may be constructed from materials which are easily obtained, or from materials specifically designed for corset construction which are available in large cities. Steel strapping, of the kind used to wrap crates for shipping, may be used instead of regular corset boning; this requires cutting and finishing the ends of the individual bones to prepare them, but the cost is next to nothing. Plastic and wire boning can frequently be purchased in fabric stores. Commercial corset stays are nice to use. They can be purchased in specific lengths, which eliminates the need to cut and finish ends before use. Any of these materials will work well for theatrical corset boning. Fabric used to create the body of the corset may vary, though densely woven washable cotton duck seems to withstand the strain of use most successfully.

Materials Needed

1. Fabric for corset and lining (may be the same fabric)
2. Corset boning
3. Grommets
4. Bias tape
5. Long shoelace or cord for lacing

Step-by-Step

1. Cut pieces of corset and lining from fabric, marking CF, CB, bone placement, and all letter markings along the top of each corset section.
2. Stitch seams of corset leaving the center back open. Do not put the lining together yet (see page 317).
3. Check for fit on the person who will wear the corset. The corset should not meet in the center back since the corset will be laced. A gap of at least two inches between center back sections is desirable.
4. Mark alterations on the corset and the lining and put each together separately.
5. Press open the seams on both the corset and the lining.
6. Place the corset on top of the lining with wrong sides together and seams matched up, top and bottom. Pin along top and bottom edges and along all seam lines.
7. Stitch along seam lines and along bottom edge through corset and lining. Do not stitch along top side.
8. Stitch along boning lines as indicated on the pattern to create casings for the corset stays. Make sure the casing is wide enough to accept the stays, which will vary in width depending on the type used (see page 317).

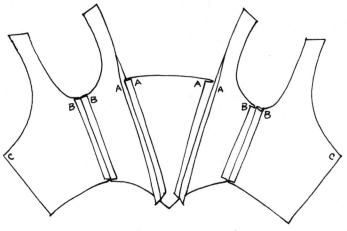

corset pieces sewn together

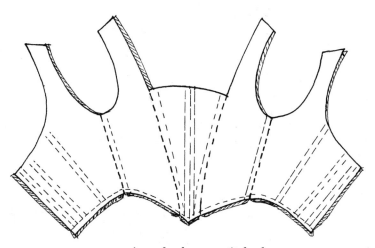

casings for bones stitched

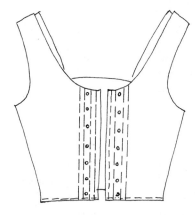

center back of corset

9. Cut boning to the proper length for each casing, making sure that the stay will not extend above the top seam line. Finish the cut end of the boning with tape, or file and dip the ends into liquid plastic to prevent stays from poking through the material of the corset. Insert bones in casings.

10. Reinforce lacing area with grosgrain ribbon or belting. It is a good idea to flank the lacing strip with boning (see page 317).

11. Install grommets every two inches by following package instructions.

12. Stitch along the top edge of the corset just above boning.

13. If corset has shoulder seams, stitch them in place.

14. Finish all edges with bias tape turned to the lining and sewn by hand.

HOOP PETTICOATS

Hoop petticoats are not difficult to construct, though storage is frequently a problem. Most hoops collapse into concentric rings and may be hung along a flat wall. They may also be stored by removing the hoops.

Materials Needed

1. Medium-weight washable fabric
2. Steel strapping (for wrapping crates) or plastic tubing
3. Bias tape

Step-by-Step

1. Cut pattern pieces from sturdy medium-weight washable fabric.
2. Label each piece for hoop and flounce location as well as placement letters.
3. Assemble all pieces, leaving a nine-inch opening in the center back.
4. Stitch casings of bias tape along hoop lines, leaving an opening large enough to insert the boning.
5. Finish the waist with waistband, elastic, or drawstring.
6. Hem petticoat to appropriate length and add flounces.
7. Insert steel or plastic tubing through casings and bind them into loops with heavy-duty tape.

HATS

Old hats should not be discarded. Even if they are in bad condition, they can be reblocked, retrimmed, and recut to create new effects. Felt hats can be dampened and restretched over various blocks and forms to change the shape of the crown. A man's felt hat can easily become a woman's cloche hat in this way. An eighteenth-century tricorne can be made by tacking up a soft-brimmed hat in three places. Artificial flowers, veils, and ribbons can perk up tired, discarded donations, and even the limp and wrinkled trims from old hats may be enlivened by steaming and pressing. Nearly all parts of old hats can be restored and reused.

When the possibilities for recycling old hats have been exhausted, new hats can be created easily and inexpensively by using the techniques described below. Most hats have two parts—the *crown* and the *brim*. By changing their shape and size, it is possible to create a wide variety of hats using the same basic construction techniques.

Crowns

Two basic types of crown are the *soft* crown and the *stretched* crown. Soft-crown hats are easy to make and inexpensive; stretched-crown hats require special equipment and a more sophisticated technique. A variety of brim shapes, including a simple decorative band, can be added to either type of crown, depending on the desired effect.

Soft Crown

Materials Needed

1. Fabric
2. Interfacing (optional)

Step-by-Step

1. Cut a circle from the hat fabric. The size of the circle will alter the final effect (see page 321).
2. If greater stiffness is required, add interfacing.
3. Gather or pleat along the outer edge until the crown opening equals the actor's head measurement plus one-half inch.

Stretched Crown

Materials Needed

1. Buckram
2. Fabric
3. Head block (or other rigid object used to create hat form such as bowl, bucket, wastebasket, or flower pot).

Step-by-Step

1. Protect the hat block or form with aluminum foil.
2. Cut a piece of buckram large enough to cover the block.

3. Place buckram in warm water for one minute. Then enclose it in a plastic bag until it becomes soft and pliable.

4. Stretch buckram over the form and pull on opposite sides to remove as many wrinkles as possible. Hold buckram in place with elastic or push pins (see page 321). Allow to dry until tacky.

5. If the hat fabric can be wetted and stretched (felt, knitted velours, some woolens), it can be stretched over the drying buckram and the two allowed to dry completely together. If not, the hat fabric may be fitted to the buckram form with pleats, gathers, or darts after the form is dry (see page 321).

6. Trim the lower edge of the buckram and fabric with heavy-duty scissors.

Brims

Brims can vary in size and shape and in the curve or sweep of the outer edge. Millinery wire may be used to strengthen the perimeter of a hat brim and to establish its direction and movement. Individualized brims can be created first in brown heavy paper and tried on the actor until the desired effect has been achieved.

Flexible Buckram Brims

Materials Needed

1. Buckram
2. Millinery wire (optional)
3. Hot-melt glue gun (optional)
4. Hat fabric

Step-by-Step

1. Cut brim shape out of buckram. To mark head opening, select a pattern one-half inch larger than the actor's head size (see pages 322 and 323). Add seam allowance to the head-opening size of the brim, but none to the outer edge.

2. Zig-zag, hand-stitch, or hot-glue milliner's wire to outer edge of brim, overlapping and carefully securing the wire ends at the center back.

3. Cut two layers of the final hat fabric to the shape of the brim, adding seam allowance to both the outer and inner edges.

4. Secure one layer of the brim fabric to the buckram frame (wrong side of fabric to brim) by using rubber cement, or by steam-ironing through the tacky buckram, or by running a stitch just inside the outer perimeter of the brim (see page 323).

5. Placing right sides of the brim together, sew both fabric pieces along the outer edge just outside the buckram edge.

6. Flip the brim fabric over the buckram frame by gently folding the buckram inside the fabric pocket.

soft crown hats

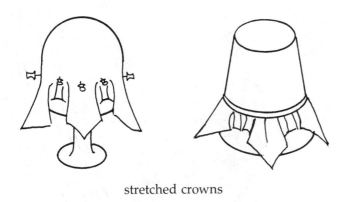

stretched crowns

crown gathered to fit buckram base

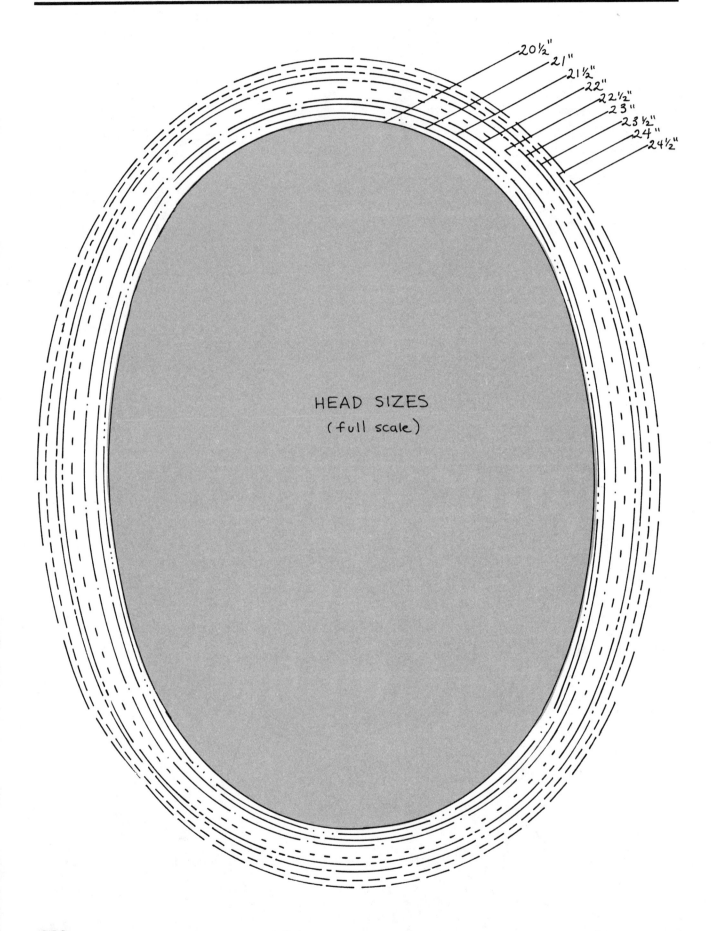

20½"
21"
21½"
22"
22½"
23"
23½"
24"
24½"

HEAD SIZES
(full scale)

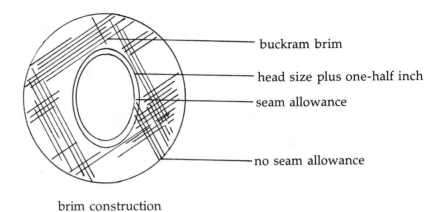

— buckram brim

— head size plus one-half inch

— seam allowance

— no seam allowance

brim construction

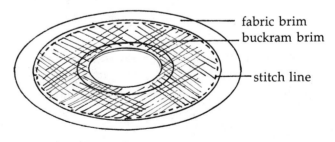

— fabric brim
— buckram brim

— stitch line

adding fabric to the brim

7. Machine-stitch all three layers along the inner head-opening line and clip all three layers to the stitching line every one-half inch. Fold these tabs up (see page 325).

Finishing

Step-by-Step

1. Join crown and brim by machine- or hand-stitching through all seam allowances. If time is critical, use hot glue.

2. Soft gathered linings (made like a soft crown) and a sweat band of ribbon may be hand-stitched inside the hat. This is particularly important if the inside of the hat will be visible to the audience.

3. Trims may be tacked loosely and freely according to the creative whim of the designer. Ribbons, flowers, buckles, and brooches greatly enhance and individualize hats.

Mob Cap

The mob cap is a useful hat and very simple to make. It resembles the soft crown, but has a soft brim as well. Varying the size of the pattern and adding ribbons and lace can greatly alter the final effect (see page 325).

Materials Needed

1. Fabric
2. Narrow bias tape
3. Elastic

Step-by-Step

1. Draw two concentric circles on the fabric—the first with a radius of nine inches, the second with a radius of seven inches (see page 325).

2. Cut along the outer-circle line and finish the edge with trim or a narrow hem.

3. Stitch bias-tape casing on the seven-inch circumference line, leaving a one-half inch opening to insert elastic (see page 325).

4. With a large safety pin secured to one end of the elastic, pull the elastic through the casing around the inner circle and back out at the starting point.

5. Fit cap to actor's head and stitch elastic ends together.

CROWNS

Like hat brims, crowns should first be made from heavy paper and fitted on the actor, then checked for necessary adjustments in size and shape.

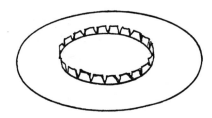

brim with inner seam allowance clipped

mob cap variation

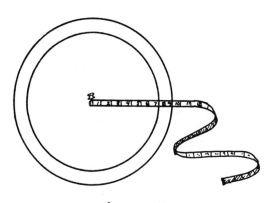

mob cap pattern

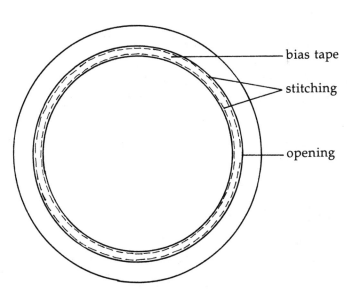

bias tape

stitching

opening

mob cap with casing for elastic

Materials Needed

1. Plastic or paper bucket
2. Celastic
3. Acetone
4. White glue
5. Enamel paint
6. Trim

Step-by-Step

1. Select a plastic or paper bucket or a wastebasket which measures less than the actor's head measurement at the small end, and which has the proper flare. Cover the bucket with aluminum foil or petroleum jelly. Surround the bucket with a strip of masking tape at the point where the bucket circumference equals the actor's head size plus one-half inch (see page 327).

2. Fit paper pattern to bucket at the tape line. Dart or slash the pattern at regular intervals to achieve correct fit (see page 327). Recheck pattern on actor's head.

3. Cut adjusted crown pattern out of celastic, allowing seam allowances for overlap at center back.

4. Immerse celastic crown in acetone. (Work with rubber gloves in a well-ventilated area.)

5. When celastic softens and becomes pliable, smooth it on the bucket, placing head opening of crown on tape line. Carefully press celastic together where it overlaps in back. Allow to dry for several hours. (For large crowns, add a second layer of celastic before the first layer dries.)

6. Remove crown from bucket by prying it loose and slipping it off the smaller end of the bucket. Trim rough edges with utility knife or heavy-duty scissors. Sand the entire surface until smooth.

7. Upholstery braid and cording may be applied with white glue or hot glue to add weight and define the crown's contour (see page 327).

8. Cover entire crown surface with white glue and allow to dry. This will give the crown a shiny surface.

9. Paint crown with enamel spray paint. By directing a dark color around and under the crown and a metallic color around and on top of the crown, shadows from the applied trim become more pronounced.

10. Gems and pearls may be applied with hot glue to the painted crown.

Using Crown Patterns

The crown patterns shown here are drawn in the correct scale for a 21" head size. (Larger sizes are indicated by additional lines.) Each crown section pattern represents one-eighth of the total crown; cut-

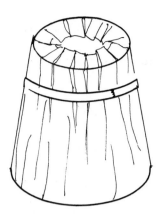

bucket marking head size

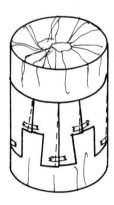
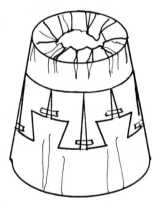

pattern fitted to bucket

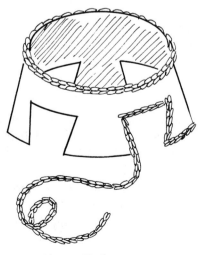

trim applied to crown

ting the pattern from folded sheets of paper will thus produce one-quarter sections.

To make the pattern for your crown, select one of the crown patterns shown here and transfer it by tracing on a folded sheet of heavy paper. Then cut out the pattern. Repeat this step to create four one-quarter crown sections.

Next, determine the degree of desired flare in the crown and select an arc line to correspond (see page 330). The arc lines on the pattern sheet represent segments of various circles with a radius of 50" down to 10 5/8". Choose an arc line with a large radius if a slight flare is desired; choose an arc line with a small radius for an exaggerated flare (see page 331). If no flare is desired, a straight line may be used for the bottom edge to create a perfectly cylindrical crown.

Arrange the pattern pieces along the arc line you selected with the bottom edge of the pattern touching the line, allowing the side edges of the pattern pieces to overlap or gap depending on the curve (see page 331). Tape the pattern pieces together and correct and smooth the curves. Add seam allowance to one side of the center back of the crown pattern (see page 331).

MASKS

Masks may be built over a plaster cast, over a prefabricated styrofoam face form, or directly on top of the actor's face. Working from a cast of the actor's face is best if time allows.

Facial Casting

Very fine, detailed casts of an actor's face may be taken from moulage and alginate, available in bulk from dental-supply stores (follow directions on label). This method is time-consuming and the fine detail is often wasted over a theatrical distance. An easier, faster, and less expensive method involves the use of plaster bandages.

Materials Needed
1. Plaster bandages
2. Petroleum jelly
3. Plaster-of-paris

Step-by-Step
1. Cover the actor's face with a thin layer of petroleum jelly. Keep hair securely pinned back. Cover facial hair (eyelashes, eyebrows, moustaches) with facial tissue for added security (see page 333).
2. Tear plaster bandages into four-inch sections and dip one at a time in water. Wring out excess moisture immediately.
3. Smooth bandages on face, overlapping edges and using the bias

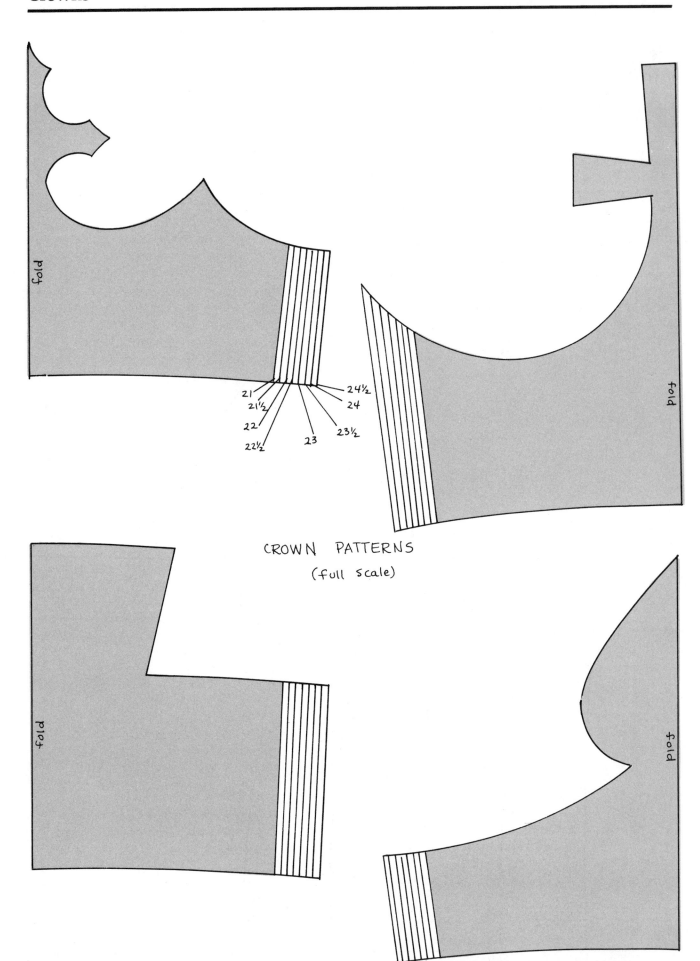

21
21½
22
22½
23
23½
24
24½

CROWN PATTERNS
(full scale)

fold

fold

fold

fold

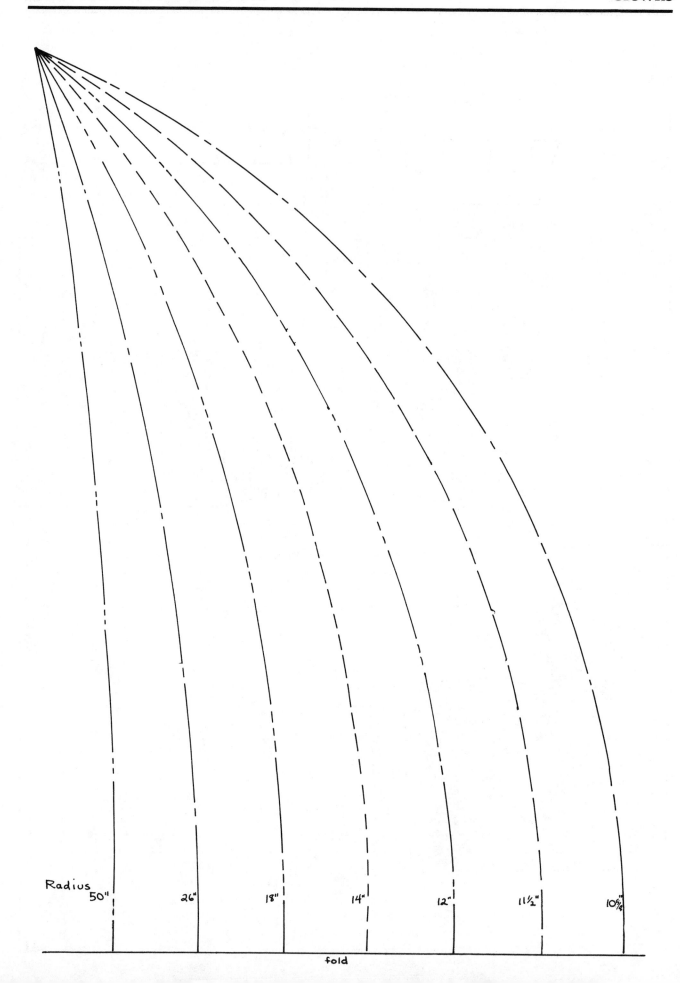

Radius
50"   26"   18"   14"   12"   11½"   10⅞"

fold

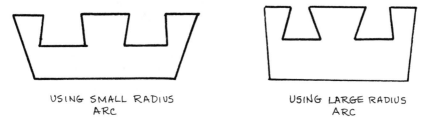

USING SMALL RADIUS
ARC

USING LARGE RADIUS
ARC

diagram of flare to crown

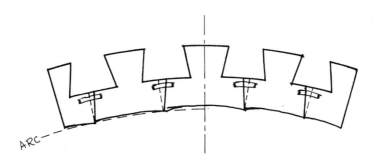

ARC

crown pattern taped together

SEAM
ALLOWANCE

crown pattern with seam allowance

(diagonal) feature of the cloth to fit the contours of nose, eye sockets, and so on.

4. Cover entire face (except nostrils) with two or three layers of bandages (see page 333).

5. Allow cast to set (about 10–15 minutes for the fast-set variety). Warn the actor that the plaster will heat slightly during the setting process.

6. Carefully remove the hardened cast from the face and discard protective tissue. This is a *negative cast* of the actor's face. The next step is to make a *positive cast* which is the form on which the mask will be built.

7. Plug nostril holes on the outside of the negative cast with additional strips of plaster bandage.

8. Mix plaster-of-paris according to package instructions. When the mixture begins to thicken and warm, pour immediately into the negative cast.

9. Allow plaster-of-paris to set. Like the plaster bandages, it will warm first, then cool before it is set. This may take several hours, depending on the specific brand, and the water-to-plaster ratio.

10. When plaster is set, pull back the sides of the negative cast very gently and push down on the face of the negative cast with your thumbs until the positive cast pops out.

The negative cast may be discarded, or if it is still intact, it may be used again to make an additional positive cast. It is helpful to have several positive casts when a large number of masks are required because of the time taken up in waiting for a mask to dry.

Creating a Mask

Masks can be made from a wide range of materials including celastic (see *crowns*), plaster bandages (see *facial casting*), and cheesecloth (described below). Cheesecloth masks are inexpensive and easy to make. They are versatile, light-weight, and comfortable to wear.

Materials Needed

1. Plaster cast
2. Modeling clay (optional)
3. Petroleum jelly
4. Cheesecloth
5. White glue
6. Paint and trim

Step-by-Step

1. The positive plaster mold may be used as is, or it may be built up with modeling clay to create animal or fantasy masks (see page 333).

2. Cover mold with a thin layer of petroleum jelly.

face protected

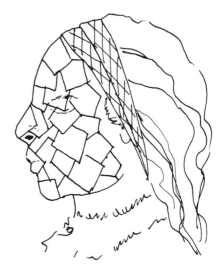

face covered with plaster bandages

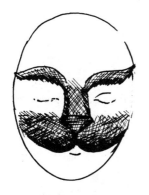

clay added to plaster cast

decorated masks

3. Place cheesecloth over face form one layer at a time and paint with a white glue slightly thinned with water to allow the glue to flow onto the form. Use three or four layers.

4. Allow mask to dry before removing it from the form.

5. Trim the outer edge of mask to desired shape with scissors or utility knife. Cut eye, mouth, and nostril openings if needed. Fit mask to actor's face and retrim or pad with felt any areas which are uncomfortable. Eye and nose areas frequently need a bit of padding.

6. Paint or decorate the mask according to specific design. Acrylic and enamel paints work well. Ribbons, sequins, feathers, hair, and so on, may be applied with white glue, hot glue, or needle and thread (see page 333).

7. An elastic band or a stick (for hand-held mask) may be stitched or glued in place if required.

WIGS

Inexpensive fashion wigs (sold in large discount department stores) may be combed, set, trimmed, and styled to suit a variety of theatrical needs and historical periods. Such wigs—made of synthetic fibers—are easily hand-washed, can be set or dyed with hair-care products, and appear tolerably realistic over a theatrical distance. Another advantage of cheap synthetic wigs is that, because they are constructed with a flexible base, they will fit a range of head sizes. It is best to style a wig on the head of the actor who will be wearing it. If the actor is unavailable for these often lengthy sittings, the wig base must be stretched and pinned to a headblock before styling.

Fantasy wigs may be constructed from a wide variety of materials. Nylon horsehair and yarn are commonly used, but fringes, furs, feathers, and tinsel can also create startling and pleasing stylized effects. The following instructions describe a suitable base to which these and many other materials may be applied. Choice of materials is limited only by the designer's imagination, and may include cotton balls, scouring pads, even steel springs! But light-weight materials work best; actors don't like to feel top-heavy.

Materials Needed
1. Buckram
2. Elastic
3. Hair substitute (yarn, tinsel, and so on)
4. Hot-melt glue gun

Step-by-Step
1. Select a head block of the same size as the actor's head.
2. Protect the block with aluminum foil or plastic wrap (dry-cleaner bags work well also).

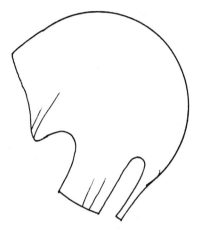

cut section from buckram form

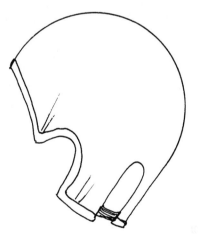

finished edges on form

3. Cut a piece of buckram large enough to cover the block.

4. Soak buckram in warm water for a minute, then place in a plastic bag until it becomes soft and pliable.

5. Stretch buckram over the form and pull on opposite sides to remove as many wrinkles as possible (see page 335). Hold buckram in place with elastic or push pins. Allow to dry overnight.

6. Remove buckram form from the block.

7. With scissors or craft knife, trim backram around ears and to establish desired hairline for the wig.

8. Cut an oval section out of the center back of the buckram form (see page 335).

9. Check fit on actor's head. Retrim where needed. Connect center back opening with elastic.

10. Sew or glue bias or felt strips around the outer edge of the buckram wig base (see page 335).

The base is now ready to accept hair or other materials, which are secured in place with hot glue. For layering, work from the bottom up. If an unusually large hairstyle is desired, dacron fiberfill or polyurethane shapes may be glued to the base, then covered with hair fiber or other materials.

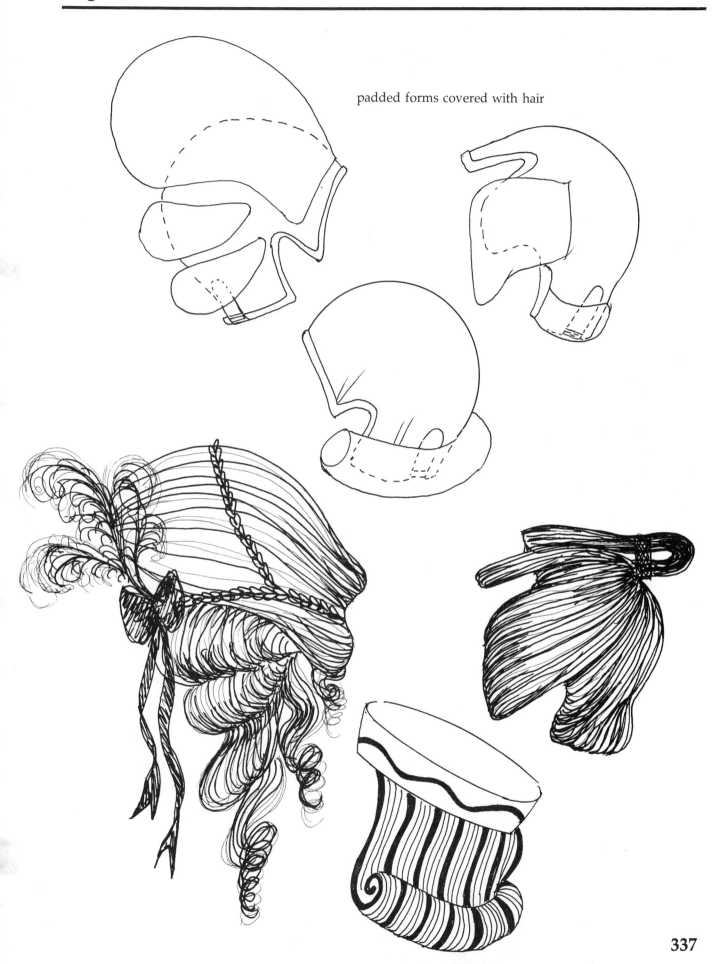

padded forms covered with hair

Index